Studies in Cor

Two week loan

Please return on or before the last
date stamped below.
Charges are made for late return.

Studies in Constitutional Law

Colin R. Munro LLB, BA

London
Butterworths
1987

346·142 M

United Kingdom	Butterworths a Division of Reed Elsevier (UK) Ltd, Halsbury House, 35 Chancery Lane, LONDON WC2A 1EL and 4 Hill Street, EDINBURGH EH2 3JZ
Australia	Butterworths, SYDNEY, MELBOURNE, BRISBANE, ADELAIDE, PERTH, CANBERRA and HOBART
Canada	Butterworths Canada Ltd, TORONTO and VANCOUVER
Ireland	Butterworth (Ireland) Ltd, DUBLIN
Malaysia	Malayan Law Journal Sdn Bhd, KUALA LUMPUR
New Zealand	Butterworths of New Zealand Ltd, WELLINGTON and AUCKLAND
Puerto Rico	Butterworth of Puerto Rico, Inc, SAN JUAN
Singapore	Reed Elsevier (Singapore) Pte Ltd
South Africa	Butterworths Publishers (Pty) Ltd, DURBAN
USA	Butterworth Legal Publishers, CARLSBAD, California, and SALEM, New Hampshire

© Butterworth & Co (Publishers) Ltd 1987
Reprinted 1989, 1990, 1992, 1993, 1994, 1995

A CIP Catalogue record for this book is available from the British Library.

British Library Cataloguing in Publication Data

Munro, Colin R.
  Studies in constitutional law.
  1. Great Britain——Constitutional law
  I. Title
  344.102   KD3989

  ISBN 0 406 26144 X
  ISBN 0 406 26145 8 Pbk

Typeset by Phoenix Photosetting, Chatham, Kent
Reprinted in Great Britain by Clays Ltd, St Ives plc

Preface

'Another book on constitutional law?' The purpose of this book is not to rival the major textbooks, whose authors are perforce obliged to try to cover the subject in all its many aspects. Instead, the aim here is to offer students a deeper perspective on some of the central themes. In the case of constitutional law, there is particular force in Sir Walter Scott's observation (in *Guy Mannering*) that: 'A lawyer without history or literature is a mechanic, a mere working mason; if he possesses some knowledge of these, he may venture to call himself an architect.' That a proper understanding of the constitution cannot be gained from legal rules alone may increase the difficulties of the subject for the student, but also adds immeasurably to the interest and enjoyment to be derived from it. If this book eases the difficulties, and helps to convey to readers some of that interest and enjoyment, it will have achieved its objects.

Parts of chapters 3 and 9 originally appeared in *Public Law*, and I am grateful for permission to reproduce the relevant material. Some of the book was prepared while I was a Visiting Scholar at Wolfson College, Cambridge in the congenial atmosphere fostered by its President, Professor D. G. T. Williams. Mr John Alder, Professor Francis Lyall and Professor Graham Zellick found time to comment on several chapters, and I benefited from their suggestions, not least when they were unable to agree with my views. My colleague at the University of Manchester, Professor Gillian White, was also kind enough to advise on one chapter.

Mary Platt, Helen Christie, Christine Johnson and Angela Wallace coped efficiently and cheerfully with my manuscript, and Butterworths were as considerate a publisher as any author could wish for. Without the help and encouragement of my wife Ruth, this book could not have been written. Without the diversions offered by Philip and Sally, it might have been written twice as quickly, and it is dedicated to them by the father they were sometimes able to persuade to come out to play.

C. R. M.
Manchester
February 1987

Contents

Table of statutes

References in this Table to Statutes are to Halsbury's *Statutes* of England (Fourth Edition) showing the volume and page at which the annotated text of the Act will be found.
Page references printed in **bold** type indicate where the section of an Act is set out in part or in full.

List of cases

1 The British constitution

Every state in the world has a constitution in the original sense of the word, by which is meant the body of rules and arrangements concerning the government of the country. In the United Kingdom, where the principal institutions of government have developed over hundreds of years, many of these rules are customary in origin.[1] Some of the rules are to be found in legislation, including such famous enactments as Magna Carta and the Bill of Rights, as well as modern statutes like the Representation of the People Act 1983 and the British Nationality Act 1981. Others reside in the judgments of the courts, although Dicey, the greatest of our constitutional lawyers, exaggerated the importance of this element when he characterised our constitution as 'judge-made'.[2] Some other matters which call for consideration are not legal at all: the government of a country could not be fully described without reference to political facts, practices and obligations.[3]

In the eighteenth century, another meaning of the word 'constitution' came into fashion. Following their success in the War of Independence, the Americans had chosen to establish a framework for national government in a single document which was called a 'Constitution for the United States of America'. Similarly, the revolutionaries in France had drawn up a Constitution in 1791 which limited the authority of the King. These were the models which the radical politician Thomas Paine had in mind when he complained that 'no such thing as a Constitution exists in England'.[4] Later the contrast with the United States and France inspired the French writer de Tocqueville to remark that our constitution was one which did not exist.[5] De Tocqueville, who was an admirer of the British constitution, was merely drawing attention to the absence of a single document referred to as 'the constitution'.

The term 'constitution' continues to be used in two senses. Of course, if we are speaking of the British constitution, only one meaning is possible. On

---

1 These include important parts of constitutional law such as parliamentary privilege (see ch 7) and the royal prerogative (see ch 8).
2 A V Dicey *Introduction to the Study of the Law of the Constitution* (10th edn) p 196.
3 Some of these are referred to as constitutional conventions: see ch 3.
4 Thomas Paine *The Rights of Man* Part the Second ch 4.
5 Alexis de Tocqueville *Democracy in America* vol 1 pt 1 ch 6.

other occasions, it is generally clear from the context which meaning is intended. Not content with that, however, some writers coined the term 'written constitution' to describe a document such as the United States Constitution of 1787. What is worse, countries were then divided by some commentators into those having a written constitution or, lacking that, an unwritten constitution. This was a singularly unhappy distinction. It suggested, wrongly, that in countries such as the United Kingdom, constitutional rules were only customary and could not be found in written form in statutes, reported cases and books, perhaps even that they were 'transmitted orally from generation to generation, like the earliest poetry of ancient Greece'.[6] It also suggested, wrongly, that in countries such as the United States, all the rules and arrangements concerning government had been reduced to writing in a single document. In practice, this is never the case. The documents called constitutions are often fairly short, and so many constitutional matters are regulated by ordinary legislation. Over the years, too, the framework in the document becomes overlaid with judicial interpretations and political practices. In other words, the constitution of a country, in the older sense of the word, includes, but is invariably larger than, the constitution in the newer sense.

The true distinction, it may be seen, is simply between states where some of the more important constitutional rules have been put in a document, or a set of associated documents, given special sanctity, and states where the constitution has many sources, none of which enjoys such recognition.

It is easy to understand why in many countries the fundamental framework of government has been set out in a document. What was more natural in post-revolutionary Russia in 1917 or newly independent Nigeria in 1960, or Zimbabwe after an independence settlement giving civil equality to the black majority was agreed in 1979? When there is a break with the past, and the institutions of government are altered, a formal embodiment of the new arrangements seems appropriate. The births of new nations and the unions of partners are aptly marked by rites of passage in the form of constitutional documents to which a special significance is attached. If later, in a state which has had such a constitution, it is desired to change some fundamentals, as in Canada in 1982, when a new constitution was adopted which could be amended without recourse to the United Kingdom Parliament, then a formal document is likely to be employed, so that the new arrangements may present as much appearance of legitimacy as did the old.

The circumstances which have led to the making of constitutions in other countries have largely been absent in this one. The British have not suffered conquest, or the loss of a major war, or revolution, for several hundred years. The United Kingdom has resulted from unions of the nations in the British

6 H W Horwill *The Usages of the American Constitution* (1925) p 1.

Isles, but the state was not organised on federal lines, for legislative and executive organs were centralised.[7]

The principal institutions of government in this country, Parliament, the Crown, and the courts, have been refashioned, and their relations with each other altered, as a result of social and political changes.[8] But they may all be traced back as far as the twelfth century (when Henry II made the Kings' Courts important) or the thirteenth (when in the reign of Edward I the English Parliament acquired something like its present form), times when constitution-making was not in fashion. Consequently, the development of governmental institutions has been evolutionary. As Sir Ivor Jennings put it, 'the British Constitution has not been made but has grown', and, mixing his metaphors: 'The building has been constantly added to, patched, and partially reconstructed, so that it has been renewed from century to century; but it has never been razed to the ground and rebuilt on new foundations'.[9]

These comments are instructive, but are perhaps misleading in one respect. The evolution has not quite been unbroken. Parliament's rebellion against Charles I in the Civil War led to the execution of the King, and experiments in republican government through Parliament. When those failed, Oliver Cromwell, preferring civil legality to the nakedness of the military sword, took office as Lord Protector in 1653 under a document called the Instrument of Government, which may fairly be considered a constitution. Provisions in the Instrument proved to be unacceptable to the Parliaments summoned under its terms, and four years later a new constitution, the Humble Petition and Advice, was accepted by Cromwell. Its currency was even shorter, for Cromwell's death hastened the Restoration.

The events which in other countries have resulted in the making of constitutions in modern times thus did so here in the turbulence of the seventeenth century. But, as the word Restoration implies, with the return of the monarchy, there was a return to the old order of things. The balance between Crown and Parliament which had existed at the commencement of the Long Parliament in 1640 was the same as that struck in 1660 when the new monarch came to the throne, and it was as if the last twenty years had never been.

Aside from the constitutions of the Cromwellian period, the government of the country has never rested upon a single framework. Why, it might be asked, do we regard the Instrument of Government as being a constitution, when we do not so regard Magna Carta or the Bill of Rights in 1688 or the Acts of Union in 1707 (when Scotland united with England and Wales to form Great Britain) and 1801 (when Great Britain united with Ireland to

---

7 See ch 2.
8 See ch 9.
9 W I Jennings *The Law and the Constitution* (5th edn, 1959), p 8.

form the United Kingdom)? Certainly, it all depends upon how we define a constitution. The Instrument of Government had certain features which are generally found in the documents regarded as constitutions. Its scope and importance were indicated by the Preamble: 'The government of the commonwealth of England, Scotland, and Ireland, and the dominions thereunto belonging'. The Instrument not only defined where executive power resided (in the Lord Protector and Council) and legislative power resided (in Parliament and Lord Protector), but specified who should be Lord Protector, how the Council was to be appointed, and the Parliament elected. Thus it was fundamental in the sense that the authority of those institutions derived from the document. It had also a higher law status, in that its provisions, unlike laws on any other matter, could not be amended by Parliament alone.

None of the other enactments mentioned is as wide in its scope. The clauses of Magna Carta were designed to check some particular royal abuses. The Bill of Rights embodied the terms upon which the Crown was offered to William and Mary, which included the establishment of certain parliamentary rights and privileges and further limitations upon the royal powers. The Acts of Union united the countries concerned, and their Parliaments, but left the Scottish courts in being and Scots law separate; they also provided for an established religion in each part of the Kingdom, and contained some provisions about trade and taxes. However, none of these enactments dealt systematically with the institutions of government and their relations with each other: in each case much was assumed. Nor has any of them been treated by Parliament as impossible to amend in the ordinary way.

For these reasons, no doubt, such enactments, important as they are in our constitutional history, have not generally been regarded as constitutions.[10] However, it is a matter of interpretation rather than anything else, for the meaning of the term 'constitution' used in this sense is, like many of the terms used in political science, inexact.[11] If we chose to define 'constitution' in a particular way, say that it is a document from which the institutions of government derive their authority, or that it is that part of a country's law which may not be altered or repealed in the ordinary manner, then we should have a certain criterion. But the difficulty in adopting such a criterion is that the variety of terms and characteristics found in documents regarded as constitutions means that no particular feature is universal.[12] By stipulating criteria such as those mentioned, one would be liable to exclude from the

---

10 There are some dissenters in respect of the Acts of Union: see ch 4.

11 See Munro 'What is a Constitution?' [1983] PL 563.

12 The documents may be studied in various collections, such as A P Blaustein and G H Flanz (eds) *Constitutions of the Countries of the World* (1971 and supplements) and A J Peaslee *Constitutions of Nations* (3rd edn, 1965–70).

category documents which in their own countries are regarded as constitutions.

The constitutions of the states of the world vary greatly in contents and in length. We may say, of course, that all are concerned with matters of government. In the main, that is true, but even as to this a reservation is necessary. Sometimes provisions are included in or added to a constitution which one would scarcely class as constitutional law, usually so as to confer on them a higher status or to impede their repeal. An example is provided by Prohibition in the United States. That misguided attempt to outlaw the consumption of alcohol was effected by the Eighteenth Amendment to the Constitution, passed in 1920 and repealed in 1933. Aside from such curiosities, constitutions display some broad similarity of subject-matter. The only other common factors are as to form: constitutions consist of rules in fixed verbal form, so that they are akin to legislation, even if the constitution is not ordinary legislation, and these are found in a single document or at most a set of associated documents.

In this country the principal rules about government have not been embodied in a single document, except during the Interregnum. One could, however, if one wished, assemble together eight or ten of this country's most important constitutional enactments, and regard them collectively as a constitution (and indeed, for purposes of comparison or exposition, some authors have done so). The result would be distinguishable from other countries' constitutions only by the number and disparateness of the enactments selected, and because of those enactments not being generally regarded as comprising a constitution.

These differences are not very important, and so it would appear that too much importance has been attached to whether a country has a constitution or not. What every schoolboy knows is that this country has no constitution; but what he knows turns out to be a distinction without a difference.

Of course, there may be a difference. The existence of a constitution in a country might be significant in a variety of ways. It may perform a symbolic or psychological role, and help to excite the reverence of the citizenry; it may have an educational value; it may simplify the task of academic exposition; and in any event its particular form and contents merit examination. But these are contingent factors, to be assessed for any country studied. They are not consequences which necessarily flow from the presence of a constitution, nor should any opposing inferences be drawn from the absence of one. The British constitution, notwithstanding its form, has been the object of more admiration than most. Sometimes it is asserted that non-legal rules and practices play a larger role in the absence of a constitution, but this is at best unproven, for in all countries legal rules are supplemented by other rules and practices. Sometimes it is suggested that the sovereignty of the United Kingdom Parliament (by which is meant that its capacity to legislate may not be restricted by any law) is a consequence of the absence of a constitution.

That this is mistaken is shown by the number of constitutional lawyers who deny that Parliament is unlimited without believing that the United Kingdom has a constitution, a position involving no logical impossibility.

The last point leads us to another example of an argument based on a fallacy. Sometimes it is said that, because the United Kingdom Parliament is sovereign, the adoption of a constitution in this country would be impossible, or at least nugatory. This is a very poor argument. Even if we accept the premise that Parliament cannot be legally restricted, it does not follow that an enacted constitution would be unrespected or worthless. There is nothing *legally* to prevent Parliament from denying used car salesmen the right to vote or making the practice of Methodism a criminal offence, but respect for the principles of universal adult suffrage and freedom of religion is such as to render the possibilities unreal.

Besides, there are many authorities on the constitution who would deny that it is impossible, as things stand, to put legal limitations on Parliament's future actions.[13] They may or may not be right. What virtually all authorities agree upon, however, is that if the will existed, some political means could be devised by which a constitution could be adopted to which the legislature would owe its existence and would be subject.

Here, of course, we are speculating about the possibility of a fundamental change in the British constitutional pattern, and it might be asked whether there is any likelihood of such a change. As we have seen, the circumstances which have given rise to the formulation of constitutions in other countries have not been present here. Other factors have combined to keep the question well down the political agenda. The British, as might be expected of an island race, display insularity, and the peculiarity of our constitutional arrangements has not troubled the country's leaders. In fact, the slow process of evolution, by which our constitution has adapted and changed as times have required, is characteristic of the dominant political pragmatism. There is pride, as well, which often shades into complacency. When we have 'the mother of Parliaments', and a far better record than most in the protection of civil and political rights, it might be thought that there is little to learn from other countries' experiences.

These sentiments may continue to prevail, but equally there are other developments which make the present period one of the most exciting in our constitutional history. Accession to the European Communities, although it has brought extensive change to our legal systems,[14] was achieved by ordinary Act of Parliament; but if the member states were ever to agree to some sort of federation or political union, this would necessitate a more fundamental restructuring. Within the United Kingdom, changes in the

13 See ch 5.
14 See ch 6.

relationship of the parts to the whole cannot be ruled out.[15] Provisions for devolution in the Scotland Act 1978 and the Wales Act 1978, receiving insufficient support in referendums, did not come into effect. But the question will not go away: a desire for greater control over their own affairs remains in those nations, in Northern Ireland, and indeed in some English regions.

Another movement which has grown in strength over the last thirty years is that which seeks the better protection of human rights. The United Kingdom government is a party to the European Convention on Human Rights, thus incurring obligations as a matter of international law, and has accepted the right of individuals to bring claims against it for violations. There are calls for it to go further and secure the enactment of a declaration of fundamental rights – a Bill of Rights, as it is usually called – as part of domestic law.

Domestic political institutions, their long evolution notwithstanding, are also under scrutiny. The members of the House of Commons are elected under a 'first past the post' system, whereas in most countries some form of proportional representation is employed. The British electoral system is under attack, on the ground of its unfairness: in the 1983 General Election, for example, the Liberal–SDP Alliance won 25% of the total votes cast, but obtained only 3.5% of the seats. The upper house of the legislature can scarcely be defended in its present form: a majority of its members are neither elected nor appointed, but take their seats by virtue of hereditary peerages.

So major changes lie on the constitutional horizon, although not all will come in with the tides. The British constitution, if not in ferment, is at least in flux. Reforms in any of the matters mentioned might be by an enactment sufficiently wide-reaching or distinctive to be considered 'a constitution' or by an instrument so designated, but it is largely a matter of nomenclature or interpretation.

In the meantime, generalisations about 'written constitutions' or 'unwritten constitutions' are unfounded, because they depend upon a distinction which is misleading and inexact. We shall see the British constitution more clearly if we look at it afresh.

15 See ch 2.

2 The United Kingdom

When undergraduates in the University of Manchester study the law of torts, the object of their study is English law. When students at the University of Aberdeen learn about the equivalent subject, the law of delict, their interest is in the law of Scotland. In constitutional law, however, these students' subject matter would be largely the same, and it would not be proper or usual to talk of 'the English constitution' or 'the Scottish constitution'.[1] The object of our study in constitutional law, whether in Manchester or Aberdeen, Aberystwyth or Belfast, is the British constitution or, more correctly, the constitution of the United Kingdom. That is because the first concern of constitutional law is with the institutions of government in a *state*, or independent political society. England and Scotland are not states, but parts of the same state. Parliament is the legislature which represents the people of that state, and the United Kingdom government, acting in Her Majesty's name, is its executive, and the study of these institutions forms a large portion of constitutional law.

Yet it would be quite erroneous to speak of 'British law' or 'United Kingdom law', for no such system exists. If the sovereign state with which we are dealing is the United Kingdom, it nonetheless comprises three distinct legal systems: English law, Scots law, and the law of Northern Ireland. That is why the land law taught in Belfast differs from that taught in Birmingham or in Glasgow. Even in constitutional law, when it comes to matters such as police powers, or public order, or remedies in administrative law, there are important differences between the three systems.

It is not unusual for states to comprise different legal systems within their boundaries, and federal states necessarily exhibit this feature. That term is generally used to denote a constitution in which the function of legislating is divided geographically, amongst federal (or central) and provincial (or regional or state) legislatures, with each enjoying some areas of autonomy. So, in the United States, there are certain matters lying exclusively within the legislative competence of Congress, as to which the fifty state legislatures may not legislate, while there are other matters reserved to the states. In fact,

---

1 Some of our greatest constitutional writers were bad exemplars in this respect. Walter Bagehot entitled a book *The English Constitution* (1867), and Dicey often used the same phrase.

federal constitutions are to be found in about a sixth of the countries of the world. But the United Kingdom is classed as a unitary, not a federal, state. The Parliament at Westminster is omnicompetent. There is no Welsh or Scottish legislature, and there is no longer a Northern Ireland legislature. There was a Northern Ireland Parliament for much of this century, but the limited powers conferred on it by the Government of Ireland Act 1920 were not exclusive and, after the imposition of direct rule, it was abolished in 1973. So, in the United Kingdom, the existence of different legal systems is not a consequence of a federal system. It is a consequence of our political history, including the arrangements made when unions were agreed and the arrangements made since for different parts of the state.

The name 'United Kingdom' should remind us, lest we forget, that the state was formed by unions between the different nations inhabiting these islands. Sadly, experience suggests that ignorance of the political history of these islands is widespread, and that misuse of terms is prevalent, even amongst those who should know better. You may be sure that only a small proportion of the persons who reside in the state would be able to name it correctly as the United Kingdom or, to give it the full title, the United Kingdom of Great Britain and Northern Ireland. Undoubtedly, many would reply 'England', a solecism which foreigners too are often guilty of committing. Many would say that it is 'Britain' or 'Great Britain'. Admittedly, the adjective 'British', when applied to the constitution or to Parliament, for example, is so convenient and widely used as to be acceptable. But, to be accurate, Great Britain comprises only the mainland of England, Wales and Scotland, and does not include the province of Northern Ireland which is part of the United Kingdom. Another term, 'the British Isles', is a geographical description, apt to include the Republic of Ireland and the small offshore islands such as the Isle of Man and the Channel Islands,[2] as well as the parts of the United Kingdom.

Perhaps, after all, it is understandable that misconceptions should abound. The state has had three different names in the last two hundred years, and its boundaries have changed with unions and disunion. An outline of these changes will be given in this chapter. The ground covered here is not difficult, and, for many readers, it will be familiar terrain. For others, it will help to fill in some of the historical background and the geographical dimensions of the United Kingdom constitution.

---

2 The Isle of Man and the Channel Islands are dependencies of the Crown. They are not part of the United Kingdom, but are treated as such for purposes of nationality law: British Nationality Act 1981. For discussion of their constitutional relationships with the United Kingdom, see the Report of the Royal Commission on the Constitution 1969–1973 (Cmnd 5460), Part XI (hereafter, *Kilbrandon Report*).

THE NATIONS UNITED

In this section we examine how the four countries which make up the British Isles developed, and consider the unions between them in 1707 and 1801 which resulted in the formation of the United Kingdom.

England

England has not been successfully invaded since 1066, but was on countless occasions before that. The earliest inhabitants had been overrun by the light-haired Celts from northern Europe in the centuries before Christ. A Roman occupation of the land corresponding to modern England and Wales began in 43 AD, and Roman rule lasted until the fifth century, when it began to yield to the repeated irruptions of the Nordic raiders. For six or seven hundred years, Angles, Saxons, Jutes, Norsemen and Danes took turns in attacking these shores. The unity of the Roman province was lost as numbers of kingdoms and tribes of the invaders were settled, especially in the eastern and southern parts of the island (where names such as Essex, Sussex and Norfolk recall them). The Danish Vikings conquered East Anglia and the large territories of Northumbria and Mercia, and so established their rule, the 'Danelaw', over a considerable area. But their attempt to conquer Wessex as well was frustrated by the young Alfred the Great, who defeated them at the Battle of Ethandune (878) and forced them to withdraw. Alfred's strengthening of Wessex enabled his descendants and successors, Edward the Elder and Athelstan, to annex the other parts of southern Britain and then to conquer the less unified Danelaw territories. When Alfred's great-grandson Edgar was King (959–975), he ruled over a land whose boundaries were not very different from those of England today.

So, from the tenth century, there was only one King of England, but for another two hundred years, there was a rich variety of laws. Some written laws were issued by the king and his advisers, but the law was predominantly administered in the local courts of shires and hundreds, where different customs prevailed and different practices emerged. These English laws were not superseded by a body of Norman law in 1066.[3] William the Conqueror confirmed that the laws of Edward the Confessor would be maintained, as did Henry I on his accession. However, the Norman instincts for political unity and administrative consolidation paved the way for change. Henry II extended the jurisdiction and increased the authority of the royal courts, and, through that means, aided by the sending of itinerant justices around the country, a native law 'common' to the whole land was shortly developed.[4] It was not until the thirteenth century that the practice began of summoning

3 See F W Maitland *The Constitutional History of England* (1908) pp 6–10.
4 Ibid, pp 10–23.

knights of the shires and representative burgesses to attend the King's Council, and during the reign of Edward I these assemblies became more regular and more important. As a 'Parliament' of the three estates of the realm, clergy, lords and commons, it was recognisably the forerunner of the institution which was to become the other major source of English law.

Wales[5]

The joinder of Wales to England was not so much a union as an absorption. It is usually said that Edward I conquered Wales, but that is an over-simplification. For a start there was no clear political entity called Wales, nor a single kingship. Instead, a few princes and upwards of a hundred lords held sway over their respective territories. Some of these, like Rhodri Mawr (in the ninth century), Hywel (tenth century), and Llewellyn the Great (early thirteenth century), did succeed in gaining authority over large parts of the country, but only temporarily and precariously. Moreover, the Welsh princes generally paid homage to the Kings of England as their overlords and, especially after Henry II's accession in 1154, were careful not to claim styles and titles which might provoke antagonism from the English crown. Llewellyn ap Griffith's title as Prince of Wales was agreed by Henry III in 1267, but when he became involved in a war with Edward I, he lost territory in 1277 and, in a second series of campaigns, his life, so that by 1283 Llewellyn's Principality of Wales had passed into the possession of the King of England. That was confirmed in the Statute of Wales 1284, which has been called England's first colonial constitution. Certainly, these events spelt the end of an independent Welsh state, but in truth one had never emerged.

The Statute of Wales applied only to the truncated principality, and not to much of what we consider Wales today. The feudal territories of the Lords of the Marches, who in blood were a mixture of Norman, English, and Welsh, were unaffected by it. Owen Glendower was one of these Marcher Lords, who led a rebellion with some success at the beginning of the fifteenth century, but the collapse of the rebellion was followed by a period of repression. In an attempt to impose firmer control over these troublesome territories, a Council of Wales and the Marches was set up in 1471, as an agency of the Privy Council. Henry VIII's centralising tendencies resulted in two Acts of 1536 and 1543, which provided for a union, which was effectively an integration. The country was divided into shires and hundreds, so as to be administered on English lines.[6] The official language was to be English.

---

5 See *Kilbrandon Report* ch 5; Dafydd Jenkins 'Law and Government in Wales before the Act of Union' and Harold Carter 'Local Government and Administration in Wales, 1536–1939' in J A Andrews (ed) *Welsh Studies in Public Law* (1970).

6 One county, Monmouthshire, was grouped with the English counties, so that its Welshness has been a subject for debate since. Under the Local Government Act 1972, it was declared to be in Wales.

English law was to be applied, although administered by a separate system of courts. There was to be representation for Wales in Parliament. The Council survived these changes, and was given a wider authority, over the English border counties too, by the Act of 1543, but it was abolished in 1689. The separate judicial arrangements were ended in 1830, when Welsh circuits were included in the English court system.

In general, a policy of assimilation was pursued from the fifteenth century to the twentieth, with only a few contrary indications. The Principality of Wales was allowed to continue in name, and it became customary for the title of Prince to be conferred upon the heir apparent to the throne. Very occasionally statutes were passed which applied to Wales only, so acknowledging that it was an identifiable country, such as the Welsh Bible and Prayer Book Act of 1563 and the Act for the Better Propagation of the Gospel in Wales 1649. However, a statute more symptomatic and symbolic of the general tendency was the Wales and Berwick Act 1746.[7] In providing that, where the word 'England' was used in an Act of Parliament, this should be taken to include Wales, it put administrative convenience above national sensitivities.[8]

Scotland[9]

There had been four kingdoms in the country we call Scotland between the fifth and the ninth centuries. In the ninth century Kenneth MacAlpin, the King of the Scots in Dalriada, became King of the Picts too. In 1018 one of his successors, Malcolm II, conquered Lothian when he defeated the Angles at the Battle of Carham, and in the same year succeeded to the Kingdom of the Britons in Strathclyde. He and his grandson Duncan I,[10] who followed him, thus became Kings of all Scotland. From that date onwards, Scotland was a recognisable country with, two or three interregnal periods apart, a continuous line of succession to the throne.

Unlike Wales and Ireland, Scotland was able to maintain its independence. The overlordship of Edward I was briefly acknowledged when he was invited to adjudge upon rival claims to the Scottish throne in 1292. But within two years his chosen man, John Balliol, and his counsellors were rebelling. Edward defeated the Scots at Dunbar, but, if he thought that he had subdued them, was soon disabused of that notion by the patriot William

---

7   The town of Berwick on Tweed had for some periods been part of Scotland, before this Act included it in England. However, its football team, Berwick Rangers, is a member of the Scottish League.

8   This was changed by the Welsh Language Act 1967, s 4.

9   See *Kilbrandon Report* ch 4; D M Walker *The Scottish Legal System* (5th edn, 1981); Robert Sutherland 'Aspects of the Scottish Constitution prior to 1707' in John P Grant *Independence and Devolution: The Legal Implications for Scotland* (1976).

10   This is the Duncan of Shakespeare's *Macbeth*, which is good drama but bad history.

Wallace. Wallace routed the English army at Stirling Bridge (1297), was defeated at Falkirk (1298), but continued to harry the English forces until his betrayal and death. Robert Bruce, who was crowned king in 1306, carried on where Wallace left off, and his campaigns culminated in a brilliant victory over Edward II at Bannockburn in 1314. The liberation of the country was complete, and its independence was recognised by Edward III in the Treaty of Northampton (1328).

Thereafter, English kings tried subtler means. Henry VII thought to bring peace to the two kingdoms by the marriage of his daughter Margaret Tudor to Scotland's King James IV in 1503. It was exactly a hundred years before his plan came to successful fruition. In the interim, Henry VIII's armies punished Scottish aggression at Flodden (1513) and punished the Scots with invasions in 1544 and 1545 after their Parliament repudiated a marriage-treaty by which his son Edward would have married Mary, the infant Queen of Scots. It was the conversion of Scotland to Protestantism, which that unhappy Queen had been powerless to prevent, which began to bring Scotland closer to England. Then in 1603, when Elizabeth I died, James VI of Scotland became King James I of England too. He was the son of Mary, Queen of Scots and the great-great-grandson of Henry VII.

What happened in 1603 was merely a personal union of the Crowns. Some trade restrictions between the two countries were abolished, and a common citizenship was introduced. But there was no union of the countries or their laws, and the English Parliament could no more make laws for Scotland than could the Scottish Parliament or Estates legislate for England. In fact, the arrangement was not popular in Scotland, as the seat of royal government had been removed to London. When discontents arose during the reign of Charles I, they were felt all the more keenly in Scotland. The Scottish Presbyterian force of Covenanters took up arms against the King before the English parliamentary forces, and, for the rest of the seventeenth century, events were to follow a broadly similar pattern in both countries. Indeed, when Cromwell's forces had succeeded in both, under the constitutions of the Commonwealth and the Protectorate, there was a single Parliament for Scotland, England and Ireland. But the brief experiment of a united Parliament was premature, and separate Parliaments met again following the Restoration. In 1689 Scotland followed the English Parliament's example and offered its Crown to William and Mary upon terms that established a limited monarchy, governing with Parliament's consent. In the seventeen years that followed, the Scottish Parliament displayed a greater authority than it had ever before possessed.[11]

11 See C S Terry *The Scottish Parliament 1603–1707* (1905).

Great Britain

It was the greater assertiveness of the Scottish Parliament after 1688, and the enhanced importance of both Parliaments as against the Crown, which brought about a more complete union. Commissioners representing the Scottish and English Parliaments had been appointed in 1604 and again in 1670 in order to negotiate on union, but the discussions had proved abortive.

However, after 1688, when it became clearer that the monarchy was to be a limited monarchy, constitutionally responsible to a Parliament, it was not easy to see how the monarch could be responsible at one and the same time to two Parliaments, each pursuing its own policies. These contradictions were exposed, and perhaps exploited, when in the midst of war against Louis XIV the Scottish Parliament passed an Act (the Act anent Peace and War of 1703) to the effect that no future Sovereign should have power to make war or peace without its consent.

By that time, feelings were running high on both sides of the border. There was resentment in Scotland of the Acts passed by the English Parliament which excluded them from trading with the English colonies. The attempt by Scots to found a trading colony of their own, the Darien scheme, had been a disastrous failure, for which the English were also blamed. In England, fearful of a Jacobite restoration, the Parliament had passed in 1700 the Act of Settlement, which declared that after Queen Anne's death the Crown would go to the Hanoverian line. But Scotland had not been consulted, and the Scottish Parliament responded with the Act of Security in 1704. Under its terms, the successor to the Scottish Crown was to be chosen by the Parliament, 'provided always that the same be not successor to the Crown of England', unless in the meantime some conditions such as freedom of trade had been established between the two countries. The English Parliament retaliated with the Aliens Act of 1705, which threatened to prohibit trade and to treat native Scots as aliens. When a Scottish ship was seized on the Thames, and an English ship captured in the Firth of Forth, the two countries seemed to be on the brink of war.

Perhaps it was that which brought them to their senses. The two Parliaments asked the Queen to appoint Commissioners on their behalf, with a view to negotiating a treaty of union.[12] The Commissioners met in Whitehall and reached early agreement on the three main points: an incorporating union, guarantees by the English of complete freedom of trade, and acceptance by the Scots of the descent of the Crown according to the Act of Settlement. With a compromise on Scottish representation in the new Parliament, the endeavour was completed in nine weeks.

12 See A V Dicey and R S Rait *Thoughts on the Union between England and Scotland* (1920); P W J Riley *The Union of England and Scotland* (1978).

Then the treaty had to be put to the two Parliaments. There was fierce debate on it within the walls of the Parliament House in Scotland, and rowdy opposition to it outside them. After three months' struggles, legislation to give effect to the treaty was accepted by 110 votes to 69. The legislation was then accepted without amendment by the English Parliament. In England, the motives were primarily political. Louis XIV was maintaining James Stewart, the legitimist King of England and Scotland, at the French court. Through union, the threat of a Jacobite succession north of the border, with its destabilising consequences, could be averted. In Scotland, the motives for union were principally economic. The trade advantages were held to be sufficient to compensate for the loss of national independence, at least provided that some of the most potent symbols of Scottish nationhood, such as the church and the legal system, could be left intact.

The legislation[13] brought about an 'incorporating' union, in that both countries merged their legislatures and identity. That was naturally seen by the statesmen of the time as the most suitable form of government. A 'federal' solution was briefly mooted by the Scottish Commissioners. What they seem to have had in mind was rather what we should call a confederation, a league of states without a supreme, central legislature, on the model of the Dutch United Provinces. But that would have been open to the same dangers as the status quo. A truly federal solution would have been a different matter, but that was scarcely in their contemplation, as there was not, until the American example in 1787, an obvious model for such a form.

Therefore, what the Acts established was a full political and economic union. As the Crowns had become one in law, the new state could justifiably be called a 'United Kingdom', and it was to be called the United Kingdom of Great Britain.[14] The Parliament of Great Britain was to take the place of the English and the Scottish Parliaments. Yet, the union was not designed to effect a complete assimilation. There were provisions included to ensure that the Scottish court system and the law of Scotland would remain distinct, and that the Presbyterian Church of Scotland would continue to be the established church in that part of the Kingdom. These were institutions more strongly rooted in the national affection than was the Parliament which was disappearing. Moreover, it was at least arguable that some of the provisions of the Acts of Union enjoyed a special status, and were not vulnerable to repeal in the ordinary way.[15]

In the years immediately following 1707, the union was not popular on either side of the border. In Scotland particularly, grievances arose over

13 The Scottish Parliament's was the Union with England Act 1707, and the English Parliament's was the Union with Scotland Act 1706. It is described more fully in ch 4.
14 The name 'Great Britain' is said to have been suggested first by Francis Bacon: *A Briefe Discourse Touching the Happie Union of the Kingdomes of England and Scotland* (1603).
15 The argument is discussed in ch 4.

taxation policies, and over breaches of some of the terms of the union legislation. In 1713, when a proposal for dissolution of the union was introduced in the House of Lords, it was defeated by only four votes. But, by the later eighteenth century, the benefits of the union were more generally appreciated. Home and colonial markets had been opened to Scottish traders as well as English, and the advances brought by the agrarian and industrial revolutions were enabling the people of North and South Britain[16] to take full advantage of them. The conditions of life were happier and more prosperous by far than in the island across the sea.

Ireland[17]

Up to the twelfth century, the land of Ireland had been divided amongst hostile and warring tribes of kinsmen, governed by their chiefs. The High Kingship was merely titular, for even such heroes as Brian Boru, who had led the defence against the Norsemen invaders, had not united the Irish Celts.

An English invasion of the island was carried out during the reign of Henry II, led not by the King, but by Marcher Lords under Richard de Clare, the Earl of Pembroke, nicknamed Strongbow. The conquest was slowly pushed westwards but, lacking proper support and control from the English Crown, was an uncertain affair. That set a pattern for English neglect, which persisted for some three hundred years. The toehold of fully English administration established in the area around Dublin known as the 'pale'[18] continued, although the pale tended to shrink. Outside it, there were parts of the west and north still dominated by Celtic tribalism, and intermediate areas of Anglo-Irish baronies.

However, England's half-hearted presence was sufficient to prevent native projects of national unity from developing. The King of England, as Lord of Ireland, assumed and exercised the power of making laws for the country. Ireland was effectively a colony. An Irish Parliament, whose membership was confined to settlers from England, had developed, but when in the fifteenth century it had pretences to home rule, Henry VII despatched Sir Edward Poynings to coerce it into obedience. By an Act known as Poynings' Law (1494), it accepted that statutes in force in England were law in Ireland too, and agreed to submit any Bills it originated to the King and his Council in England for approval. The title of Lord of Ireland was altered to King of Ireland by Henry VIII in 1541, and his religious policies were imposed there as in England. Under Elizabeth I, the northern province of Ulster was subdued more effectively than before, and Protestants from Scotland and England were then settled on lands forfeited to the Crown. Ireland was

16 Some enthusiastic unionists hoped that the names 'Scotland' and 'England' would fall into disuse, to be replaced by terms such as these.
17 See *Kilbrandon Report* ch 6; Harry Calvert *Constitutional Law in Northern Ireland* (1968) ch 2.
18 This is the origin of the expression 'beyond the pale'.

inevitably the setting for a great deal of religious bitterness and strife during the seventeenth century, but, by the end of it, the ascendancy of the Protestants was ensured, both by the course of events on the mainland and by the defeat of the deposed James II by his successor William of Orange at the Battle of the Boyne in 1690. The attempted suppression of the Catholic religion was energetically pursued by the Irish Parliament during the reigns of William and of Anne.

So, at the beginning of the eighteenth century, the government of Ireland remained firmly under the control of the English or, as it became, the British Crown. A dispute over the respective judicial powers of the Irish House of Lords and the British was settled, in favour of the latter, by an Act of the British Parliament in 1720. The same Declaratory Act confirmed that the British Parliament retained full power to legislate for Ireland.

Later in the century there was a brief flowering of reform. Henry Grattan, a great and broad-minded Irish politician, led a movement for a greater Irish say in their own affairs. In 1782 the Declaratory Act was repealed, and in 1783 the British Parliament passed an Act recognising the right of the people of Ireland to be bound only by laws enacted by the king and the Irish Parliament.[19] 'Grattan's Parliament' thus enjoyed an apparent, but not a real, autonomy. The Parliament was unrepresentative; it was riddled with rotten boroughs and other forms of corruption; and Catholics were still ineligible for membership. There had been no change in the position of the monarchy, and so the executive remained British, and generally able to manipulate it.

United Kingdom of Great Britain and Ireland

Grattan's reform movement, the United Volunteers, had achieved some of its demands. In 1791 a second reform movement, taking note of that success, but also inspired by radical ideas in the spirit of the French Revolution, was formed by Wolfe Tone and Lord Edward Fitzgerald, converts from the English garrison. The Society of United Irishmen had the aims of parliamentary reform and of 'uniting Irishmen of all religions against the unjust influence of Great Britain'. These were no doubt laudable objectives in themselves, but the movement was seen by the government as subversive, especially when its leaders showed willingness to take up arms against the British forces and to accept aid from France. The government's repression of the movement was an exercise in calculated brutality. But their excesses provoked a reaction, while the involvement of France was arousing old antipathies between Protestants and Catholics. In 1798 there was a rebellion against the British government, but it was put down in a pitched battle at Vinegar Hill, and a French force which landed two months later was soon defeated.

To the British government, already alarmed by Napoleon's imperialist

19 Irish Appeals Act 1783.

ambitions, an Ireland which was demonstrating separatist tendencies represented a danger, and a separately functioning Parliament might increase it. Mindful of the success of the 1707 union, the Prime Minister, William Pitt, began to think that a solution to the problems of Ireland might lie in the same direction. He hoped above all to restore order, but also intended to provide for religious toleration, and tacit promises of Catholic emancipation were made in exchange for Irish acceptance of full political union. At first, the Dublin Parliament would not agree to the union proposals. But the government was not to be thwarted, and with some changes in its membership arranged and a good deal of bribery, the Irish Parliament was induced to acquiesce. In 1800, following messages from the Crown, and the passing of resolutions, the two Parliaments both enacted the union legislation.[20]

In these events there were some similarities to the earlier union, but also some differences. Unlike Scotland in 1706, Ireland in 1799 was not an independent state. The Crowns of Great Britain and Ireland were already united, not because the same person had become entitled under the respective laws of two different states, but because of Ireland's status as a lesser kingdom under the English, and later the British, Crown. This difference, as well as the quite different course of history, explains why Irish institutions did not receive similar protection to the Scottish.

The new state which came into being on 1 January 1801 was the United Kingdom of Great Britain and Ireland. The British and Irish Parliaments ceased to exist, and in the new Parliament of the United Kingdom at Westminster, there were to be 100 members for Irish constituencies in the House of Commons, and four Lords Spiritual and 28 representative Lords Temporal from Ireland. There was to be free trade within the enlarged Kingdom. The established church in Ireland, as in England and Wales, was to be Anglican, the United Church of England and Ireland. The language of some of the provisions was such as could indicate that they were intended to have a special constitutional status.[1] The union itself was to last 'for ever', according to the Acts.

DISSOLUTION AND DEVOLUTION

After 1800, therefore, the four nations of the British Isles were united in full political and economic union. Government was carried on in the name of the Sovereign by the ministers of the Crown. The people of the United Kingdom, who shared a common citizenship, were represented by a

20 The Irish Parliament's was the Act of Union (Ireland) 1800, and the British Parliament's was the Union with Ireland Act 1800.
1 See ch 4.

Parliament at Westminster, which was the supreme law-making authority, and there were no legislatures representing parts of the whole. There were some differences in the legal and judicial systems obtaining in different parts of the Kingdom. But, generally, the United Kingdom had the appearance of a highly centralised, unitary state.

Since then, however, there have had to be changes. The nations which united have sometimes regretted their loss, or at least their lack, of autonomy. This has led to a partial dissolution of the union, and to some measures of devolution. Besides, there have been intermittent demands for more devolution, or sometimes federalism or independence. These were of sufficient strength in 1969 to cause a Royal Commission to be appointed in order to examine these constitutional relationships. These changes, and the prospects for others, have to be borne in mind, when considering the state of the union.

Dissolution

The union between Great Britain and Ireland was never a happy one. Pitt failed to persuade George III of the necessity of Catholic emancipation. The King, contending that it would be a breach of his coronation oath, refused to co-operate, and the Prime Minister resigned over the issue in 1801. For another 28 years, Roman Catholics were prohibited from sitting in Parliament.[2] That delay was probably fatal to whatever slim chances of success the arrangement had.

In fact, the failure of the union was probably inevitable. The deep-rooted hatred of the Irish people for English rule was not extinguished by the union, which they could scarcely see as anything other than a perpetuation of it. There were other grievances as well as the religious disabilities, such as the land question. Most of Ireland, apart from a section west of the Shannon, had been settled on Protestant British landlords as a reward for their military services. There was resentment of these alien, often absentee, landlords, who did little to improve the lot of their tenants and workers. Then in 1845 and 1846 the Irish potato crop, on which more than half the population depended almost entirely, was ruined by blight. About a million people died as a result, and the perception of the government's response as inadequate and uncaring added an additional bitterness to nationalist demands.

The Liberal Prime Minister Gladstone did try to rectify some of these injustices. In 1869 the Irish Church Act disestablished the Protestant church in Ireland. By Acts of 1870 and (during his second administration) 1881, some provision was made for rent regulation and security of tenure.[3]

However it was too little, too late. From the 1870s, for fifty years, the

---

2 Until the passing of the Roman Catholic Relief Act 1829.
3 Landlord and Tenant (Ireland) Act 1870; Land Law (Ireland) Act 1881.

'Irish question' was to dominate British domestic politics.[4] A Home Rule League had been formed in 1870, with the aim of securing internal self-government through constitutional means. By 1874, the movement had 59 supporters at Westminster. By 1886, this had increased to 89. Under the skilful leadership of Parnell, their obstructionist tactics were impeding the government in the House of Commons. Finally Mr Gladstone, and some other Liberals, became converted to the necessity of a home rule measure, and with the return of a Liberal government in 1886, such a Bill was introduced. But his late conversion had split the party. The Bill was defeated in the Commons and caused the downfall of his government. A second Home Rule Bill was introduced during Gladstone's fourth ministry in 1893, but was defeated in the House of Lords.

[margin note: Home Rule league]

The political ramifications of these events were considerable. In Britain, the Liberal party had been split irrevocably, if not quite fatally, and the Conservatives had become associated with the unionist position. In Ireland, there were strong currents of nationalism, especially in the south. However, the unionist faction, mainly consisting of Protestants in the northern counties, who feared that they would be an oppressed minority in a Catholic-dominated Ireland, had closed ranks more tightly than ever. This meant, although British opinion was slow to appreciate it, that there was not one 'Irish question', but two.

A crisis was inevitable when the issue revived. The Liberal government in 1912, whose majority depended upon the Irish Nationalists with 82 seats, introduced a third Irish Home Rule Bill. The House of Lords rejected it, but under the Parliament Act 1911 procedure, it could despite that become law after two years. The King was pressed by the Bill's opponents to withhold the royal assent and, if necessary, dismiss the government. Volunteer forces were formed to fight against the provisions in the north of Ireland, and for them in the south. Civil war seemed entirely possible, when the possibility was suddenly displaced by a greater quarrel. On the day when the Bill, delayed by two years, received the royal assent as the Government of Ireland Act 1914, the Suspensory Act 1914 prevented its coming into effect, in view of the outbreak of war.

The 1914 Act provided for an internally self-governing, undivided Ireland, with its own Parliament subject to the overriding paramountcy of the United Kingdom Parliament. But it never took effect. It was superseded by the Government of Ireland Act 1920, which resorted to partition, providing as it did for two separate, subordinate Parliaments, one for six counties of the north,[5] and one for the remainder of Ireland.

4 See Vernon Bogdanor *Devolution* (1979) ch 2.
5 Historically, Ulster comprised nine northern counties, but the name is often used to refer to the six counties, an artificial province designed by the Ulster Unionists as an area in which their majority would be secure.

However, the 1920 Act was not destined to come fully into operation itself. In 1916, there had been a minor rebellion in Dublin, known as the Easter rising. The summary execution of 14 of its leaders did more than anything else to mobilise support for Sinn Fein, a revolutionary independence movement founded eight years before. In the general election of 1918, the Sinn Fein party won all but four of the 128 seats outside the six counties. The elected representatives did not take their places at Westminster, but instead established the first Dail or Irish Parliament and set up a Provisional Government of the Irish Free State. The British government's attempted repression encountered resistance from the Irish Republican Army, and for two years there was a bitter and disgraceful civil war.

Sinn Fein had simply ignored the 1920 Act, and eventually the British government wearied of the conflict and met to negotiate with the leaders of the Provisional Government. In December 1921, the 'Articles of Agreement for a Treaty' which were concluded provided for the establishment of an Irish Free State, with Dominion status within the British Commonwealth. There was an option for the six northern counties to opt out, using the institutions provided for them under the 1920 Act, which they did at the earliest opportunity. In 1922 the United Kingdom Parliament enacted legislation to give effect to the agreed arrangements.[6] From that date onwards (and arguably earlier, from an Irish perspective), the Irish Free State was effectively an independent state. After Mr Eamonn De Valera became its Prime Minister, it took further steps to dissociate itself from the United Kingdom, and in 1948 left the Commonwealth.

The union, intended to last 'for ever', had been dissolved. Northern Ireland remained part of the state which became the United Kingdom of Great Britain and Northern Ireland. Northern Ireland had also, rather by accident, become the setting for an experiment in devolved government.

Devolution

As was noticed earlier, in a federal state there are central and regional legislatures, with each having some areas of exclusive competence, and neither being subordinate to the other. As a definition which rests on legal form, that is not too difficult to apply. However, in political practice, the distinction between federal and non-federal (or unitary) states becomes one of degree. The United Kingdom is not classified as federal, but the legislative and executive powers exercised in Northern Ireland under the provisions of the Government of Ireland Act 1920 afforded that province a greater degree of autonomy than is enjoyed by the provinces in some nominally federal states.

The governmental arrangements brought about under that legislation, or

---

6 Irish Free State (Agreement) Act 1922, Irish Free State (Constitution) Act 1922, Irish Free State (Consequential Provisions) Act 1922.

the process by which it was done, would normally be termed 'devolution', and so it might be said that the advanced forms of devolution approximate to federalism. 'Devolution' is an inexact term. The Royal Commission on the Constitution, which reported in 1973, defined it as 'the delegation of central government powers without the relinquishment of sovereignty'.[7] That description, apart from its exclusion of federalism, was advisedly imprecise. There are different kinds of powers which might be distributed, and different ways of distributing them.[8] It is a type of devolution when powers with regard to a particular function or service are distributed, as for example to the National Coal Board or to the Arts Council. But, in this country recently, devolution has normally been used to describe a distribution of powers on a geographical basis to the different parts of the United Kingdom.

In that context, the Royal Commission went on to describe and discuss three models of devolution.[9] Under 'legislative devolution', the power to legislate, to settle policies and to administer might be devolved on elected assemblies in respect of specified subjects, with the central legislature retaining ultimate power to legislate on all matters. Under 'executive devolution', directly elected regional assemblies might be responsible for devising regional policies and administering regional affairs, in accordance with laws and general policies made by the legislature and central government. A third type, 'administrative devolution',[10] would involve the central government, without the creation of new regional institutions of government, arranging for aspects of its work to be conducted on a regional framework or in a regional setting.

These were only working definitions, but they suffice to show something of the variety of possible arrangements. If we were to adopt them, we could say that there was legislative devolution to Northern Ireland after 1920, which ended in 1972, and there have been measures of administrative devolution to Scotland and Wales, and to Northern Ireland since 1972. Perhaps we shall leave some of the terminological difficulties behind, if we simply describe what these developments entailed. Then, with that background, the Royal Commission's proposals and the subsequent history can be considered.

Legislative devolution

The Government of Ireland Act 1920 was the post-war Lloyd George government's attempt to solve the Irish question. It was conceived in the hope that the partition would be temporary, with the north and south

7   *Kilbrandon Report* para 543.
8   See Harry Calvert 'Devolution in Perspective' in Harry Calvert (ed) *Devolution* (1975).
9   *Kilbrandon Report* para 546 and chs 17, 18 and 21.
10 The phrase has been criticised as a misnomer: see A W Bradley 'Devolution of Government in Britain – Some Scottish Aspects' in Harry Calvert (ed) *Devolution* (1975).

reuniting as a self-governing part of the United Kingdom. However, as we saw, the Act was rejected as irrelevant in the south. By that stage in events, it was virtually forced on the north, for which, if it did not choose to be part of the Irish Free State, it was the only means on offer by which the union with Great Britain could be maintained. Ironically, the British government was insisting on home rule for that part of Ireland where the unionist majority had so strenuously opposed the Irish home rule movement, with the encouragement of many British politicians. So, it has fairly been said that the constitutional arrangement for Ulster was one

> which nobody had ever wanted; which was doing a radically different job from that for which it had been intended; and which was more apt, in form and substance, for an adolescent British territory trying out its wings prior to flying away rather than for an advanced metropolitan territory in which the prevailing political forces were centripetal.[11]

Under the provisions which came into effect, Northern Ireland had its own legislature and executive.[12] The Parliament was composed of two Houses, one directly and one indirectly elected, which sat at Stormont, near Belfast. The royal assent to its legislation was given by a Governor, representing the Crown. The executive was headed by a Prime Minister and Cabinet, responsible to the Parliament, and aided by the province's civil service. The Parliament was given power 'to make laws for the peace, order and good government' of Northern Ireland. However, certain subjects such as foreign relations, defence, nationality and external trade, were 'excepted' or 'reserved' as being exclusively within the United Kingdom Parliament's competence, and legislation in excess of the Northern Ireland Parliament's competence could be held void by the courts.[13]

The United Kingdom Parliament, in which the Northern Ireland representation was reduced,[14] retained supreme and plenary powers to legislate in respect of Northern Ireland. The government's powers were not restricted either. But, in practice, the Northern Ireland Parliament and government were able to enjoy a substantial degree of autonomy in domestic affairs after 1922, as Westminster and Whitehall became disinclined to intervene, except upon request.

The devolution of administrative and executive powers was generally regarded as advantageous in the province. Ministers and their officials were closer to each other and to local authorities, local business and the public,

---

11 Harry Calvert 'Northern Ireland – What Went Wrong?' in J A Andrews (ed) *Welsh Studies in Public Law* (1970) p 88.

12 The leading commentary is Harry Calvert *Constitutional Law in Northern Ireland* (1968).

13 See eg *R (Hume) v Londonderry Justices* [1972] NI 91.

14 From 17 to 13 seats. It became 12 in 1948, when the university constituencies were abolished, and remained at that until increased to 17 by the House of Commons (Redistribution of Seats) Act 1979.

and the quality and speed of administration seemed to benefit accordingly.
The devolved legislative powers were used in a variety of ways. Sometimes,
Westminster legislation was enacted by Stormont in more or less identical
terms. Sometimes, Northern Ireland would follow more slowly and be able
to improve on the corresponding British legislation in the light of some
years' experience of it. Sometimes, as with education in schools, a different
approach to the mainland's was preferred, and in a few matters such as
abortion and homosexuality, Westminster's reforms were deliberately
rejected. Sometimes, as on the parole of offenders and the protection of
wildlife, initiatives in Northern Ireland were later followed at Westminster.

In one important respect, it must be said, the province's autonomy was
eroded. The financial provision made in the 1920 Act shortly proved
inadequate, as did some subsequent adjustments. In consequence, finance
had to be regularly renegotiated with the United Kingdom Treasury, and
the corollary of this was a measure of central control. For example, under an
agreed parity principle, the people of Northern Ireland were to be entitled to
the same benefits as people in Great Britain. But this effectively meant that
legislation on social security had to be identical. Thus, in areas involving
substantial expenditure, the freedom to differ became rather illusory.

The Stormont system of legislative devolution came to an end in 1972. In
1968, the grievances of the Catholic minority spilled out into civil
disturbances. The British government abandoned its policy of *laisser faire*,
and intervened in order to hasten reforms and keep order. However,
terrorism and strife worsened, and in 1972 the Northern Ireland Parliament
and executive ceased to exist when direct rule over the province was
resumed.[15]

What went wrong? The answer seems to lie rather in the inpropitious
circumstances surrounding the experiment, rather than in devolution itself.
The divisions between the province's million Protestants, overwhelmingly
unionist in persuasion, and half million Catholics, mostly opposed to the
union, were not ended or mended, but were aggravated by the border with
the south. The community problem was reflected in political life. Ulster's
political history was such that every election there had the appearance of a
constitutional referendum. The mainland political parties did not emerge as
important actors on the scene, and every election for Stormont from 1921
onwards resulted in victory for the Unionist party. The Catholic minority
had no prospect of attaining political power in Ulster through the ballot box,
and had legitimate complaints of discrimination. The beneficial effects of
devolution were less obvious to the minority than some of its unintended
side-effects.

It is interesting to note that a system of proportional representation was
originally employed for elections to the Northern Ireland Parliament.

15 Northern Ireland (Temporary Provisions) Act 1972.

However, in 1929, Sir James Craig's Northern Ireland Government succeeded in having this changed,[16] having already achieved the same for local government elections. In retrospect, it is probably easy to conclude that the constitutional arrangements made for Northern Ireland were flawed in several respects, and that the financial implications of devolution were not properly thought out. But the Royal Commission was surely right to conclude that 'the fact that devolved government did not provide a lasting solution to a political and community problem which has persisted for several centuries, and is peculiar to Ireland, in no way implies a defect in the concept of devolution which was there applied'.[17]

Administrative devolution

After the political union in 1707, there was no reason of principle why special arrangements should be made for Scotland in the matter of executive government. However, in 1885, just when the Irish home rule issue had become pressing, it was decided to differentiate the government of Scottish affairs more clearly. A Scottish Office was created, whose minister, the Secretary for Scotland, was to be responsible for law and order, education, and a few other matters. Since 1892, wartime apart, the relevant minister has had a seat in the Cabinet, and in 1926 the office became that of a Secretary of State, with the full status and powers that implies. The principal base of the Scottish Office became St Andrew's House in Edinburgh in 1939.

Over the years, the functions and importance of the Scottish Office have gradually increased.[18] On the recommendations of the Gilmour Committee on Scottish Administration in 1937,[19] a number of statutory boards with particular functions were abolished, and their powers vested in the Secretary of State. Some more functions were allocated to the minister as a result of recommendations made by the Royal Commission on Scottish Affairs which reported in 1954,[20] and others from time to time. Today the minister, with the Scottish Office organised in five departments, is responsible for agriculture and fisheries, the arts, crofting, education (including higher education), electricity, the environment, the fire service, forestry, health, housing, industrial assistance, some legal matters,[1] local government, police, prisons, roads, rural and urban development, social work, sport, transport (excluding road freight and rail), tourism and town planning, as

---

16 House of Commons (Method of Voting and Redistribution of Seats) Act (NI) 1929.
17 *Kilbrandon Report* para 548.
18 See David Milne *The Scottish Office* (1957); A G Donaldson 'Administrative and Legislative Devolution' in John P Grant (ed) *Independence and Devolution: The Legal Implications for Scotland* (1976).
19 Report of the Committee on Scottish Administration (Cmd 5563).
20 Report of the Royal Commission on Scottish Affairs (Cmd 9212).
1 Other functions in connection with the Scottish legal system fall to the Lord Advocate's Department and the Crown Office, for which the Lord Advocate is responsible.

well as some minor departments and some public corporations operating in Scotland.

Even that, however, is only part of the story. There are some other matters for which the Scottish Secretary is jointly responsible with an 'English' colleague. More importantly, it is recognised that in a more general sense he is 'Scotland's Minister' and has an interest in all matters affecting Scotland. As the Gilmour Committee put it, 'there is a wide and undefined area in which he is expected to be the mouthpiece of Scottish opinion in the Cabinet and elsewhere'.[2]

Scotland has probably profited from the Secretary of State system. Certainly, it has enjoyed a higher expenditure per head of population than other parts of Great Britain, and it is reasonable to attribute this in part to the advantage of having a spokesman at Cabinet level. Administration has probably been better by reason of the Scottish Office civil servants being closer to the country's concerns and its people. Policies formulated in areas such as social work services and education have often compared favourably with the English equivalents. Policies which apply to the whole kingdom may be applied with Scottish conditions in mind. The scope for administrative initiative has increased since 1978, when a change in the method of allocating public funds enabled the Secretary of State to have greater freedom of action within the total budget.

At the same time, it is difficult to form an accurate picture. The collective responsibility of governments, and the secrecy surrounding British government, prevent us from knowing when, for example, the Secretary of State has been instrumental in winning something for Scotland or when he has been frustrated or defeated by a Cabinet majority. It can be argued that, although the system has eased access to local officials, it has only produced marginal gains.[3]

Besides, there is a weakness at the heart of the system, in that the administrative powers are not properly matched by a political base. The Northern Ireland executive under the Stormont system was drawn from, and responsible to, the Northern Ireland Parliament. But the Secretary of State is a United Kingdom government minister. When the majority in the House of Commons and the majority of Scottish MPs come from different parties (as they have between 1959 and 1964, between 1970 and 1974, and since 1979), then, as has been observed, 'a Conservative Secretary of State's claim to be Scotland's Minister becomes rather transparent when his government persists with policies affecting Scottish domestic administration which would be rejected by Scotland's elected representatives'.[4] There are problems

---

2 Cmd 5563, para 37.
3 John P Mackintosh 'Regional Administration: Has it Worked in Scotland?' (1964) 42 Public Administration 253.
4 A W Bradley 'Devolution of Government in Britain – Some Scottish Aspects' in Harry Calvert (ed) *Devolution* (1975) p 100.

of accountability as well as of legitimacy. The Scottish Office's appearance on the parliamentary question rota once every three weeks is hardly commensurate with the scale of their activities. The establishment of a Select Committee on Scottish Affairs as part of the specialised select committee system instituted in 1979 has improved matters, but it is still obvious that the House of Commons has insufficient time for scrutiny of Scottish administration.

Incidentally, with regard to Scottish legislation, the position is rather better. Since, in accordance with intentions in 1707, the Scottish legal system has remained distinct, Parliament has of necessity to enact frequently measures for Scotland. In practice, there are some special legislative arrangements to ensure that Scottish business is largely in the hands of Scottish MPs, and does not overly trouble other MPs. Two Scottish Standing Committees are designed for the Committee Stage of Bills which will apply only to Scotland. The Second Reading debates and Report Stages of such Bills may be referred to the Scottish Grand Committee, which is composed of all the Scottish MPs with some others so as to reflect the party balance, and which also has a few additional sittings for debate and discussion of Scottish affairs. Of course, on politically contentious subjects, the government of the day will wish to get its own way, and that is allowed for in the composition of these committees, but there is otherwise some willingness to leave Scottish legislative business to Scottish members.

Enough has been said to explain something of the Secretary of State system of administrative devolution. It has been justified usually upon the ground of efficiency. A senior civil servant, discussing the transfer of functions to the Scottish Office, explained to the Royal Commission on the Constitution that 'on every occasion within government the question is looked at whether a particular development would be better handled as a Great Britain matter or as separate Scottish and English ones without any preconceived notions about the decision to be reached'.[5] Nevertheless, the devolution of administrative powers, the historical separateness of some of Scotland's institutions, and the special arrangements for Scottish legislation, have combined to satisfy some of the demands for separate treatment.

Administrative devolution on a similar pattern has occurred with regard to Wales, if rather more slowly. The process began with the creation of some regional sub-departments or offices. A Welsh Department of the Board of Education was established in 1907. The Health Insurance Commission of 1913 was followed by the formation of the Welsh Board of Health in 1919 and, in the same year, a Welsh Department of the Ministry of Agriculture. For twenty years or so after that, there was little more decentralisation, but in wartime and in the post-war years, the number of departments with

5 Sir Douglas Haddow, the Permanent Under-Secretary at the Scottish Office: Royal Commission on the Constitution 1967–1973, Minutes of Evidence II (Scotland) p 8.

administrative units in Wales increased, although more as a result of changes in departmental organisation than in furtherance of any policy of dispersing power.

In 1948, the government established the Council for Wales and Monmouthshire. Conceived of as a body for consultation and advice, the Council began to operate as a pressure group for greater devolution to Wales. There had been attempts to secure a minister for Wales from the later nineteenth century onwards, and finally in 1951 an office of Minister for Welsh Affairs was created. Even then, however, the office was one held in common with another ministerial appointment, at first that of Home Secretary, and later that of Minister for Housing and Local Government.

The creation of a separate Department of State, with a Secretary of State for Wales, occurred only in 1964, in fulfilment of an election promise, on Labour's return to power. The Welsh Office, which is based principally in Cardiff, has been given additional responsibilities at various times since its inception. The Secretary of State's functions today extend to agriculture, the arts, education (excluding universities), the environment, health, housing, local government, roads, rural and urban development, social work, tourism, town and country planning, and a few other areas. In two or three of these, his responsibilities are less extensive than the Scottish Secretary's, and he is not responsible for police, prisons, or legal matters.

In addition, the minister has some joint responsibilities with other ministers. Also, with regard to the United Kingdom ministries, many of which continue to have departments in Wales, he has, as the Prime Minister put it when the office of Secretary of State was first instituted, 'oversight within Wales of the execution of national policy', enabling him 'to express the voice of Wales'.[6]

As with the Secretary of State system in Scotland, it is reasonable to conclude that this arrangement has brought benefits to Wales. For example, according to a former junior minister at the Welsh Office, the Secretary of State was instrumental in the transfer of the Royal Mint to Wales and, during the Labour administration from 1966 to 1970, was successful in opposing the building of a reservoir in the Dulas valley, and the closure of the railway line from Llanelli to Shrewsbury.[7] A seat in the Cabinet brings influence. Of course, there must be other, undisclosed occasions when the Secretary of State's influence does not prevail against the more heavyweight members of the government, but the members of the Royal Commission on the Constitution had no doubt that the Welsh Office had been 'effective in securing additional benefits for . . . Wales'.[8] It may be presumed that there

6 702 HC Official Report (5th series) col 627.
7 Edward Rowlands 'The Politics of Regional Administration: The Establishment of the Welsh Office' (1972) 50 Public Administration 333.
8 *Kilbrandon Report* para 385.

are also gains in allowing administration to be better geared to local
conditions and rendering administrators more accessible.

As with Scotland, too, there is the same flawed political base. Back in
1955, a future Secretary of State for Wales, Mr Cledwyn Hughes, had
commented that he did not 'like the idea of bureaucracy being projected into
the Principality without simultaneous answerability to an elected body
there'.[9] But, that is just what happened. There has at least been a Select
Committee on Welsh Affairs since 1979, but, that apart, no doubt because
so few Bills apply exclusively to Wales, the special arrangements made for
Welsh affairs in Parliament are very limited. Moreover, since the Labour
Party invariably wins the most parliamentary seats in Wales, whenever
another party forms the government, the Secretary of State for Wales has
different policies from the majority of Welsh MPs.

On examination, the Secretary of State system turns out to be a clumsier
compromise than is perhaps generally recognised. However, it has merits.
Scotland and Wales, in acknowledgement of their nationhood, receive some
special consideration which is denied to regions of England, and benefit as a
result. The United Kingdom remains a unified entity, with one Parliament
and one government. Of course, that may not be what everyone wants. In the
1960s and 1970s, many seemed to want something different.

The Royal Commission and its aftermath

The Scottish National Party (SNP) and Plaid Cymru, the Welsh Nationalist
Party, were for long perceived as being on the lunatic fringe of British
politics. But, in the 1960s, these parties began to attract substantial
support, as economic grievances were felt more keenly, and dissatisfaction
increased with what were seen as remote and uncaring governments in
London. By-election victories for Mr Gwynfor Evans at Carmarthen in 1966
and Mrs Winifred Ewing at Hamilton in 1967 heralded spectacular advances
over the following ten years. By 1974, the SNP had become the second
largest party in Scotland, and in the October General Election won 11 seats.
Plaid Cymru, with three seats and 10.7% of the vote in Wales at that
election, seemed to have a narrower appeal. But, in both countries, the major
parties had been put on guard.

The two main parties were diffident, and rather defensive, in their
response to the threat posed by these nationalistic stirrings. The
Conservatives, in opposition, set up in 1968 a committee chaired by Sir Alec
Douglas-Home, which reported two years later in favour of the creation of an
elected Scottish Convention, which would deal with the Scottish Bills
initiated at Westminster, but would not have its own legislative powers.[10]

---

9 537 HC Official Report (5th series) col 2449.
10 Scotland's Government (1970).

The Labour Party, with more seats to lose in Scotland and Wales, was more concerned. However, in 1969 Mr Wilson's government resorted to a favourite method of sidelining troublesome issues: it set up a Royal Commission.

The Royal Commission on the Constitution had unusually wide terms of reference. It was asked 'to examine the present functions of the central legislature and government in relation to the several countries, nations and regions of the United Kingdom; and to consider . . . whether any changes are desirable . . . in the present constitutional and economic relationships . . .'. Under that remit, almost any constitutional question could have been considered, but the majority of the Commissioners largely confined themselves to issues geographical in character.

The Commission was singularly ill-starred in its fortunes, and its Report did not appear until October 1973, four-and-a-half years after its appointment.[11] Its first chairman, Lord Crowther, and another member died, and no fewer than three others resigned during its deliberations. Lord Kilbrandon, who took over the chairmanship, was unable to deliver anything approaching unanimity. Two members, Lord Crowther-Hunt and Professor Alan Peacock, regarded their disagreement with the others as so fundamental that they did not sign the majority Report, and wrote a substantial Memorandum of Dissent.[12] The eleven others signed, but were far from agreed on the course to follow.

On two points there was agreement. Independence for Scotland and Wales, or 'separatism', as it was perhaps more pejoratively described, was flatly rejected, because 'the political and economic unity of the United Kingdom should be preserved',[13] and 'the vast majority of people simply do not want it to happen'.[14] Surprisingly, there was an equally quick dismissal of federalism. It was considered that 'the United Kingdom is not an appropriate place for federalism',[15] and noted that 'there was very little demand for federalism in Scotland and Wales, and practically none at all in England'.[16] It was asserted that 'only within the general ambit of one supreme elected authority is it likely that there will emerge the degree of unity, co-operation and flexibility which common sense suggests is desirable'.[17]

Beyond that, the Commissioners found it difficult to agree. It was

---

11 See T C Daintith 'The Kilbrandon Report: Some Comments' and D G T Williams 'Wales and Legislative Devolution' in Harry Calvert (ed) *Devolution* (1975).
12 Royal Commission on the Constitution 1969–1973, vol 2, Memorandum of Dissent (Cmnd 5460–1).
13 *Kilbrandon Report* para 431 and see generally chs 11 and 12.
14 *Kilbrandon Report* para 497.
15 Ibid, para 539.
16 Ibid, para 498.
17 Ibid, para 539.

accepted that the administrative devolution of the Secretary of State system had been carried about as far, or at least almost as far, as it could reasonably go, and that something different was needed. Eight of the Commissioners supported a scheme of legislative devolution to Scotland, with a directly elected assembly having power to legislate on subjects largely co-extensive with those for which the Scottish Office had responsibility previously, and an executive drawn from the assembly. Six of the eight also favoured legislative devolution to Wales, but the other two recommended only an elected Advisory Council for Wales, with scrutinising and advisory functions. A ninth member would have given Scotland and Wales a Council of that sort, with the Scottish one having additional functions in relation to Parliament's Scottish Bills.

Two Commissioners signing the majority Report favoured a scheme of executive devolution, under which directly elected assemblies, not only in Scotland and Wales, but also in eight regions of England, would have responsibility for subordinate policy-making and administration within the framework set by Parliament and the central government. Eight other Commissioners would have established regional councils, with lesser responsibilities, for those eight regions.

Lord Crowther-Hunt and Professor Peacock also advocated a form of executive devolution. They believed that the causes of dissatisfaction with government were common to all parts of Great Britain, and in their view the claims of Scotland and Wales to nationhood did not 'entitle the people in Scotland and Wales to be better governed or to have more participation in their own affairs than is offered to the people of Yorkshire or Lancashire'.[18] Their concern for equality of rights led them to propose in their Memorandum of Dissent a scheme of 'intermediate level government', allowing for seven directly elected assemblies and governments, for Scotland, Wales, and five regions of England. They also interpreted the terms of reference more widely, and made a number of other suggestions, including reform of the House of Lords, a new system of specialised parliamentary committees, and the creation of a strengthened Prime Minister's Department.

Perhaps the most conspicuous characteristic of the Commissioners' work was their diversity of views, and it was small wonder that it was initially received with disappointment and some bafflement. Besides, the Heath government which was in office at the time of publication had more pressing problems, and within four months there was a General Election, in February 1974.

In that election the Scottish Nationalists gained six seats, and Plaid Cymru two. When Mr Wilson took office at the head of a minority Labour government, it was announced in the Queen's Speech that proposals on

18 Memorandum of Dissent (Cmnd 5460–1) para 129.

devolution would be brought forward in the light of consideration of the Report. Labour continued in government with a tiny majority after the October 1974 election, and, after a succession of White Papers, the Scotland and Wales Bill 1976 was introduced. The Bill was unpopular with MPs and poorly drafted. It was progressing so slowly that the government proposed a guillotine motion to limit the time spent on it. That was defeated, and the government was ignominiously obliged to shelve its intended enactment.

In 1977, the government made a parliamentary pact with the Liberals, and tried again. This time there were two Bills, which after protracted proceedings in both Houses became law as the Scotland Act 1978 and the Wales Act 1978. These would have given directly elected asssemblies to Scotland and Wales, the Scottish one having legislative powers, and the Welsh only executive powers. However, amongst the amendments which the government had been forced to accept, was one which proved fatal. The government planned to hold referendums in Scotland and Wales, so as to give electors an opportunity to say whether they wanted the proposals to come into effect. Mr George Cunningham, a backbench Labour opponent of devolution, successfully proposed that if less than 40% of those *entitled to vote* were to vote 'Yes', then Orders for the repeal of the legislation would have to be laid before Parliament.[19] The polls took place on 1 March 1979. In Scotland, a majority of those voting were in favour, for 32.9% of the electorate said 'Yes' and 30.8% said 'No', but that was not enough to satisfy the Cunningham provision. In Wales, only 11.9% of the electorate voted 'Yes'. There had been insufficient enthusiasm for further devolution, or at least for the degree of it on offer.

Prospects

The Royal Commission had been deliberating while Northern Ireland's troubles had worsened, and did not choose to make any recommendations with regard to the government of that part of the United Kingdom.[20]

Where there had been legislative devolution, after the imposition of direct rule in 1972, Northern Ireland was given a species of administrative devolution. The office of Secretary of State for Northern Ireland was created, and that minister effectively assumed the functions of the Government of Northern Ireland.[1] At the time of writing, that is still the position. The minister carries out executive functions, and legislation for the province is made by Her Majesty in Council, which for practical purposes is the government.[2]

In the years in between, a number of constitutional experiments have been

19 Scotland Act 1978, s 85; Wales Act 1978, s 80.
20 *Kilbrandon Report* chs 28 and 30.
 1 Northern Ireland (Temporary Provisions) Act 1972.
 2 Northern Ireland Act 1974, as amended.

tried. One of the more significant, an attempt to restore devolved powers to an Assembly and Executive operating on a power-sharing basis,[3] collapsed in 1974 after less than a year. In 1982 there were new Assembly elections, and by legislation in that year[4] it was reconstituted as part of a plan for so-called 'rolling devolution'. It was hoped that the Assembly, given deliberative and consultative functions at first, could propose legislative and executive powers for itself when this would 'command widespread acceptance throughout the community'. However, the refusal of some of the elected representatives to participate in the Assembly's work frustrated these hopes.

In 1985, the 'Anglo-Irish Agreement' or 'Hillsborough Agreement' was announced, in which the United Kingdom and Republic of Ireland governments agreed inter alia on consultation over Northern Ireland affairs and closer co-operation in security arrangements. This provoked anger amongst the Protestant community, and in these conditions the resumption of legislative devolution to Northern Ireland seems remote. Nevertheless, it remains the policy of all the main political parties to devolve powers again to the province, as soon as circumstances permit. The Labour Party, in its manifesto for the General Election in 1983, said that its aim was 'to establish an agreed, devolved administration', but also expressed its belief 'that Ireland should by peaceful means and on the basis of consent be united'.[5]

As for Scotland and Wales, following the referendum results, there was a natural loss of enthusiasm for devolution amongst politicians and people. The subject had claimed a lion's share of parliamentary time; it had engendered jealousies between different parts of the Kingdom, and caused divisions within as well as between the parties; and, in the end, it had come to nothing. Legislation on the subject was not likely to be attempted again for some time.

In any event, the matter had led indirectly to a change of government. For, when the SNP withdrew its support from the Labour government in 1979, the government was defeated on a vote of confidence, and obliged to resign. Since then, the governments led by Mrs Thatcher have not shown much interest in legislative devolution for Scotland and Wales. That is only to be expected, for the reason of principle that the party's philosophy is historically opposed to it, and perhaps for the practical reason that the party enjoys its strongest support in England.

However, true to the traditions of the Liberal Party, which has consistently favoured either federalism or legislative devolution, the Liberal–SDP Alliance in the 1980s was advocating a Scottish Parliament, with Welsh and English regional assemblies being phased in afterwards.[6]

3 Northern Ireland Assembly Act 1973, Northern Ireland Constitution Act 1973.
4 Northern Ireland Act 1982.
5 *The New Hope for Britain* (1983).
6 *Working Together for Britain* (1983).

After some vacillation, the Labour Party also seemed to be supporting further devolution, and in 1986 Mr Kinnock committed himself to the introduction of an elected assembly for Scotland in the early stages of a Labour government. Reports of the death of devolution have almost certainly been exaggerated.

3   Constitutional conventions

Many matters which are of interest to students of the British constitution are not matters of law at all. Nobody need be surprised by this, other than a few lawyers who naively imagine that law is what makes the world go round.

Most of us know better. One man who certainly did was A V Dicey, who wrote more often of politics than of law, and devoted much of his life to a political cause, opposing Home Rule for Ireland.[1] His *Introduction to the Study of the Law of the Constitution*, first published in 1885, is still the Authorised Version for students of constitutional law. In it he advised them to pay due heed to 'those constitutional understandings which necessarily engross the attention of historians or of statesmen'.[2] These non-legal matters he referred to as 'the conventions of the constitution', and in this country that has become the accepted term for them, or for at least the most important of them.

A few illustrations are in order. Consider the giving of the royal assent to legislation. As a matter of law, Acts of Parliament are made by the Queen-in-Parliament (or King-in-Parliament, as the case may be), and the Sovereign may either give or withhold assent when presented with a Bill passed by the two Houses. However, that assent has not been withheld since 1708, when Queen Anne declined to approve a Scottish Militia Bill, and on that occasion she was acting upon the advice of her ministers. It is safe to assume that monarchs have not invariably wished for Bills to become law, but have felt obliged to assent regardless of their own feelings; so we may say that there is a non-legal rule, or convention, to that effect.

That convention would fall within Dicey's formulation of the scope of conventional rules, which was that 'they are all, or at any rate most of them, rules for determining the mode in which the discretionary powers of the Crown . . . ought to be exercised'.[3] Certainly it is in that area that the operation of conventions is most conspicuous. Notably, the power of executive government has effectively been transferred from the Sovereign to ministers responsible to Parliament. This has been achieved largely by the growth of conventional limitations on the royal prerogative, for in law the

1 See Richard A Cosgrove *The Rule of Law: Albert Venn Dicey, Victorian Jurist* (1980).
2 *Law of the Constitution* (10th edn, 1961), p 417.
3 Ibid, p 422.

power of executive government is still vested in the Crown, so that our whole system of Cabinet government rests upon rules and practices which have no legal force.

Thus, to take a particular example from that sphere, the office of Prime Minister is a creation of convention.[4] There is no law which requires that a Prime Minister be appointed, or specifies how one is to be chosen. According to law, the Queen may appoint or dismiss ministers at her pleasure. However, it is well established by convention that the Sovereign must invite one person to be the chief minister and head a government. Sir Robert Walpole, who normally presided at meetings of the Cabinet from 1721 to 1742, is generally regarded as having been the first Prime Minister, although the office acquired its present form only with the strengthening of the party system and of representative government in the nineteenth century. Every Prime Minister since Walpole has been a member of either the House of Commons or the House of Lords, and we may say that there is another well established convention to that effect, which has ensured that governments have been responsible to Parliament. No peer has been Prime Minister since the resignation of Lord Salisbury in 1902,[5] and arguably the Sovereign is nowadays obliged to choose from the ranks of the Commons. That view is supported by the choice of Stanley Baldwin rather than Lord Curzon in 1923, and by the Earl of Home's renunciation of his peerage in 1963 in order to assume the leadership of the Conservative Party when Mr Macmillan, the Prime Minister, fell ill. By convention, the Sovereign should choose as Prime Minister that person who appears best able to command the support of a stable majority in the House of Commons. Where one party has an absolute majority of seats, and has chosen a leader under whatever party procedures are in force, the Sovereign is probably left without any personal discretion in the matter. The Queen had to exercise a discretion upon the resignations of Sir Winston Churchill in 1955, Sir Anthony Eden in 1957, and Mr Macmillan in 1963, but in 1965 the Conservative Party adopted a new procedure for leadership elections, in order to obviate this.

As another example of the operation of conventions, we might focus on something which has been mentioned, ministerial responsibility. That concept involves a group of conventional rules regulating the relationship of government to Parliament. A brief explanation of ministerial responsibility is 'that Ministers are responsible for the general conduct of government, including the exercise of many powers legally vested in the Monarch; and ultimately, through Parliament and parties, to the electorate'.[6] One part of

---

4 However, the existence of the office is recognised in a few statutes, eg Chequers Estate Act 1917.

5 Excepting the Earl of Home for four days in 1963, before the disclaimer of his peerage took effect.

6 G Marshall and G C Moodie *Some Problems of the Constitution* (5th edn, 1971), p 37.

the doctrine is the individual responsibility of ministers, which makes them politically answerable in Parliament in respect of matters lying within their fields of responsibility. They are responsible not only for their personal acts but for the conduct of officials in their departments, and the principle is said to be that a minister takes the praise for the successes of his department and the blame for its failures. The sanction for misconduct of government is that a minister is exposed to criticism or censure in the House, and, if the misconduct is serious, may be expected to resign.

There have been a few instances of resignation on these grounds in recent years. In 1982 the Foreign Secretary, Lord Carrington, resigned following Argentina's invasion of the Falkland Islands, when there was criticism of the government's failure to anticipate the crisis, for which his department was responsible. In 1986 Mr Leon Brittan, the Secretary of State for Trade and Industry, became the second minister to resign following differences within the government over the difficulties of the helicopter makers Westland. Mr Michael Heseltine resigned because of his objections to the handling of the issue. Mr Brittan later felt obliged to resign, when he was held responsible for the leaking of advice confidentially provided by the Solicitor General.

Some of the most important conventions, therefore, are, as Dicey said, concerned with 'the discretionary powers of the Crown' and how they should be exercised. But it is not only in connection with executive government and legislature-executive relations that we find such rules and practices in operation. They may be found in other spheres of constitutional activity too; for example, in relations between the Houses of Parliament and in the workings of each House, in the legislative process, in judicial administration and judicial behaviour, in the Civil Service, in local government, and in the relations with other members of the Commonwealth. Some will be encountered in later chapters.

Enough has been said to show something of the nature and the importance of non-legal rules in the constitution. When rules such as these become relevant, the actors in their constitutional settings are expected to behave in a particular way. If they do not, they are exposed to the charge of acting 'unconstitutionally'. That term, as it is used in this country, generally involves the allegation that a non-legal constitutional principle or rule of behaviour has been infringed, whereas in countries with a written constitution, an unconstitutional act is one in breach of the terms of that document. So it may be said that 'for the Americans, anything unconstitutional is illegal, however right or necessary it may seem; for the British, anything unconstitutional is wrong, however legal it may be'.[7]

From even a few illustrations, it may be seen that any description of the British constitution which omitted to refer to the non-legal rules and facts of government would be incomplete. Indeed, the same may be said of any other

7 J R Mallory *The Structure of Canadian Government* (1971) p 2.

country. For example, in the United States,[8] according to the Constitution (Article II and Amendment XII), the President is indirectly elected, by representatives of the states in electoral colleges. In practice, however, the President is elected by popular vote, and the members of the electoral colleges are obliged to cast their votes accordingly. In Australia,[9] the Constitution provides for the appointment of the Governor-General by the Sovereign of the United Kingdom, but by convention the Sovereign is obliged to act on the advice of the Australian Prime Minister. If that is a straightforward convention, many others are not. The Australian Governor-General in 1975, Sir John Kerr, dismissed Mr Gough Whitlam's government, on the ground that, as it had been refused supply by the Senate, it did not command the confidence of the Parliament, and should have resigned or advised dissolution. However, his action was controversial, to say the least, and in that constitutional crisis there was ample scope for debating whether the Prime Minister and the Governor-General respectively had acted consistently with, or contrary to, what conventions required.

It is simply a natural process for other rules and practices to develop alongside the laws of the constitution. As Sir Ivor Jennings put it:

> The laws provide only a framework; those who put the laws into operation give the framework a meaning and fill in the interstices. Those who take decisions create precedents which others tend to follow, and when they have been followed long enough they acquire the sanctity and the respectability of age. They not only are followed but they have to be followed.[10]

There were rules and practices of this sort at earlier periods of British constitutional history, just as there are today.[11]

For that matter, it should not be thought that the phenomenon is peculiar to the constitutional field. One has to look beyond rules of law in order to obtain a complete picture of the operation of the constitution. But, in just the same way, if we were to give a complete account of the control of criminal behaviour, we should have to go beyond the rules of criminal law and would want to consider police practices and interpretation, prosecutorial discretion, penal policy, and so on. It is interesting that, in criminal and other fields, commentators have not found it difficult to distinguish between what is law and what is not. There is no good reason why particular difficulty should be experienced in the constitutional field, and Dicey saw none, but

8 See H W Horwill *The Usages of the American Constitution* (1925); Charles A Miller *The Supreme Court and the Use of History* (1969).
9 See G Evans (ed) *Labour and the Constitution. 1972–1975* (1977); L J M Cooray *Conventions, the Australian Constitution and the Future* (1979).
10 *Cabinet Government* (3rd edn, 1959), p 2.
11 See eg W S Holdsworth *A History of English Law* vol 6; G H L Le May *The Victorian Constitution* (1979).

some later constitutional lawyers have presented it as a problematic or ill-conceived exercise.

LAWS AND CONVENTIONS DISTINGUISHED

Dicey was an admirer of John Austin, who, in his writings on jurisprudence, was concerned to map out the province of legal studies by defining 'law strictly so called' and differentiating it from international law and non-legal rules.

In the same way, Dicey was concerned to demarcate the lawyer's special preserve in the study of the constitution. He was fully aware that the rules of the constitution comprised different classes;[12] he conceded that some conventions and practices were as important as laws,[13] and observed that 'a lawyer cannot master even the legal side of the constitution without paying some attention to the nature of those constitutional understandings',[14] and he devoted Part III of *Law of the Constitution* to the discussion of conventions. It is quite unjust, although regrettably not unknown, for Dicey to be accused of promoting a narrowly legal approach to study. But he did say that the lawyer's proper function was the exposition of legal rules, whereas 'with conventions or understandings he has no direct concern'.[15]

However, his distinguishing between laws and conventions has been criticised. Unless the distinction is abandoned, according to one modern writer, 'it is impossible to present constitutional law as a coherent subject or relate it in a meaningful way to the functions it has to fulfil or the social and political context in which it has to operate'.[16] To this it may be answered that if in fact laws and conventions are different in kind, then an accurate and meaningful picture of the constitution will only be obtained if the distinction *is* made. If the distinction is blurred, analysis of the constitution is less complete, which cannot be to the benefit of lawyers or political scientists.

But are laws and conventions different in kind? Sir Ivor Jennings doubted it. His conclusion, that there was 'no distinction of substance or nature'[17] between the two, may astonish us. But Jennings liked to shock students out of complacency and little of Dicey's work (which had enjoyed an unchallenged position for fifty years) escaped his critical eye. Often Jennings

---

12 Dicey pp 23–30.
13 Ibid, p 27.
14 Ibid, p 417.
15 Ibid, p 30.
16 Geoffrey Wilson *Cases and Materials on Constitutional and Administrative Law* (1st edn, 1966), p v.
17 *The Law and the Constitution* (5th edn, 1959), p 117.

went too far, in his enthusiasm to knock down the Diceyan edifice, but his criticisms are invariably stimulating.

One technique employed by Jennings was to point to certain kinds of similarity or interaction between laws and conventions. Both sorts of rule rested upon general acquiescence, he suggested, and the major conventions were as firmly fixed and might be stated with almost as much accuracy as principles of common law.[18] The late Professor J D B Mitchell built up further arguments of this sort:

> Conventions cannot be regarded as less important than rules of law. Often the legal rule is the less important. In relation to subject-matter the two types of rule overlap: in form they are often not clearly distinguishable . . . very many conventions are capable of being expressed with the precision of a rule of law, or of being incorporated into law. Precedent is as operative in the formation of convention as it is in that of law. It cannot be said that a rule of law is necessarily more certain than is a convention. It may therefore be asked whether it is right to distinguish law from convention . . .[19]

These statements appear to be of varying acceptability, but are apt to mislead. For example, there seems to be only a small number of conventions in this country whose existence and precise formulation are generally agreed, so that the statements about precision and certainty are very questionable.[20] Sometimes there seems to be force in the assertion that the convention is more important than the law, but it is hard to see how their relative importance can be measured. In the United States, in the 1930s, the convention that a President should not stand for re-election more than once might have been considered more important than the law, which imposed no restriction. But what would we say in retrospect, knowing that in 1940 Franklin D Roosevelt was elected for a third term, and in 1944 for a fourth?

Besides, the important point is that none of Mitchell's propositions, even if accurate, would entail the conclusion which he went on to derive from them, that any effort to distinguish laws and conventions is bound to fail. This is readily illustrated by applying some of the comparisons to other bodies of rules:

> *Rules of morality* cannot be regarded as less important than rules of law . . . in relation to subject-matter the two types of rules overlap . . . Very many *religious edicts* are capable of being expressed with the precision of a rule of law, or of being incorporated into law. Precedent is as operative in the formation of *etiquette* as it is in that of law. It cannot be said that a rule of law is necessarily more certain than is a *rule of cricket*.

---

18 *Ibid*, pp 72, 117.

19 *Constitutional Law* (2nd edn, 1968), p 34.

20 This is discussed further below. See also S A de Smith *The New Commonwealth and its Constitutions* (1964) pp 82–90; Geoffrey Marshall *Constitutional Theory* (1971) ch 1.

These new statements are just as accurate as the others, to put it no higher. We cannot draw from them the conclusion that laws are *indistinguishable* from rules of morality, religion, etiquette or cricket. In fact, the explanation of why conventions, and all these, reveal some similarities to laws is simple: they are all rules operating in society, and certain similarities, especially of form, are only to be expected.

A ginger ale, however, is not the same as a whisky, merely because each is amber in colour and liquid in form. The critical question is whether laws may be *differentiated* from conventions. Dicey, who was in no doubt that they might be, also suggested a means:

> The rules which make up constitutional law, as the term is used in England, include two sets of principles or maxims of a totally distinct character.
>
> The one set of rules are in the strictest sense 'laws', since they are rules which (whether written or unwritten, whether enacted by statute or derived from the mass of custom, tradition, or judge-made maxims known as the common law) are enforced by the courts; these rules constitute 'constitutional law' in the proper sense of that term, and may for the sake of distinction be called collectively 'the law of the constitution'.
>
> The other set of rules consist of conventions, understandings, habits or practices which, though they may regulate the conduct of . . . officials, are not in reality laws at all since they are not enforced by the courts. This portion of constitutional law may, for the sake of distinction, be termed the 'conventions of the constitution', or constitutional morality.[1]

Thus Dicey provides a simple working test by which laws and conventions may be distinguished: laws are enforced by courts, conventions are not. However, critics such as Jennings and others following him have doubted whether all laws may be said to be court-enforced, and have questioned whether the courts are as unable or unwilling to deal with conventions as Dicey implied. Their arguments require examination.

Laws and enforcement

Are all laws court-enforced? To begin with, I think that what Dicey meant would have been better expressed as 'court-enforceable'. He would not, presumably, have denied legal status to, for example, a recently enacted statute which had yet to come before the courts. It is susceptibility to court enforcement that he was surely thinking of, and so we might allow him a small amendment to that effect.

But there are some categories of legal rules which might appear not to be enforced or enforceable at all, or not enforced in courts. The difficulty here is that it rather depends what one means by a 'court', and what one means by

---

1 Dicey p 23.

'enforced'. Dicey did not say what he meant by either term, although neither is easily defined.

So, it might be said that the law and custom of Parliament, concerning matters such as parliamentary privileges and procedure, is enforced and applied within the Houses of Parliament, not in the courts.[2] In answer to that, the rejoinder might be that the Houses comprise the High Court of Parliament, so that the law in question is court enforced. That is technically correct, but perhaps not a very satisfactory answer, for Dicey was almost certainly thinking of the *ordinary* courts of law. However, the ordinary courts do play a role in relation to these rules. They adjudicate upon their existence and extent, as in *Stockdale v Hansard*.[3] They enforce them on suitable occasions, as in *Bradlaugh v Gossett*[4] or *Stourton v Stourton*.[5] It is a better answer, I think, to point to this: the laws of Parliament may be principally applied within Parliament, but they are treated as law by the ordinary courts when occasion arises.

Rather similar arguments apply in respect of those areas of modern public law which Sir Ivor Jennings and Professor Goodhart observed were generally enforced by administrative tribunals or authorities, and not by courts.[6] On a functional view, bodies given a specialised jurisdiction by statute may readily be viewed as enforcing the law in the way that Dicey envisaged, and, had he adverted to the point, it would not have caused him much difficulty. Besides, there is again the role of ordinary courts alongside. The decisions on law of tribunals and other authorities are in most cases appealable to the ordinary courts, and in any event subject to review under the High Court's supervisory jurisdiction.

So, with one or two refinements, Dicey could have met these criticisms. What about the claims that some laws are not susceptible to enforcement at all? Sir Ivor Jennings said that most of constitutional law related to the government, and law could not be enforced at all against the government.[7] That argument sounds strange indeed today, when courts quite frequently hold that ministers have acted ultra vires, and when we have almost forty years' experience of the Crown Proceedings Act 1947. What Jennings did was to confuse enforcement with execution.

What many have regarded as a more serious challenge to Dicey's test is posed by areas of law where the jurisdiction of the courts is apparently excluded, perhaps by an explicit provision that a duty may not be enforced in court proceedings or by the provision of an administrative channel as the

2 Jennings *The Law and the Constitution* (5th edn, 1959), pp 115–117.

3 (1839) 9 Ad & El 1.

4 (1884) 12 QBD 271.

5 [1963] P 302, [1963] 1 All ER 606.

6 Jennings *The Law and the Constitution* (5th edn, 1959) pp 103–105; A L Goodhart (1959) 75 LQR 112.

7 *The Law and the Constitution* (5th edn, 1959) pp 131–132.

exclusive remedy. Sometimes there are provisions of written constitutions in other countries which are expressed as non-justiciable, or are interpreted as such.[8]

Take the example that Jennings gives, a statutory duty upon local authorities to provide adequate sewers and sewage disposal works, which was, under a statute, only remediable by means of complaint to the Minister of Housing and Local Government. When proceedings were brought in court, the House of Lords held that Parliament had deprived the courts of jurisdiction in that area, and that the complaint to the Ministry was the sole means of redress (*Pasmore v Oswaldtwistle UDC*).[9] The error that Jennings makes is in using the case as evidence that the law concerned was not court-enforced. The case is the best evidence possible that the law *was* court-enforced. Certainly a statutory duty was not judicially enforced, but that was precisely because the *law* said it should not be, and the courts obeyed the law and put it into effect. Other such examples may be explained in the same way. When provisions are unsusceptible to judicial enforcement, the correct analysis is either that no obligation is involved, as with some of the ideological pronouncements found in written constitutions, or is that an imperfect obligation has been created. None of this should surprise us. A legal system does not consist only of obligations for breach of which there is redress.

The difficulty felt is partly linguistic. 'Enforcement' may not be the most appropriate way to describe a court's role in respect of some of its functions or with regard to some kinds of law. Perhaps Dicey's test might be better reformulated in terms of a court's capacity to deal with rules, and its roles in respect of them. Take another frequently cited example, the provisions in the Parliament Act 1911 concerning Money Bills and the effects of the Speaker's certificate. According to a leading textbook, these are 'non-justiciable'.[10] But there is no reason to doubt that the Parliament Act 1911, enacted by the Lords and Commons with the assent of the King, is law. There is no reason to doubt that its provisions, including the ones mentioned, fall to be interpreted by the courts, if the occasion arises. When once the intention of the legislature, as expressed in the statute, is ascertained, there can be no doubt that the duty of the court is to give that effect. These matters may be only clumsily captured in the word 'enforced', but there is no difficulty in concluding that recognition of the legal quality of rules causes courts to react in characteristic and *distinctive* ways.

---

8 Eg the Directive Principles of State Policy in the Constitution of India, which Art 37 declares not enforceable by any court.

9 [1898] AC 387, HL.

10 S A de Smith *Constitutional and Administrative Law* (5th edn by Harry Street and Rodney Brazier, 1985) p 44.

Conventions in the courts

Conversely, when rules are not legal rules, courts of law will not respond to them in the same way, if indeed they respond to them at all. That is what Dicey meant when he said that the 'conventions, understandings, habits or practices . . . are not in reality laws at all since they are not enforced by the courts'.[11]

The evidence of case law seems to vindicate Dicey's view. On the rare occasions when courts have been asked to enforce conventional rules, they have refused. In *Adegbenro v Akintola*, the Privy Council, discussing the argument that a Regional Governor in Nigeria had acted contrary to convention in reaching a decision, held that these were 'not legal restrictions which a court of law . . . can . . . make it his legal duty to observe'.[12] A few years later, the Privy Council took the same line when it was suggested to them that it was contrary to constitutional convention for Parliament to legislate for Southern Rhodesia except with the colony's consent:

> It is often said that it would be unconstitutional for the United Kingdom Parliament to do certain things, meaning that the moral, political and other reasons against doing them are so strong that most people would regard it as highly improper if Parliament did these things . . . Their Lordships in declaring the law are not concerned with these matters.[13]

The Crossman Diaries case[14] provides another helpful illustration of the court's attitudes. Richard Crossman, a minister in the Labour governments from 1964 to 1970, had kept a political diary with a view to its publication. After his death in 1974, his literary executors went ahead with plans to publish the diaries in book form and also in extracts in *The Sunday Times*. The Attorney General of the day decided to try to prevent publication. But on what basis might he obtain an injunction? The convention of collective ministerial responsibility involved, amongst other aspects, an obligation to preserve Cabinet secrecy, as the Attorney General was at pains to demonstrate. However, Lord Widgery CJ accepted that 'a true convention [is] . . . an obligation founded in conscience only',[15] so that, he said, the Attorney General would have to fail if the convention were all that he could rely on. In fact the Attorney General had another strand to his argument, which was derived from the developing case law on confidence. In appropriate circumstances, the courts will act to prevent a breach of confidence, when information has been imparted under an obligation of confidentiality. Lord Widgery held that Cabinet proceedings could be

11 Dicey p 24.
12 [1963] AC 614 at 630, PC.
13 *Madzimbamuto v Lardner-Burke* [1969] 1 AC 645 at 723.
14 *A-G v Jonathan Cape Ltd* [1976] QB 752, [1975] 3 All ER 484.
15 [1976] QB 752 at 765.

protected by the law of confidence, but only for a limited period, and the publication of the diaries ten years after the events had taken place was unobjectionable.

These cases suggest that courts will not provide redress simply because there has been a breach of a conventional rule. There are no instances which controvert that proposition, and it was specifically approved by the Supreme Court of Canada, when it had occasion to consider a convention concerning the circumstances in which the United Kingdom Parliament would legislate for Canada.[16] Further, the majority had this to say:

> In contradistinction to the laws of the constitution, [the conventional rules] are not enforced by the courts . . . [T]o enforce them would mean to administer some formal sanction when they are breached. But the legal system from which they are distinct does not contemplate formal sanctions for their breach.[17]

For the sake of completeness, a couple of reservations must be made, although they do not affect the cardinal test of enforcement. First, it has to be acknowledged that, in appropriate circumstances, the courts in some jurisdictions may treat conventions as justiciable and may be prepared to give an opinion as to their existence and extent. The cases in the Canadian provincial courts and the Supreme Court,[18] which arose out of their Prime Minister's determination to introduce a new constitution, notwithstanding some provincial dissent, are good examples of that. However, the relevant statutes there were drawn in wide terms which permitted non-legal matters to be placed before the courts, whereas English courts would be unlikely to assume a similar jurisdiction. Besides, it would be quite wrong to infer that the Canadian courts treated a convention as law or in the same way as law. The existence of the particular convention was a question of *evidence*, to be established on the basis of historical events and expert factual submissions. In their effect, the decisions were essentially advisory. They did not change the character of the obligation, and although the Federal Government was persuaded to alter its proposals, it is not difficult to conceive of circumstances in which a government in a stronger position than Mr Trudeau's might rest on the strict legality of its proposed action and disregard a court's opinion, for on a matter of this sort a court's opinion need not be regarded as uniquely authoritative, or indeed as authoritative at all.

The second reservation is that, in a number of cases, the courts have taken notice of constitutional conventions, and sometimes used them, for example, to aid in the interpretation of statutes or Commonwealth

16 *Re Resolution to Amend the Constitution* [1981] 1 SCR 753 at 783. See O Hood Phillips 'Constitutional Conventions in the Supreme Court of Canada' (1982) 98 LQR 194.

17 *Re Resolution to Amend the Constitution*, n 16 above, at 880.

18 In a second case, the Supreme Court further clarified the convention: *Re A-G of Quebec and A-G of Canada* (1982) 140 DLR (3d) 385.

constitutions.[19] In the Crossman Diaries case, the convention of collective responsibility was recognised and discussed, and, it might be said, employed in order to show that the quality of confidentiality attached. But there is nothing significant in this. The existence of facts or of mental states is commonly relevant to the existence or extent of legal rights and duties.

It is true that at one point in his book Dicey referred to conventions as 'customs, practices, maxims or precepts which are not enforced or recognised by the courts'.[20] But the sense of the passage and other indications suggest that he meant that conventions were not *recognised as law* by courts, rather than not recognised as existing, which would have been to attribute to judges an improbable state of ignorance.[1]

It would appear, on the whole, that Dicey's test may be defended. There are some marginal cases of laws which do not fit happily within the language of 'courts' or 'enforced', but these hardly strike at the root of Dicey's distinction. But, if his test is defensible and useful, that is not to say that it offers the best or the only way by which laws and conventions may be differentiated. There are other contrasts which could be drawn for that purpose.

For example, instead of being concerned with the practical effects of breaches of rules, we might consider how the rules come into being. In a legal system, a certain number of sources are recognised as law-constitutive. So there are rules specifying what counts as law (or what, by implication, does not). In England, for instance, the courts accept as law only legislation made or authorised by Parliament and the body of rules evolved by the courts called common law. There are formal signs, such as the words of enactment used for Acts of Parliament, denoting that rules have passed a test for being laws. The point here is not merely to reiterate that conventions fall outside the categories recognised as law (which it has been the object of this section so far to show). Rather, what is significant is that conventions do not share the same qualities as laws. They do not come from a 'certain' number of sources: their origins are amorphous, and there are any number of dramatis personae whose behaviour may later be taken as evidence for the existence of a constitutional rule or practice. No body has the function of deciding whether conventions exist. There is no formal sign of their entitlement to be so regarded, and there are no agreed rules for deciding.

These points are related to a larger contrast which may be drawn. Rules of law form parts of a system. Included in the system are rules about the rules: there are provisions about entry to, and exit from, the system, and procedures for the determination and application of the rules. We cannot

---

19 See eg *Liversidge v Anderson* [1942] AC 206, [1941] 3 All ER 338; *Ibralebbe v R* [1964] AC 900, [1964] 1 All ER 251, PC.

20 Dicey p 417.

1 I have argued this more fully in 'Laws and Conventions Distinguished' (1975) 91 LQR 218.

conceive of a single legal rule, in isolation from a system. However, conventions do not form a system. There is no unifying feature which they possess, and no apparatus of secondary rules. They merely evolve in isolation from each other.

Here, incidentally, lies the answer to Jennings's specious argument that laws and conventions are the same because both 'rest essentially upon general acquiescence'.[2] That is quite misleading. Conventions rest entirely on acquiescence, but individually. If a supposed convention is not accepted as binding by those to whom it would apply, then there could not be said to be a convention, and this is a test on which each must be separately assessed. Laws do not depend upon acquiescence. Individual laws may be unpopular or widely disobeyed, but it does not mean that they are not laws. No doubt the system as a whole must possess some measure of de facto effectiveness for us to recognise it as valid, although it might be stretching language to describe the citizens of any country occupied by enemy forces, or the black majority in the Republic of South Africa, as 'acquiescing' in the laws which govern them. In any event, it is obvious that the comparison is inapt.

When 'acquiescence' is properly analysed, another means of distinguishing emerges. Breaches of a legal rule do not bring into question the existence or validity of the rule; for example, however frequently motorists might exceed the speed limits, the road traffic laws are no less laws for that. However, according to a generally accepted definition, conventions are supposed to be 'rules of political practice which are regarded as binding by those to whom they apply'.[3] If such rules are broken, it becomes appropriate to ask whether they are still 'regarded as binding', and if they are broken often, surely one cannot say that any obligatory rule exists? In other words, the breach of a convention carries a destructive effect, which is absent with laws. The reason for this is that 'feeling obliged' is a necessary condition for the existence of a convention, whereas it is neither a necessary nor a sufficient condition for the existence of laws.

Here these points have been little more than sketched, but it is perhaps sufficient to demonstrate that Dicey's test by no means exhausts the differences which enable us to distinguish conventions and laws. The question, since it concerns the nature of law, is really jurisprudential. It would be instructive to consider, keeping this question in mind, what legal philosophers such as Hans Kelsen, Alf Ross and H L A Hart have to say about what characterises law. The student who does so will find that other distinguishing features are uncovered.[4]

2 *The Law and the Constitution* (5th edn, 1959) p 117.
3 O Hood Phillips *Constitutional and Administrative Law* (6th edn by O Hood Phillips and Paul Jackson, 1978) p 104.
4 As students of legal theory will realise, the preceding discussion has been influenced by H L A Hart's *The Concept of Law* (1961).

This, after all, should scarcely surprise us. It is not much more than a truism to say that non-legal rules are different from legal rules, and it would not be necessary to say it, had not writers such as Jennings and Mitchell mischievously suggested otherwise.

The superficial attractions of their argument lay in the fact that there are some similarities and connections between the rules that are conventions and the rules that are laws, as there are between laws and some other sorts of rules. Indeed, we may go further. It is perfectly possible that in some countries political rules or constitutional practices might be recognised as a species of customary law, *if* the rules about what constitutes law are to that effect. But they should then be laws, and not non-legal rules. In this country as well as in others, what was formerly a non-legal rule might by legislation become a legal rule, as is explained below. But, in the absence of either of those processes, the rules are non-legal, and while they are non-legal, it is quite wrong to deny or neglect the differences this entails.

CONVENTIONS BECOMING LAW

What has been demonstrated is that conventions, while conventions, are to be distinguished from laws. This does not mean, of course, that what was formerly a convention may not later become a matter of law. A comparison may be made with the relationship of law to morality. One should distinguish moral rules from legal rules, but this does not mean that there are no connections or similarities between the two or that moral rules may not become legal rules. The same applies to conventions, which the legal historian Maitland actually called 'rules of constitutional morality'.[5]

A distinction must, however, be drawn between the two categories of legal rules found in English law. Parliament, the representative law-making body, is unrestricted and may legislate on any matter and in any terms which it chooses. By contrast, the courts are law-interpreting bodies; while their role includes the declaration and the development of the common law as well as the interpretation of legislation, it does not extend to the creation of laws de novo. The law may be developed on the back of earlier law, even if there are only threads, but it cannot be spun out of nothing. Therefore, at least in England and in countries with similar legal systems, non-legal rules may only be converted into legal rules by the process of legislation.

It is important to emphasise this, because at first sight it might appear otherwise. The common law includes an element of law which is customary in origin, and in constitutional law this element is prominent, because it includes rules concerning the legislature known as the law and custom of Parliament and, in the royal prerogatives, rules concerning the Crown. As

5 F W Maitland *The Constitutional History of England* (1908) p 398.

we have seen, many of the non-legal rules of the constitution are also customary in origin, in so far as they evolve from past practice into obligations, and they are established, often, by pointing to a chain of precedents. Superficially the processes may look similar, and it is tempting to infer that if customary rules have been recognised by courts as law, then constitutional conventions might become laws in this manner or, as it is sometimes put, crystallise into laws.

Some writers on constitutional matters have jumped to that conclusion. 'Convention can become law also by judicial recognition', stated Sir Kenneth Wheare.[6] Sir Ivor Jennings put forward a sociological hypothesis that 'the citizen from Hoxton' had a mixture of motives for obedience to law, amongst which the enforcement process was not paramount. He concluded that, 'The constitution of a country, whatever it be, rests upon acquiescence. Constitutional laws and constitutional conventions are in substance the same . . .'[7]

Because of the differences already noticed in the nature of law and convention, views such as these are fundamentally flawed. To say that laws and conventions are 'in substance the same' neither corresponds to reality nor conduces to proper analysis. It is not even likely that Jennings's hypothetical Everyman would make the same mistake. The American judge and jurist Oliver Wendell Holmes was probably closer to the truth with his observation that what mattered to the ordinary man was 'what the courts will do in fact'.[8] The blurring together of different categories of rules, when matters of practical and social importance turn upon the differences, is indefensible.

Besides, students of the English legal system will know that the comparison between custom as a source of law and conventions is fallacious. The origins of the common law as applied in Norman courts lay in customs. But customs are 'no longer regarded as a separate source of law since they have either become part of the common law or been incorporated in statute'.[9] In other words, the role of custom as a source is only historic. The constitutional conventions operative today are mostly products of nineteenth and twentieth century thinking, and cannot be candidates for recognition as customary law. So far it has been argued on grounds of principle that conventions may not become laws by way of judicial recognition. There is nothing in case law to suggest otherwise. The courts have not treated conventions as a species of law which lies at the bottom of the hierarchy; as we have seen, they have treated them as not being law. In two cases recently, courts have had to consider whether a convention had become law. In *Re*

---

6 K C Wheare *Modern Constitutions* (2nd edn, 1966), p 135.

7 *The Law and the Constitution* (5th edn, 1959), p 346.

8 O W Holmes 'The Path of the Law', in Max Lerner (ed) *The Mind and Faith of Justice Holmes* (1943) p 71.

9 R J Walker and M G Walker *The English Legal System* (6th edn by R J Walker, 1985) p 64.

Resolution to Amend the Constitution, it was suggested that a convention might have crystallised into a matter of law. The majority (numbering seven out of nine as to this) of the Canadian Supreme Court noted that no instance of such a happening had been produced, and observed:

> The attempted assimilation of the growth of a convention to the growth of the common law is misconceived. The latter is the product of judicial effort, based on justiciable issues which have attained legal formulation and are subject to modification and even reversal by the courts which gave them birth . . . No such parental role is played by the courts with respect to conventions.[10]

Again, in the case of *Manuel v A-G*[11] which reached the English courts, it was suggested that a convention (that the United Kingdom Parliament should not legislate for Canada except with its consent)[12] might by formal recognition or by long acceptance have crystallised into a law. The submission was given short shrift. Slade LJ, giving the judgment of the Court of Appeal, observed that they were being asked to vary or supplement the terms of the law 'by reference to some supposed convention', and they found the argument 'quite unsustainable in the courts of this country'.[13]

On grounds of principle, and on the evidence of these cases, it may safely be concluded that conventions are unable to make the leap from being rules of political obligation to being part of the common law.

Nothing, however, prevents a convention from being enacted as legislation. In some countries the process is familiar, for at some stage a deliberate attempt may have been made to formulate the conventions and include them in a Constitution. This has been done in many Commonwealth countries, and in those some of the conventions may be derived from British constitutional practice. Sometimes, indeed, their incorporation has been achieved by providing that certain powers were exercisable as nearly as possible in accordance with the constitutional conventions applicable to the exercise of similar powers in the United Kingdom.[14] Sometimes the conventions which it was desired to include have been spelt out. In either event, conventions of the British constitution have been incorporated in legislation, although it is not this country's legislation.

There are few instances of conventions becoming law in this country. Section 4 of the Statute of Westminster 1931 provided that no future Act of the United Kingdom Parliament was to extend, or be deemed to extend, to a Dominion as part of its law unless the request and consent of that Dominion

10 [1981] 1 SCR 753 at 775.
11 [1983] 1 Ch 77, [1982] 3 All ER 822, CA.
12 The convention was recognised in the Preamble to the Statute of Westminster, but words in a Preamble yield to an express provision in the body of an Act, and section 4 dealt with the matter rather differently, as explained below.
13 [1983] 1 Ch 77 at 107, [1982] 3 All ER 822 at 831.
14 See S A de Smith *The New Commonwealth and its Constitutions* (1964) ch 3.

were expressly declared in that Act.[15] This did not precisely reproduce the convention which was operating (by which real consent was a precondition), but may be said to incorporate it in a modified form. The enactment of the Parliament Act 1911 is interesting in this respect. In 1909, when the House of Lords refused to accept the Liberal government's Budget proposals, it was thought to have acted in breach of convention, there being a general convention that it should not obstruct the policy of an elected government with a majority in the House of Commons, and a more specific convention that matters of national finance were for the Commons to decide. The consequences, two general elections later, were that the House of Lords lost the power to prevent the enactment of a measure certified by the Speaker as a 'Money Bill', being given only the power to delay its enactment for a month; and a procedure was created by which other Bills could become law, notwithstanding the dissent of the House of Lords, after a longer suspensory period.

The enactment of those provisions illustrates that sometimes the consequence of a breach of convention is a change in the law. Another illustration of this may be found in the United States where, as we saw, the convention that Presidents should not seek re-election after a second term was disregarded by President Roosevelt in 1940, when he stood successfully for a third time. Later the Twenty-Second Amendment to the Constitution was passed, forbidding re-election for a third term.

When there is a legislative sequel to the breach of a convention, it does not invariably consist in the enactment of the convention as such. That might be a reasonable way of describing the Twenty-Second Amendment. Section 4 of the Statute of Westminster was rather a refinement or modification of the convention. The Parliament Act provisions were designed so as to achieve the same end as the convention. They did not replicate it, however, but provided means for avoiding or circumventing future breaches of it.

The general effect of legislating on such matters is the strengthening of the rule. Some writers have underplayed the importance of this. Jennings regarded as a difference between laws and conventions 'of some, though not fundamental, importance'[16] that 'it is the recognised duty of certain persons, especially of judges, to consider whether acts are legally valid and to take such steps as they can to see that the law is obeyed'.[17] But consider the effect of the Twenty-Second Amendment. It is to make further breaches impossible, which is surely an important difference. Sometimes, as in the Parliament Act example, the legislation does not guarantee obedience, but provides a formal remedy for disobedience. Even this is sufficient to show the relative weakness of conventional rules. If such a lesson were needed, it

15 Whether this involves a limitation on Parliament is discussed in ch 5.
16 *The Law and the Constitution* (5th edn, 1959), p 132.
17 *Cabinet Government* (3rd edn, 1959) p 3.

was brought home to that government in 1909, and appropriate action was taken.

Is there an argument here for codifying or putting into legislative form all the conventions of the constitution? As well as strengthening the obligations, this would lead to greater certainty, as they would have to be precisely formulated, and there could be authoritative judicial interpretation of them when necessary. However, conventions are adaptable to changing ideas and circumstances, and have been a useful means of evolving the constitution, so there would be losses as well as gains. As de Smith succinctly put it, 'codification would purchase certainty at the expense of flexibility'.[18] There are some conventions, too, for which judicial enforcement seems inappropriate. Ministerial responsibility, for example, concerns essentially political relationships, and judicial enforcement of the rules would completely alter their character.

An ad hoc approach is preferable. In so far as constitutional goals depend on mere conventions, it would be imprudent to overrate their strength (and this is another reason why it is dangerous to blur the distinction with laws).[19] Therefore, when it is important to secure obedience to rules and there is a danger of disobedience, the case for enactment as law is strong. Often, it is not.

Two final points may be made. First, we should realise that, by making conventions into law, we would not avoid disputes about what the rules ought to be, but would merely have put a particular formulation into statutory form. Secondly, even if the attempt were made to incorporate all the conventions in legislation or into a constitution, this would not, in the nature of things, prevent the growth of further non-legal practices and rules.

WHAT ARE CONVENTIONS?

So far in this discussion we have adopted Dicey's term, conventions, for the non-legal elements of the constitution. It has been convenient, in distinguishing the legal from the non-legal, and in observing that the non-legal may become legal, to employ a single and familiar term.

But questions so far glossed over must now be addressed. Does the term serve to distinguish a particular group of political precepts and, if so, which are included in the group? What in fact constitutes a convention?

Perhaps the best way of starting to tackle these questions is by examining how various authorities on the constitution have treated the subject. There are subtle, but significant, differences in approach which have scarcely been noticed.

18 *Constitutional and Administrative Law* (5th edn by Harry Street and Rodney Brazier, 1985) p 46.
19 See Nevil Johnson *In Search of the Constitution* (1977) pp 31–33.

Dicey introduced the subject in his preliminary chapter, the Outline. Having criticised the lawyers' view of the constitution for its unreality, he proceeded to criticise the political theorists for their neglect of rules of law. The study of constitutional law therefore required attention to two sets of rules. One set comprised the laws, enforced by the courts. The other set he described as:

> conventions, understandings, habits, or practices which, though they may regulate the conduct of the several members of the sovereign power, of the Ministry, or of other officials, are not in reality laws at all since they are not enforced by the courts[20]

and, in a second formulation:

> the other element, here called the 'conventions of the constitution', consists of maxims or practices which, though they regulate the ordinary conduct of the Crown, of Ministers, and of other persons under the constitution, are not in strictness laws at all.[1]

and later they are said to consist of 'customs, practices, maxims, or precepts'.[2] Several things about these passages deserve notice. First, the distinction being made is between the legal and the non-legal. That is what he was concerned to do. Secondly, the non-legal matters are given six different descriptions (conventions, understandings, habits, practices, maxims, precepts), and if Dicey regarded these as different, or at least not identical, categories, he did not bother to explain the distinctions between them. Thirdly, when Dicey for convenience fastened upon a single term for the non-legal elements, he called them 'the conventions', selecting one of the descriptions to cover all the categories. We may be sure that he did mean this to cover all the categories, for at one point he said that 'the invariableness of the obedience to constitutional understandings is itself more or less fictitious' and that only 'some few of the conventions of the constitution are rigorously obeyed'.[3] As a marginal note indicates, he was content to include amongst conventions even those which were 'often disobeyed'.[4]

To sum up, Dicey's approach was to postulate one class of non-legal rules. He had no need to (and did not) offer a definition of conventions. They were illustrated by examples, and negatively defined by the fact that they were not court-enforced. Any non-legal matters relevant to the constitution were, for Dicey, conventions.

Sir Ivor Jennings, perhaps unconsciously, took a different path. At the beginning of his account of the topic in *The Law and the Constitution*, he

---

20 Dicey p 24.
 1 Ibid, p 24.
 2 Ibid, p 417.
 3 Ibid, p 441.
 4 Ibid, p 440.

explained how rules of practice developed alongside the law, remarked that these had been variously designated by Mill, Dicey and Anson, and, because of its prevalence, adopted Dicey's term, conventions, for the purpose of his discussion.[5] The implication was that the class being discussed was coextensive with Dicey's. The same inference might be drawn from the initial treatment of the topic in his *Cabinet Government:*

> There is a whole complex of rules outside 'the law', nowhere inconsistent with it but nowhere recognised by it, which can be stated with almost as much precision as the rules of law. Such rules have been set out by many authorities; they are discussed in Parliament; they are appealed to whenever dispute arises. They are called by various names, but are now commonly referred to as 'constitutional conventions'.[6]

However, Jennings later proceeded to ask the question, 'When is it possible to say that a convention has been established?' His answer was that a test had to be used:

> We have to ask ourselves three questions: first, what are the precedents; secondly, did the actors in the precedents believe that they were bound by a rule; and thirdly, is there a reason for the rule?[7]

The point is given more emphasis by a section headed 'Mere Practice is Not Enough'. Jennings, by stipulating the conditions for the existence of a convention, as Dicey had not, had implicitly divided the non-legal into *two* classes, those rules which amounted to conventions, and those which did not.

Sir Kenneth Wheare more explicitly divided the non-legal rules into two relevant classes:

> These non-legal rules are given a variety of names, as has been indicated. It appears convenient to adopt two terms, usage and convention. By convention is meant an obligatory rule; by usage, a rule which is no more than the description of a usual practice and which has not yet obtained obligatory force. A usage, after repeated adoption whenever a given set of circumstances recurs, may for a sufficient reason acquire obligatory force and thus become a convention. But conventions need not have a prior history as usages. A convention may, if a sufficient reason exists, arise from a single precedent. Or again it may result from an agreement between the parties concerned, declared and accepted by them as binding.[8]

Later writers have, on the whole, followed the same approach. Thus, Hood Phillips adopted a definition of conventions which enabled him to distinguish 'mere practice, usage, habit or fact, which is not regarded as

5 *The Law and the Constitution* (5th edn, 1959) p 80ff.
6 *Cabinet Government* (3rd edn, 1959) p 2.
7 *The Law and the Constitution* (5th edn, 1959) p 136. See also *Cabinet Government* (3rd edn, 1959) pp 5–13.
8 *The Statute of Westminster and Dominion Status* (5th edn, 1953) p 10.

obligatory, such as the existence of political parties (fact) or the habit of Chancellors of the Exchequer in carrying from Downing Street to the House of Commons a dispatch case supposed to contain his Budget speech'.[9] Mitchell acknowledged that 'it is necessary that conventions should be distinguished from mere practices'.[10] For de Smith, the conventions were 'forms of political behaviour regarded as obligatory', to be distinguished from 'non-binding usages'.[11]

However, Wheare's approach has been effectively criticised by two authors, in a passage which merits careful consideration:

> There is . . . a difficulty in the commonsense distinction which is involved in saying that it is a convention that the Monarch should give her assent to any bill duly passed by both Houses of Parliament, but that her agreement to dissolve the House of Commons when requested to do so by the Prime Minister is a matter of usage, in that her consent is not mandatory under all circumstances. Not all authorities would agree that the first of these alone provides an example of an obligatory rule; but if the second may be assumed to be a 'usage', it could not with equal justice be referred to as a 'rule'. A rule must *prescribe* something if it is to guide action or state obligations, whereas, according to [Wheare's] definition, a usage would only describe actual behaviour. But the reasons why a particular action is not mandatory cannot lie in the fact that any statement about it is [to quote Wheare] 'no more than description'. A description is not a weak kind of prescription.[12]

There is considerable force in these arguments, and their implication is that, while other matters of political facts and behaviour may also be of interest, the non-legal *rules* relevant to the constitution are best viewed as being of one type, even if their precision and obligatoriness are variable. If that is accepted, then the exercise of stipulating tests for the establishment of a convention seems misconceived.

We might be encouraged in this approach to the subject by recalling that it was also Dicey's. Remember that he treated the non-legal rules as being of one class, some of which might be rigorously obeyed, but others not:

> . . . the invariableness of the obedience to constitutional understandings is itself more or less fictitious. The special articles of the conventional code are in fact often disobeyed. A Minister sometimes refuses to retire when, as his opponents allege, he ought constitutionally to resign office . . . in 1784 the House of Commons maintained, not only by argument but by repeated votes, that Pitt had deliberately defied more than one constitutional precept, and the Whigs of 1834 brought a like charge against Wellington and Peel. Nor is it doubtful that anyone who searches

---

9 *Constitutional and Administrative Law* (6th edn by O Hood Phillips and Paul Jackson, 1978) p 105.

10 *Constitutional Law* (2nd edn, 1968) p 39.

11 *Constitutional and Administrative Law* (5th edn by Harry Street and Rodney Brazier, 1985) p 52.

12 G Marshall and G C Moodie *Some Problems of the Constitution* (5th edn, 1971) p 26.

through the pages of *Hansard* will find other instances in which constitutional maxims of long standing and high repute have been set at nought. The uncertain character of the deference paid to the conventions of the constitution is concealed under the current phraseology, which treats the successful violation of a constitutional rule as a proof that the maxim was not in reality part of the constitution.[13]

These are astute observations. Dicey's contemporary, the constitutional historian Maitland, regarded the conventions of the constitution in the same way: 'We find them of every degree of stringency and of definiteness', he said.[14]

Of course, it is not sufficient to say that we prefer the approach of Dicey and Maitland, even if there are some difficulties inherent in the other approaches. The question has to be looked at in relation to the subject-matter, too.

It would only seem sensible to have what we might call a two-class approach if some number of the non-legal rules may be picked out as being of a uniform and high degree of 'stringency and definiteness'. But reflection suggests rather that the non-legal rules are of every degree. There is hardly space to demonstrate this with respect to all of the conventions, but the point may be illustrated by reference to the conventions mentioned at the beginning of the chapter, concerning the royal assent, the selection of a Prime Minister, and individual ministerial responsibility. All of these matters are regarded as important and as involving conventions, not practice or usage only, when that distinction is made. The matter of the royal assent was chosen by Maitland to exemplify the higher end of his scale of 'stringency and definiteness'.

In fact, when we examine it, there are doubts about what precisely the convention concerning the royal assent is, what degree of obligation exists, and what its limits are. The convention is usually stated to be that 'the Queen must assent to Bills duly passed'. But it may be that a different formulation is more accurate: 'the Crown cannot refuse assent except on advice'. It is really impossible to choose between the two versions since there are no instances in modern times of legislation being presented for assent against the wishes of the government (although the situation might arise with minority governments or when there is a change of government without a dissolution of Parliament). However, it is arguable that the Sovereign has more discretion than these formulations of the convention imply. In 1913 the Government of Ireland Bill was being put through Parliament under the provisions of the recently enacted Parliament Act of 1911. The Conservatives and Unionists, who had a majority in the House of Lords, were opposed to the Bill, and it appears that the King, George V, was too. The

13 Dicey p 440.
14 F W Maitland *The Constitutional History of England* (1908) p 398.

King sought advice, and received conflicting views as to the courses open to him. In the end, so as to avoid seeming to intervene on behalf of one side, he neither dismissed the government nor refused assent to the Bill. But he considered those courses, and, according to Sir Ivor Jennings's account, 'it was assumed by the King throughout that he had not only the legal power but the constitutional right to refuse assent'.[15] In other words, the supposed convention was not regarded as binding by the person to whom it applied.

Another way of viewing this might be to say that there is a general rule which is subject to exceptions, so that in certain instances assent may properly be withheld. It has been argued that it would be right to refuse assent to any Bill which altered the position of Northern Ireland as part of the United Kingdom without the consent of the people of Northern Ireland.[16] It has been suggested that the Sovereign might not agree to the abolition of the House of Lords.[17] Would the Sovereign agree to a Bill by which the government in office, without any mandate from the electorate, sought to prolong the duration of a Parliament beyond five years? Or a Bill altering matters which in the Coronation oath the Sovereign pledged to protect? Or a Bill abolishing the monarchy? The answers are uncertain, so the convention is neither so definite nor, arguably, is it so stringent, as is generally made out.

Take the matter of the appointment of a Prime Minister. Here there are a number of different rules involved, which well illustrate the variations of strength and precision which conventions exhibit. We may say with absolute confidence that the Sovereign is expected to appoint a Prime Minister. It is practically inconceivable that anyone would be appointed who was not a member of either House of Parliament, although it could just possibly happen in an emergency. It is improbable that a member of the House of Lords would be selected, but not inconceivable. For example, it has been asked, 'does anyone believe that the Labour Party would have refused to accept Winston Churchill as P.M. in 1940 if he had happened to be a peer?'[18] In recent years Viscount Whitelaw, a member of the Lords, has been Deputy Prime Minister; and it is thought that, if the Prime Minister had been killed in the Brighton hotel bombing, he would have been asked to become Prime Minister, for an interim period at least.

Then again, while the Sovereign's choice may admittedly be little more than formal when one party enjoys an overall majority in the Commons and has an elected leader, in the absence of either of those conditions, the

---

15 *Cabinet Government* (3rd edn, 1959) p 400. See also Harold Nicolson *King George V* (1952) p 234. Dicey, in a letter to *The Times*, quoted with approval Burke's view that the royal power of negative 'extends to all cases whatsoever' and might be 'the means of saving the constitution itself on an occasion worthy of bringing it forth': *Cabinet Government* App III.
16 Harry Calvert *Constitutional Law in Northern Ireland* (1968) pp 30–32.
17 Eg Hugo Young, The Sunday Times, 8 November 1981.
18 J A G Griffith [1963] PL 401.

convention becomes rather cloudy. In 1931, when the economic crisis led to the disintegration of Mr Ramsay MacDonald's minority Labour government, King George V took the initiative, after consultation with the party leaders, in the formation of a coalition called the 'National Government' and asked MacDonald to head it in spite of the defection of most of his own party. But, even if he acted according to his perception of the national interest, the King was criticised for his role in the affair. After the first general election in 1974, there was no majority party in the new House, although the Labour Party held the largest number of seats. The Prime Minister, Mr Edward Heath, did not immediately resign, for he might have been able to form a coalition with the Liberals. (He was not, shortly resigned, and Mr Harold Wilson was asked to become Prime Minister.) Mr Heath was accused by some persons of acting unconstitutionally. Others regarded it as perfectly proper for the sitting Prime Minister to have the first entitlement to attempt to form a government. The conclusion must be that in circumstances such as these it is not unambiguously clear how the Sovereign, or others involved, should act, because there is room for dispute over the rules. Moreover, it may be that 'hung Parliaments', where no single party possesses an overall majority in the House of Commons, will occur more frequently than in the past fifty years. That will happen if the two-party system which has dominated British politics is weakening, as supporters of the Liberal–SDP Alliance hope, and it would be facilitated if a form of proportional representation were to be adopted for parliamentary elections. In the setting of multi-party politics, if it should come about, it may readily be imagined that the Crown's role in choosing a Prime Minister, and in other matters such as the dissolution of Parliament, would cease to be a mere formality. There is a growing industry of speculation concerning these possibilities,[19] which in itself tells us a good deal about the nature of constitutional conventions.

What is entailed in the convention of individual ministerial responsibility is not clear either. In particular, it is not easy to say when the ultimate sanction of resignation is expected of ministers. Before 1982, when Lord Carrington resigned, the last instance of resignation on these grounds was in 1954. Then the Minister of Agriculture, Sir Thomas Dugdale, resigned over the Crichel Down affair, when there was maladministration by officials in his department. Yet other equally or more serious instances of maladministration did not have the same consequence. In 1964 a lack of communication within the Ministry of Aviation led to Ferranti being overpaid by more than £4 million on defence contracts. In 1968 the Parliamentary Commissioner for Administration found the Foreign Office to

19 See eg Vernon Bogdanor *Multi-Party Politics and the Constitution* (1983); David Butler *Governing Without a Majority: Dilemmas for Hung Parliaments in Britain* (1983); Rodney Brazier 'Choosing a Prime Minister' [1982] PL 395.

be seriously at fault in the handling of compensation claims from war prisoners who had been detained in the Sachsenhausen concentration camp; but the Foreign Secretary, Mr George Brown, while agreeing to alter the decision, continued to deny fault. When the Vehicle and General Insurance Company collapsed in 1971, a statutory tribunal of inquiry was appointed, which found that some named officials in the Department of Trade and Industry had been negligent in the exercise of their supervisory powers. On none of these occasions did the minister feel obliged to resign.

What are we to make of this? Certainly an obligation to resign cannot be asserted in unqualified terms. Professor S E Finer, in an examination of individual responsibility, has shown how the punitive effect of the convention is often avoided, because a minister who resigns may be appointed to another post, or there may be a timely ministerial reshuffle rendering resignation unnecessary, or collective solidarity may be exerted to protect a minister against the Opposition. The only generalisation which may be made, according to Finer, is that 'If the Minister is yielding, his Prime Minister unbending, and his party out for blood – no matter how serious or trivial the reason – the Minister will find himself without Parliamentary support'.[20]

Of course, one way out of this would be to say that there is no convention of resignation at all. But surely that would be an example of the fallacious thinking Dicey criticised, 'which treats the successful violation of a constitutional rule as a proof that the maxim was not in reality part of the constitution'. After all, Lord Carrington felt an *obligation* to resign (and the Prime Minister, to judge by her reply to him,[1] was not 'unbending', but most reluctant to accept his resignation), and likewise Mr Brittan in 1986. In everyday political discourse, too, the rule continues to be treated as if it had practical content,[2] and Opposition members not infrequently call for the resignation of a minister 'in accordance with parliamentary precedent'. So it seems preferable to say that there is a rule of some sort here, even if it cannot be stated with precision and is not invariably obeyed.

When those matters regarded as conventions are examined, the conclusion that stares one in the face is that it does not make sense to set particular standards for a sub-class of the rules. As Geoffrey Marshall says, 'it is doubtful if there is any area in which this can be done'.[3] Once acknowledge that the non-legal rules are 'of every degree of stringency and of definiteness' – and this is what consideration of them shows – and the way is open to a less mystical, and more accurate, approach. The non-legal rules, call them what

20 S E Finer 'The Individual Responsibility of Ministers' (1956) 34 Public Administration 377 at 394.
1 The Times, 6 April 1982.
2 See R K Alderman and J A Cross *The Tactics of Resignation* (1967).
3 *Constitutional Theory* (1971) p 12.

we will, may be viewed as on a continuum. Some few may be stated with precision, others are harder to formulate. Some are more or less invariably obeyed, while there are others to which, by degrees, a lesser sense of obligation adheres.

When this is appreciated, then we might agree with the suggestion that we should 'delete those pages in constitutional textbooks headed Conventions, with their unreal distinctions and their word puzzles'.[4] Of course, that does not mean that the student of the constitution should ignore the matters which have been put under that label. Political rules and practices deserve study in their own right, and should be viewed alongside the law when relevant. To accuse Dicey, or other constitutional lawyers since, of encouraging a narrow approach, is not merely unjust but absurd, because constitutional lawyers for a hundred years or more have been studying law in its context, a perspective which has only recently become fashionable in other fields.

4 Was Parliament born free?

The principle which A V Dicey, who was our greatest constitutional lawyer, described as the keystone of the British constitution was the sovereignty of Parliament. By the term sovereignty, he meant legislative supremacy: 'Parliament has the right to make or unmake any law whatever.'

The proposition has not, however, commanded universal acceptance, and those who deny it have employed a variety of real or hypothetical examples in rebuttal. Generally, Dicey's critics seek to show that Parliament can legislate in such a way as to bind later Parliaments, or indeed that it has done so (and these contentions will be examined in the following chapter). Some critics of Dicey, however, attack him on a rather different ground. Their argument is that Parliament suffers from a disability not self-inflicted but inborn, so that in the late Professor Mitchell's memorable phrase, it was 'born unfree'.

In many other countries, where there are written constitutions, and the authority of the legislature is derived from the constitution, there may be found, alongside the grant of legislative power, restrictions placed upon it. In the United Kingdom, as we know, there is usually taken to be no written constitution, but there are laws which constituted a new Parliament for Great Britain (in 1707) and for the United Kingdom of Great Britain and Ireland (in 1800), and so it is at least conceivable that those laws, being antecedent to the Parliaments created by them, might have contained limitations upon the powers of the Parliaments which followed.

This is the possibility seized upon by a number of constitutional lawyers, who have suggested that the union legislation of 1707 and 1800 does in fact restrict Parliament which, in their view, is unable to alter some of its more important terms. Curiously, this view has been canvassed more vigorously in the last thirty years or so than it was before. Not so curiously, the view has been most widely held in Scotland and in Ireland, countries which lost Parliaments within their own lands upon entering into union, and whose representation in the United Kingdom Parliament at Westminster is dwarfed by the much larger number representing constituencies in England and Wales.

The proposition that Parliament was born unfree has been argued most strongly (concerning the Anglo–Scottish union) by J D B Mitchell,[1] T B

---

1 *Constitutional Law* (2nd edn, 1968) pp 93–98; [1956] PL 294.

Smith[2] and Neil MacCormick,[3] and (with regard to the British–Irish union) by Harry Calvert.[4] We may begin by examining the arguments they use to persuade us that the Acts of Union should be regarded differently from other enactments, so as to have this exceptional effect.

WHAT MAKES THE ACTS OF UNION DIFFERENT

They find support for their case in two ways. The first argument derives from the special nature of the legislation in question.[5] The terms of the Anglo–Scottish union were negotiated by commissioners representing the two Parliaments. With a few amendments, and the addition of provisions protecting the established Presbyterian Church (which had not been negotiable), these terms were passed by the Scottish Parliament or Estates as the Union with England Act 1707. The terms of the Scottish Act, with the addition of provisions to safeguard the established Church of England, were then passed by the English Parliament as the Union with Scotland Act 1706. (The apparently inconsistent chronology is explained by the fact that while Scotland and the rest of Europe had adopted the Gregorian calendar, England did not do so until 1752, so that the year 1707 did not commence there until 25 March.) Two features of these events should be noticed. First, the resulting terms, which emerged from a freely negotiated bargain, may be viewed as a contract or a treaty, perhaps even a treaty in the technical sense understood by international law, although unenforceable as such because the two parties to it have ceased to exist as separate entities, 'like whisky polluted with soda', as T B Smith says.[6] Secondly, it needs to be emphasised that the union legislation was not contained in an Act, but in *Acts* of Union, and these were enacted by the Scottish and English Parliaments which were effectively signing their own death warrants, not by the Parliament of Great Britain. So the Acts of Union were not only antecedent to the Great Britain Parliament, but may be regarded as constituent: they brought into being a new state, and with it a new Parliament. The proposition is that the legislation may be regarded as 'a fundamental written constitution'[7] or 'a constitutional act, which created and limited a Parliament'.[8]

The British–Irish union was negotiated by commissioners from both countries, but there was no formal treaty, and fewer constitutional

2 *A Short Commentary on the Law of Scotland* (1962) pp 49–60; *British Justice: The Scottish Contribution* (1961) ch 5; 'The Union of 1707 as Fundamental Law' [1957] PL 99.
3 'Does the United Kingdom Have a Constitution?' (1978) 29 NILQ 1; [1972] PL 174.
4 *Constitutional Law in Northern Ireland* (1968) ch 1.
5 On the significance of which in constitutional history, see ch 2.
6 *British Justice: The Scottish Contribution* (1961) p 204.
7 Ibid, p 207.
8 J D B Mitchell [1956] PL 294 at 296.

guarantees were given to Ireland than had been given to Scotland. However, the terms again were separately enacted by statutes of each of the two Parliaments concerned in 1800, when the Irish Parliament yielded to pressures and inducements from the British government, having rejected union in the previous year. A new state, the United Kingdom of Great Britain and Ireland, came into being with a corresponding legislature; and for the Irish union legislation too, it is urged that its exceptional and constituent nature gives it the character of fundamental and unalterable law.

A second and connected argument points to the language of the union legislation. That the legislation was antecedent to the Parliaments indicates a theoretical possibility that they might be bound by it. That it was intended that succeeding Parliaments should be so restricted is suggested by the wording of the Acts, in which a number of provisions are expressed to be 'fundamental', or to govern 'for ever' or something similar. In the 1800 legislation, the union of the two countries, the existence of a Parliament of the United Kingdom and Ireland, the succession to the Crown as then laid down, and the union of established churches into the United Church of England and Ireland, were all amongst the provisions expressed to 'be in force and have effect for ever'. In the 1706–07 Acts, there are some provisions which are transitional and some which envisage their own alteration, so that it has not been claimed that the Acts in their entirety are sacrosanct, but only that some portions are, which are marked out as of particular importance. For example, the union of the two countries was 'for ever after'. The Court of Session and Court of Justiciary, Scotland's higher courts, were to remain as they were then constituted 'in all time coming', although 'subject nevertheless to such regulations as shall be made by the Parliament of Great Britain'. While the Parliament of Great Britain might legislate freely upon matters of public rights, it was provided that 'no alteration be made in laws which concern private right except for evident utility of the subjects within Scotland'. The Protestant Religion and Presbyterian Church Act 1707 was to be 'held and observed in all time coming as a fundamental and essential condition of any treaty or union . . . without any alteration thereof or derogation thereto in any sort for ever'. Language of this sort seems to leave little room for doubt concerning the intentions of those who framed the legislation, and, in construing legislation, it is the duty of the courts to give effect to the intentions of the legislator.

However, these arguments are not so compelling as they first appear. Even if it is correct that the framers of the union legislation intended that some parts would be unalterable, this would not ensure the fulfilment of their hopes. Legislation which purports to bind future Parliaments will, on Dicey's view of the matter, simply be ineffective: 'That Parliaments have more than once intended and endeavoured to pass acts which should tie the hands of their successors is certain, but the endeavour has always ended in failure'.[9] The Acts of Union were grist to Dicey's mill, for they afforded 'the strongest proof of the futility'. We may refer to more recent cases such as *Vauxhall Estates Ltd v Liverpool Corpn*[10] and *Ellen St Estates Ltd v Minister of Health*[11], where it was contended that a phrase in the Acquisition of Land (Assessment of Compensation) Act 1919 to the effect that inconsistent provisions 'shall not have effect' was an attempt to tie the hands of later Parliaments. The courts' view was that, even if Parliament had so intended, it could not be done. 'The constitutional position', according to Scrutton LJ in the later case, was that 'Parliament can alter an Act previously passed'.[12] Similarly, Maugham LJ declared that 'the Legislature cannot, according to our constitution, bind itself as to the form of subsequent legislation'.[13]

A capacity to bind subsequent Parliaments should not, therefore, be too readily inferred from the terminology of the Acts. Besides, the language used, unusual as it may sound to our ears, was not exceptional, measured against other enactments of the times. In 1688 the provisions of the Bill of Rights were declared to 'remaine and be the law of this realme for ever', but that had not prevented the English Parliament from altering the succession to the Crown as there laid down twelve years later in the Act of Settlement. The Act of Settlement purported to regulate the coronation oath for all future Kings and Queens, but this has not prevented its amendment. Phrases similar to those found in the Acts of Union were also, as Professor Mitchell admits, 'of common occurrence in the Acts of the Parliament of Scotland',[14] but had been ineffective there. In view of this, there is much to be said for a Scottish writer's view that 'the experienced politicians and lawyers of the two countries who drew up the Articles of Union must have been well aware that both parliaments had attempted in the past without success to bind subsequent parliaments, and that the legislature of the United Kingdom would find itself under the same disability'.[15] Indeed, the lack of any legal bar to a British Parliament's destruction of the treaty guarantees was a point to which attention had been drawn by pamphleteers in Scotland, when they were campaigning to prevent the members of the Estates from agreeing to the union.[16]

Later in the eighteenth century, we still find Parliament using terms which purport to bind its successors. In 1783 the British Parliament, in an attempt to assuage Irish doubts, enacted that:

9 *Law of the Constitution* (10th edn) p 65. Dicey's views were somewhat modified later: see A V Dicey and R S Rait *Thoughts on the Union between England and Scotland* (1920).
10 [1932] 1 KB 733.
11 [1934] 1 KB 590, [1934] All ER Rep 385, CA.
12 [1934] 1 KB 590 at 595.
13 Ibid at 597.
14 *Constitutional Law* (2nd edn, 1968) p 70.
15 K W B Middleton 'New Thoughts on the Union' 1954 JR 37 at 57.
16 G M Trevelyan *Ramillies and the Union with Scotland* (1932) p 272: Geoffrey Marshall *Parliamentary Sovereignty and the Commonwealth* (1957) p 52.

The Right claimed by the People of Ireland to be bound only by Laws enacted by his Majesty and the Parliament of that Kingdom, in all Cases whatever . . . shall be, and it is hereby declared to be established and ascertained for ever, and shall, at no time hereafter, be questioned or questionable.

It is ironical that some constitutional lawyers ask us to believe that phrases like 'for ever' and 'at no time hereafter', when used in 1707 or 1800, have an effect which they conspicuously failed to achieve when used to the opposite end in 1783.

It remains true that the circumstances of the enactment of the Acts of Union were unique. They differ from subsequent statutes in so far as they were passed by different legislatures and, on each occasion, by two legislatures which thereupon ceased to exist. It is undeniable that the Acts of Union brought, in each case, a new state into being, although it may be noted that a number of other Acts have also changed the boundaries of the state by addition or subtraction. It seems but a short step further to say, along with Smith, that 'the British Parliament is the creation of the terms of Union',[17] or, with Mitchell, that the Acts 'created . . . a Parliament'.[18] However, we might falter at that last step. It is true, of course, that there was no Parliament of Great Britain before 1707, but another writer from Scotland concedes that 'it would be far-fetched to say that either in form or in substance a new Parliament came into being at Westminster in 1707'.[19] It is difficult to picture 1707 as a completely fresh start. Legislation enacted earlier by the English and Scottish Parliaments continued to be applied as law in the courts. The British Parliament met in the same building as the pre-union English Parliament, and its privileges and procedures were the same as had adhered in that body. Rather than say that Parliament was 'born' in 1707 (or born again in 1800), it would be more accurate to say that some aspects of the institution are regulated by statute (including those Acts), whereas others are not. Thus, while matters such as composition of the Houses, territorial jurisdiction, duration and frequency may all be regulated by statute, the *existence* of a Parliament under English law (and perhaps under Scots)[20] and certain other matters are not, and seem rather to be products of custom. We may establish this by posing some questions. From where comes the rule that Parliament is composed of three parts, each of which must consent for a measure to be enacted? By what authority did the Lords Spiritual, or the peers of England, or the members representing English constituencies, sit in Parliament in 1708? The answers to these questions do

17 [1957] PL 99 at 111.
18 [1956] PL 294 at 296.
19 K W B Middleton 'New Thoughts on the Union' 1954 JR 37 at 53.
20 This might not be so clear, in view of its earlier history. But such thinking underlies the view sometimes expressed that the Scottish Parliament could be summoned again. See J T Cameron 'Summoning the Estates' 1961 SLT (News) 98.

not lie in the Acts of Union. This suggests that the Acts of Union cannot be regarded as the sort of fundamental law for our Parliament in the way that the United States Constitution is for Congress. The correctness of this analysis is confirmed by examining the union legislation itself. The natural reading of the 1707 Acts (and, even more clearly, the 1800 Acts) is that aspects of an existing institution were being changed, not that an institution was being established de novo.

Thus, the arguments that Parliament was 'born unfree' are less than compelling. We may say, in any event, that arguments about the special nature of the legislation at most show that limitation of Parliament by it is a theoretical possibility, and reference to the language employed at most reveals the aspirations of those who framed the documents.

There is, however, better evidence than this to hand. The question is whether Parliament is restricted by the Acts of Union. It is surely relevant to see whether Parliament has felt able to amend them, or has been inhibited from doing so.

PARLIAMENT AND THE UNION LEGISLATION

The Irish union legislation, far from being treated as inviolate, has been severely mauled. An important feature of it was Article 5, which enacted that

> the churches of England and Ireland as now by law established be united into one Protestant Episcopal Church to be called the United Church of England and Ireland and that the doctrine, worship, discipline and government of the said United Church shall be and shall remain in full force for ever, and that this be deemed and taken to be an essential and fundamental part of the Union.

These fine words did not save the provision from being torn up by the Irish Church Act 1869 when Gladstone bowed to the strength of feeling in Ireland and disestablished and disendowed the Episcopal Church in Ireland. The very union of the two countries and their political institutions, although it was to 'be in force and have effect for ever' was dissolved by legislation in 1922 when, following a period of civil strife, most of Ireland gained independence as the Irish Free State, and only six northern counties remained part of the United Kingdom.

The result is that every Article and section in the Union with Ireland Act 1800 (or the corresponding Act of the Irish Parliament) has been repealed or amended. In the light of this, it is, to say the least, difficult still to regard the 1800 legislation as having a binding character. Indeed, the Royal Commission on the Constitution in 1973 used as evidence of the supremacy of Parliament that 'the creation of the Irish Free State in 1922 was made possible by an ordinary Act of Parliament, despite the declared intention of the Act of Union of 1800 that the union of Great Britain and Ireland should last for ever'.[1]

The Anglo–Scottish union legislation is not so obviously in tatters. Certainly the union of the countries, their Crowns, and the Parliaments, is still intact, and the Church of Scotland retains its position as the established church in Scotland. But a closer examination reveals that almost all of the articles and sections of the legislation have been repealed in whole or in part. Not all of these repeals constitute 'breaches' of the legislation, of course. Some of the provisions in the Acts of Union were only transitional in duration. Others have been repealed as spent, such as those concerning the first meeting of the new Parliament (in Article XXII) and the amount of the Scottish contribution when land tax was being raised (in Article IX). There are a number of provisions in which future legislation by the Parliament of Great Britain was contemplated and authorised, such as with regard to the coinage of the realm (Article XVI) and the Scottish Privy Council (Article XIX), abolished in 1708.

Many parts of the legislation neither authorise nor expressly forbid alteration. For example, Article XII and section 6 provide for sixteen peers of Scotland, elected by the larger total number, to sit in the House of Lords and 45 representatives for Scottish constituencies in the House of Commons. But changes in the electoral law from 1832 onwards have resulted in redrawn constituencies and a greater number of MPs, while the Peerage Act 1963 provided that all peers of Scotland might thereafter sit in the House of Lords.

There are some matters where no alteration is expressly contemplated, and it is arguable that none was intended. Article XXI provides 'That the rights and privileges of the royal burghs of Scotland as they now are do remain entire after the union and notwithstanding thereof' and Article XX required that heritable offices and jurisdictions 'be reserved to the owners thereof as rights of property in the same manner as they are now enjoyed by the laws of Scotland notwithstanding this treaty'. Whether clauses such as these were intended to be susceptible to alteration or to be binding is a matter for interpretation. It is a matter of record, however, that the heritable jurisdictions were abolished in 1748 and that the royal burghs lost their functions in 1975.

Finally, there are those parts of the legislation where the terms employed seem more evidently to point to intended entrenchment. There is Article I: the union of the kingdoms is to be 'for ever after'. Article II provides for a common succession to the monarchy, and the barring of Roman Catholics and persons marrying Catholics is 'for ever'. Article VI requires that 'all parts of the United Kingdom for ever from and after the union shall have the same allowances, encouragements and drawbacks, and be under the same prohibitions, restrictions and regulations of trade . . .', and Article VII that

1 Report of the Royal Commission on the Constitution 1969–1973 (Cmnd 5460) para 56.

the excises upon liquors shall be uniform in all parts of the new Kingdom 'for ever from and after the union'. Article XVIII, after authorising the new Parliament to alter matters of public right, lays down that 'no alteration be made in laws which concern private right except for evident utility of the subjects within Scotland'. Article XIX deals with the courts: the Court of Session was to 'remain in all time coming within Scotland as it is now constituted by the laws of that kingdom' but 'subject nevertheless to such regulations for the better administration of justice as shall be made by the Parliament of Great Britain', and the Court of Justiciary similarly; the Court of Admiralty in Scotland was to remain as it was 'until the Parliament of Great Britain shall make such regulations and alterations as shall be judged expedient for the whole United Kingdom so as there be always continued in Scotland a Court of Admiralty . . . subject nevertheless to such regulations and alterations as shall be thought proper to be made by the Parliament of Great Britain'. By Article XXIV the Scottish regalia and parliamentary and other records and rolls were to remain in Scotland 'in all time coming'.

The Protestant Religion and Presbyterian Church Act 1707, which was incorporated in the union legislation by both Parliaments, was declared to be 'a fundamental and essential condition of the . . . union in all times coming', and in that Act it was provided that 'the true Protestant religion and the worship, discipline and government' of the established church were 'to continue without any alteration to the people of this land in all succeeding generations'.

Since some parts of the Acts were clearly not intended to be permanent, those who maintain that Parliament is restricted by the union legislation confine their claim to some of the matters just mentioned. What portions may be included in the category of 'intended to be binding' is a question upon which authorities may disagree. Not only is it doubtful whether Articles XX and XXI were intended to be unalterable, but some of the Articles where phrases implying permanence are employed are nevertheless far from unambiguous. It is interesting, for example, to consider the clauses concerning the courts in Article XIX. Scots lawyers and judges have tended to regard these as fundamental, and therefore forbidding the abolition of the higher Scottish courts. However, it is certainly a possible interpretation of these clauses that reform, or even abolition, by Parliament is authorised if it is 'for the better administration of justice'. Mitchell argues that 'the essential point of a distinct court may be regarded as fundamental', and cites an opinion to the effect that the destruction of the Court of Session cannot have been within the Commissioners' contemplation.[2] But, in answer to this, it must be observed that neither English nor Scottish judges may consult *travaux préparatoires*, and it is the will of the legislature as expressed in the language of the Act to which courts are bound to give effect.

2 *Constitutional Law* (2nd edn, 1968) pp 72–73.

Even the provisions which seem more obviously intended to be binding have not survived unscathed. Scotland and England are still united, but not in the same form. It was accepted without question in 1800 that the Parliament of Great Britain could merge the country into a wider union with Ireland, which at the same time altered the name of the state and the design of the national flag as they had been specified in Article I of the union legislation of 1707. There have been encouragements to trade and industry in particular parts of the country, despite the words of Article VI, and, it might be added, to the considerable benefit of Scotland. There have, of course, been numerous alterations to the law of Scotland in matters of 'private right' since 1707, and only persons of an exceptionally trusting or uncritical nature could regard them all as being of 'evident utility'. The Court of Admiralty, the continuing existence of which, upon my reading of Article XIX, was more clearly ordained than that of the other courts mentioned, was abolished in 1830; its jurisdiction in prize having earlier been transferred to the English Court of Admiralty, its remaining civil jurisdiction was then merged in the Court of Session, and its criminal jurisdiction in the Scottish criminal courts. The Court of Session and the High Court of Justiciary have undergone a number of reorganisations and reforms since the union.

Nor have the provisions concerning the established religion been untouched.[3] Within a few years of the union, the British Parliament legislated for toleration in the Scottish Episcopalians Act 1711 and restored lay patronage in the Church Patronage (Scotland) Act 1711. These measures were regarded in Scotland as violations of the spirit of the union agreement, and the latter was a violation of its letter as well. A requirement in the 1707 Act that professors and masters in universities, colleges and schools had to subscribe to the Confession of Faith did not survive nineteenth century liberalism: the tests were modified or abolished by the Universities (Scotland) Act 1853, the Parochial and Burgh Schoolmasters (Scotland) Act 1861, and later enactments. Subscription of the confession by ministers was required by the 1707 Act in the form laid down in a 1693 Act, but the Churches (Scotland) Act 1905 provided a means of amending the formula, which within a few years was employed. Considerable changes in church organisation and government were made in the Church of Scotland Act 1921.

This adds up to a substantial number of amendments and repeals in supposedly unalterable legislation. It is quite astonishing that Professor Mitchell was prepared to assert that 'it is doubtful if there has as yet been any breach',[4] but his arguments, skilful as they are, convey an impression of casuistry. T B Smith admitted that 'many changes have been made, even of the most fundamental clauses'.[5]

---

3 See Francis Lyall *Of Presbyters and Kings* (1980).
4 *Constitutional Law* (2nd edn, 1968) p 73.
5 Two Scots Cases' (1953) 69 LQR 512 at 515.

In the face of such overwhelming evidence of Parliament's willingness to override provisions in the Acts of Union, one might think that their lack of binding effect would have to be conceded. Yet it is not. Those who maintain that the Acts limit Parliament have a number of answers, when confronted with these breaches.

First, Neil MacCormick seeks to persuade us that 'there is at least some evidence . . . that in legislative . . . practice there has been acceptance of the Treaties of Union as imposing limits on Parliamentary competence'.[6] His evidence is no more than a single instance. In 1872–73 when reform of the English court system was being considered, a proposal that the appellate jurisdiction of the House of Lords be abolished and that an enlarged Court of Appeal should hear appeals from Scotland and Ireland was abandoned, partly because of the objection that it was precluded by the terms of the union legislation. Frankly, it is difficult to attach much significance to this solitary example, if we put it in the scales against the numerous occasions when Parliament has blithely legislated in disregard of the union provisions.

Another argument is that what are apparently breaches in fact happened with the consent of those whom the provisions were designed to protect. Because of that, the argument goes, such breaches do not really count, as they tell us nothing about whether Parliament may legislate contrary to the union legislation without the relevant consent. Thus, as Mitchell says, the abolition of the test in universities was 'in effect carried out at the request and with the consent of the body most able to express national opinion upon the topic',[7] for the Church of Scotland acquiesced in its removal. Similarly, as Smith observes, the reforms of the Court of Session were 'instigated by Scottish interests'.[8] However, the examples are selective. Some of the breaches may have been uncontroversial and welcome, but this cannot be true of all of them. Some of the breaches and possible breaches in the early years of union, such as the restoration of lay patronage in the church, were so unpopular as to cause great anger, and other alterations such as the abolition of the heritable jurisdictions were presumably against the wishes of those affected. Amongst other difficulties with the consent argument, we may observe that it is not clear whose consent is supposed to be required, whether majority consent would suffice, or how it is to be signified or recognised. Is it the consent of those affected which is relevant? Or of the Scottish or Irish people? Or their parliamentary representatives? Or the courts? We do not receive any clear answer. But the fatal weakness in the argument is that once it is conceded that in the appropriate political circumstances the Acts of Union are alterable, it cannot consistently with that be argued that they

---

6 'Does the United Kingdom Have a Constitution?' (1978) 29 NILQ 1 at 11.

7 *Constitutional Law* (2nd edn, 1968) p 73.

8 'Scottish Nationalism, Law and Self-Government' in Neil MacCormick (ed) *The Scottish Debate* (1970) p 38.

contain provisions which are legally unalterable. It is an attempt to have things both ways. Breaches or potential breaches which you dislike you may complain about, and describe as unconstitutional and illegal. Alterations which you like, increased parliamentary representation or the removal of an outdated and inconvenient religious test, are somehow converted to being lawful despite their inconsistency with the Acts. This really will not do.

There is another answer sometimes given to contest the breaches, and that is that 'the fact that Parliament has done something cannot prove that it was entitled to do it'.[9] The implication here could be that some of the breaches, if challenged, would be held illegal, but that they have not been challenged. However, I do not think that is the implication; there is no support for such a bold proposition in the cases. The implication is rather that a breach is still an unlawful act even if courts lack the power (as we shall see that they do) to hold legislation illegal. As T B Smith puts it, 'Parliament may, of course, by usurpation of power, alter the Constitution . . . A lawyer is not, however, concerned with those changes which naked power could achieve . . .'[10] With respect, however, a constitutional lawyer has to be concerned with just such matters as these. When we ask what Parliament can or cannot do, we are going to the very root of the legal system, and in that proximity legal theory depends upon political fact.[11] Take the creation of the Republic of Ireland, which in purely legal terms was made possible by an Act of the United Kingdom Parliament in 1922, which was in breach of the Acts of Union in 1800. If we adopt Smith's approach, we shall have no more to say concerning the Republic than that it rests upon an unlawful foundation. This cannot be sensible. Rather it is the law which must come into step with reality. The reality is that there has been an effective legal system in the Irish state for more than fifty years, and the validity of their laws may be traced back to the Constitution of 1922.[12]

THE ATTITUDE OF THE COURTS

The activities of Parliament with regard to the Acts of Union, according to Sir Ivor Jennings, 'at best . . . show what Parliament thought of its own powers'.[13] However, there may be no better evidence than that, if it is beyond the capacity of other bodies to limit those powers. It is in the courts, however, that issues of legality are adjudicated upon, in the normal way. Moreover, in many countries the courts have the power to hold legislation

9 K W B Middleton 'New Thoughts on the Union' 1954 JR 37 at 49.
10 *A Short Commentary on the Law of Scotland* (1962) p 59.
11 This is discussed further in the following chapter.
12 On the Irish view, it would be traced back further, to the formation of a Provisional Government in 1918: see Harry Calvert *An Introduction to British Constitutional Law* p 6.
13 *The Law and the Constitution* (5th edn, 1959), p 169.

invalid on the ground that it is unconstitutional. If, as we are asked to believe, the Acts of Union are to be looked on as constitutions, imposing limitations, we should expect to find evidence of this in judicial decisions, and perhaps even a power of judicial review by which enactments contrary to their terms may be declared void.

In fact, there is no instance of legislation being held invalid as being contrary to the Acts of Union; no court in the United Kingdom has ever claimed that it could exercise such a power; and on some occasions courts have expressly denied that such a power exists under our constitution.

Nevertheless, there are dicta in a few Scottish cases, especially *MacCormick v Lord Advocate*[14] and *Gibson v Lord Advocate*[15], which give some support to the proposition that parts of the union legislation are binding and may not be altered. In fact, it might be more accurate to say that the proposition has been largely inspired by some unexpected remarks from Scottish judges in the 1953 case. It is interesting, for example, to notice that a Scottish writer on constitutional law, in his textbook which was in use at that time, quite happily assented to the Diceyan view that Parliament was unlimited.[16]

The case of *MacCormick v Lord Advocate* arose from the designation of the present Queen, who had just succeeded to the throne upon her father's death, as 'Elizabeth the Second'. The numeral caused offence to some Scots of nationalist sympathies, for Elizabeth the First had been Queen of England only, and so it was argued that on historical and legal grounds the designation adopted was wrong. The objectors were led by John MacCormick, a prominent Scottish nationalist who had been elected Rector of Glasgow University (the MacCormick already referred to is his son, which may indicate a very natural filial bias!). They petitioned the Court of Session, seeking to prevent Her Majesty's Ministers and Officers of State from publishing a proclamation entitling the Queen as Elizabeth the Second, or alternatively that the court should make an order declaring the unlawfulness of such a designation. It was part of their argument that, since a new state had come into existence in 1707, the enumeration of sovereigns should have begun afresh then; that some of the provisions of the 1707 Acts were fundamental and unalterable, including Article I which created the new state of Great Britain; and that the designation proposed was in conflict with Article I, and should therefore be held illegal.

The Lord Ordinary (Lord Guthrie) who first heard the case found the petitioners' propositions to be 'unsound and indeed extravagant'.[17] The Royal Titles Act 1953 empowered Her Majesty to adopt such style and titles as she

---

14 1953 SC 396.
15 1975 SLT 134.
16 W I R Fraser *Outline of Constitutional Law* (2nd edn, 1948) p 12ff. The writer later became a Lord of Appeal as Lord Fraser of Tullybelton.
17 1953 SC 396, 403.

thought fit, and in the judge's view, any challenge to that position was incompetent, since he accepted as an accurate exposition of the law Dicey's statement that any law might be altered by our legislature. Secondly, the petitioner's case was irrelevant: since Article I did not contain any provisions as to style and titles of the monarch, there was no breach of it. Thirdly, since no rights of the petitioners would be infringed by the royal designation, they had no legal title or interest to sue.

On appeal, three judges in the First Division of the Court of Session reached the same result. They agreed with the Lord Ordinary that the petition was irrelevant, since nothing in the Acts of Union dealt with royal numerals. They agreed that the petitioners lacked title to sue. As to the Royal Titles Act, the Lord President, Lord Cooper, observed that the designation 'Elizabeth the Second' had been adopted and used before the Act came into force, and so that Act was not really in issue; the new royal title, like others before it, had actually been adopted without statutory authority.

The decision on relevancy would have been sufficient to dispose of the case, and may be considered the ratio decidendi. But Lord Cooper made some observations upon the union legislation:

> The principle of the unlimited sovereignty of Parliament is a distinctively English principle which has no counterpart in Scottish constitutional law. It derives its origin from Coke and Blackstone, and was widely popularised during the nineteenth century by Bagehot and Dicey . . . Considering that the Union legislation extinguished the Parliaments of Scotland and England and replaced them by a new Parliament, I have difficulty in seeing why it should have been supposed that the new Parliament of Great Britain must inherit all the peculiar characteristics of the English Parliament but none of the Scottish Parliament, as if all that happened in 1707 was that Scottish representatives were admitted to the Parliament of England. That is not what was done. Further the Treaty and associated legislation by which the Parliament of Great Britain was brought into being . . . contain some clauses which expressly reserve . . . powers of subsequent modification, and other clauses which either contain no such power or emphatically exclude subsequent alteration by declarations that the provision shall be fundamental and unalterable in all time coming, or declarations of a like effect. I have never been able to understand how it is possible to reconcile with elementary canons of construction the adoption by the English constitutional theorists of the same attitude to these markedly different provisions.

The Lord Advocate conceded this point by admitting that the Parliament of Great Britain 'could not' repeal or alter such 'fundamental and essential' conditions.[18]

These remarks (with which Lord Carmont and Lord Russell expressed agreement) are interesting, but not altogether easy to interpret. Their force is weakened in several ways. First, as has been said, the observations were obiter. Secondly, the point was conceded by the Lord Advocate. The judge's views would carry more weight if an opposing submission had been argued. Thirdly, the judge's attack on Dicey seems to rely upon a false premise. There is obviously sensitivity in Scotland over the supposition that the Great Britain Parliament should have assumed all the attributes of the pre-union English Parliament and none of the Scottish Parliament. But Dicey does not put things that way, and the more important point is that the theory of unlimited sovereignty is not necessarily based on that premise at all. It is not entirely clear either that the Scottish Parliament lacked such an attribute before 1707 (for its authority had grown rapidly since 1688) or that the English Parliament had it. It might well be, for example, that events of the seventeenth century culminating in the Glorious Revolution established the supremacy of Parliament in both countries, a proposition which seems to have the distinguished support of Lord Reid.[19] Another view might be that sovereignty was not fully developed and recognised until the nineteenth century, when Parliament was more truly representative and constitutional principles better understood. Neither of these views, and others are possible, depends upon the premise which Lord Cooper puts into the mouths of 'English constitutional theorists'.

Despite these qualifications, the view emerges from the judgments in *MacCormick* that some provisions in the Anglo-Scottish union are to be regarded as fundamental and unalterable. However, Lord Cooper continued in this way:

> But the petitioners have still a grave difficulty to overcome on this branch of their argument. Accepting it that there are provisions in the Treaty of Union and associated legislation which are 'fundamental law', and assuming for the moment that something is alleged to have been done – it matters not whether with legislative authority or not – in breach of that fundamental law, the question remains whether such a question is determinable as a justiciable issue in the Courts of either Scotland or England, in the same fashion as an issue of constitutional *vires* would be cognisable by the Supreme Courts of the United States, or of South Africa or Australia. I reserve my opinion with regard to the provisions relating expressly to this Court and to the laws 'which concern private right' which are administered here. This is not such a question, but a matter of 'public right' . . .
>
> This at least is plain, that there is neither precedent nor authority of any kind for the view that the domestic Courts of either Scotland or England have jurisdiction to determine whether a governmental act of the type here in controversy is or is not conform to the provisions of a Treaty, least of all when that Treaty is one under which both Scotland and England ceased to be independent states and merged their identity in an incorporating union.[20]

With these remarks, our difficulties are apt to be compounded. The court

19 *British Railways Board v Pickin* [1974] AC 765 at 782, [1974] 1 All ER 609 at 614, HL.
20 1953 SC 396 at 411.

disclaimed jurisdiction to determine whether 'a governmental act of the type here in controversy' conformed to the union legislation. It is unclear whether this was intended as a disclaimer with regard to questions of royal title, or breaches of Article I, or breaches in the field of public law, or all breaches, to name but a few of the possibilities. Although some English commentators chose to interpret it as a general disclaimer of jurisdiction, it should be noted that Lord Cooper expressly reserved his opinion with regard to possible breaches of parts of Articles XVIII and XIX, and Lord Russell with regard to Article XIX and the provisions concerning the church.[1]

Nonetheless, there is a difference between reserving your opinion and claiming that a court may treat the matter as justiciable, and there is an even greater difference between what was said and claiming a power of judicial review. T B Smith extracts from Lord Cooper's judgment the implication that 'legislation may be illegal and unconstitutional without necessarily being subjected to scrutiny and restraint by the judiciary'.[2] This is a possible interpretation, certainly, for those who find comfort in it, but in the absence of a remedy for its breach, the supposedly binding quality of the legislation would not seem in that event to count for much. Lord Cooper himself appreciated the point, for he actually said: 'it is of little avail to ask whether the Parliament of Great Britain "can" do this thing or that, without going on to inquire who can stop them if they do.'[3] On reflection, it is difficult to place too much weight on Lord Cooper's Janus-like dicta.

The case of *Gibson v Lord Advocate* in 1975 concerned EEC Regulations giving member states equal access to fishing grounds, which had become law in this country by virtue of the European Communities Act 1972. The pursuer's argument was that the law was in breach of Article XVIII which forbade 'alteration . . . in laws which concern private right except for the evident utility of the subjects within Scotland', and therefore invalid. As in *MacCormick*, the action failed on the ground of relevancy. Lord Keith, the Lord Ordinary, held that the 'branch of law which is concerned with the control of fishing in territorial waters round the coasts of Scotland is a branch of public law',[4] so that Article XVIII did not restrict Parliament's power to alter it. This meant that the broader constitutional questions were 'not live issues', but he did not resist the temptation to comment upon them, which he did in these terms:

> Like Lord President Cooper, I prefer to reserve my opinion on what the question would be if the United Kingdom Parliament passed an Act purporting to abolish the Court of Session or the Church of Scotland or to substitute English law for the

---

1 Lord Russell says Articles XIX and XXV. But he probably meant not Article XXV, but the Church provisions which immediately follow it.
2 *British Justice: The Scottish Contribution* (1961) p 209.
3 1953 SC 396 at 412.
4 1975 SLT 134 at 136.

whole body of Scots private law. I am, however, of opinion that the question whether a particular Act of the United Kingdom Parliament altering a particular aspect of Scots private law is or is not 'for the evident utility' of the subjects within Scotland is not a justiciable issue in this court. The making of decisions upon what must essentially be a political matter is no part of the function of the court, and it is highly undesirable that it should be.[5]

Most of this is reminiscent of Lord Cooper's approach, and it is scarcely less equivocal. However, Lord Cooper had left open the question of the justiciability of breaches of Article XVIII, whereas here such issues (with the exception of the substitution of English law for the entire body of Scots private law, which is inconceivable) are classified as not justiciable. Incidentally, in *Gibson* the Lord Advocate, far from conceding the special nature of the Acts of Union, denied in his argument that the Court of Session had jurisdiction to interfere with an Act of Parliament on the ground of its inconsistency with the legislation.

Naturally, some Scottish writers make much of the dicta in these two cases, but they remain problematic. On the one hand, some provisions are said to be fundamental and unalterable; on the other hand, even with regard to breaches of those provisions, no power of judicial review is asserted.

In my submission, it ought to be doubted whether these obiter remarks should really be taken to represent Scots law on the subject. In matters of civil law, appeal lies from the courts in Scotland to the House of Lords. In *Edinburgh and Dalkeith Rly Co v Wauchope*,[6] the House of Lords, on an appeal from the Court of Session, heard an argument that a purported Act of Parliament, because of a procedural defect during its passage, could and should be held invalid. The argument was roundly condemned. Lord Campbell declared that 'All that a Court of Justice can do is look to the Parliament Roll',[7] and expressed the hope that Scottish courts would not again feel able to make any inquiry into the validity of Acts of Parliament. In *Mortensen v Peters*,[8] a Danish fisherman challenged his conviction for an offence made under the authority of the Herring Fishery (Scotland) Act 1889, on the ground that the enactment was contrary to international law. A Full Bench of twelve judges was convened in the High Court of Justiciary, but all were in agreement. The Lord Justice General, Lord Dunedin, said: 'For us an Act of Parliament duly passed by Lords and Commons and assented to by the King is supreme, and we are bound to give effect to its terms.'[9] Of course, the Acts of Union were not involved in that case, but Lord Dunedin's statement was made without any qualification, and would hardly have been

5 Ibid at 137.
6 (1842) 8 Cl & Fin 710.
7 Ibid at 725.
8 1906 14 SLT 227.
9 Ibid at 230.

phrased in such terms if it was the view of the Scottish judiciary that
Parliament's legislative powers were limited by a constitutional instrument.
In *Pickin v British Railways Board v Pickin*[10] in 1974, the House of Lords
unanimously and decisively rejected another attempt to impugn the validity
of an Act on the ground of a procedural defect. Lord Reid, a Scottish Lord of
Appeal and probably the most respected judge of the post-war period,
approved Lord Campbell's dictum as a correct statement of the constitutional
position, and accepted the supremacy of Parliament without qualification.
In *Sillars v Smith*[11] in 1982, the High Court of Justiciary was faced with an
argument that Parliament's authority to legislate had been lost when it failed
to bring into force the devolution provisions of the Scotland Act 1978
despite the wishes of a majority of those in Scotland who voted. In dismissing
the contention, the court referred again to Lord Campbell's speech, and also
to that part of Lord Cooper's judgment in *MacCormick v Lord Advocate* in which
he disclaimed 'jurisdiction to determine whether a governmental act of the
type here in controversy is or is not conform to the provisions of a Treaty', as
an illustration of the same principle. If it were truly part of Scots law that
Parliament is 'unfree', one would not have anticipated the tenor of the
remarks in these various decisions.

There are no counterparts to *MacCormick*'s case in England or in Ireland.
Calvert argues, perhaps with more hope than conviction, that a court in
Northern Ireland, if seized of a corresponding issue, might take a similar
view to Lord Cooper's.[12] But Irish courts have not had the opportunity.

It has not been squarely argued before an English court that the Acts of
Union are a limitation upon Parliament. However, in *Ex p Canon Selwyn*,[13] a
clergyman attempted to question the validity of the Irish Church Act 1869
on the ground that the disestablishment was contrary to the Queen's
coronation oath made under the Act of Settlement. Thus, the argument was
not based on inconsistency with the Acts of Union as such. Nevertheless, the
Court of Queen's Bench, in dismissing his action, stated that 'there is no
judicial body in the country by which the validity of an act of parliament
could be questioned,'[14] without adding any reservation. There are many
other dicta to the same effect, and no English court has ever attributed any
exceptional effect to the union legislation. In *Moore v A-G for the Irish Free
State*,[15] it was necessary to decide whether the Irish Free State Parliament
could competently prohibit appeals from the Irish Supreme Court to His
Majesty in Council. The Privy Council, in deciding that it could, simply

10 [1974] AC 765, [1974] 1 All ER 609, HL.
11 1982 SLT 539.
12 *Constitutional Law in Northern Ireland* (1968) ch 1.
13 (1872) 36 JP 54.
14 Ibid at 55.
15 [1935] AC 484, PC.

assumed that the 1922 Acts contrary to the union legislation were valid. There was no hint of a suggestion in the Lord Chancellor's speech that Parliament was limited by the union legislation, nor any hint of support for the argument mentioned earlier, that Parliament might have acted 'unlawfully'. The question may be taken as closed, with regard to English law.

Coda

On the back of Lord Cooper's obiter dicta, a small number of constitutional lawyers have skilfully put together an argument that the Acts of Union act as a limitation upon what Parliament may do. In fact, whatever was intended by the makers of the union legislation, the evidence is overwhelming that Parliament will not be hindered by it from passing any legislation it likes.

One of the ironies in the debate is that the view of the Acts of Union as binding is often urged by those sympathetic to Scottish nationalism, while the realisation of the aim of Scottish National Party politicians, independence from England, would itself be a breach of the Acts.

However, the realities are clear enough. When a Royal Commission on the Constitution was set up in response to demands in the 1960s for greater devolution of power to Scotland and Wales, independence or separatism was one of the possibilities considered by it under its terms of reference. The government obviously thought that legislation to that effect was perfectly possible. So did the Royal Commission, which in its later stages was chaired by a Scottish judge, Lord Kilbrandon. 'The supremacy of Parliament,' they said, 'has the consequence that it is not bound by the acts of its predecessors . . . No special procedures are required to enact even the most fundamental changes in the constitution.'[16]

16 Report of the Royal Commission on the Constitution 1969–1973 (Cmnd 5460) para 56.

5 The sovereignty of Parliament

In the last chapter, we considered the argument that Parliament was born unfree, but had to conclude that it was not proven. There are other arguments to the effect that Parliament is, or can be, limited in its powers to legislate, which will be considered in this chapter. One argument, that the European Communities Act 1972 limits Parliament, will be discussed in the following chapter, when the relationship of the United Kingdom to the European Communities is considered.

All these arguments are put in opposition to Dicey's view of Parliament as being illimitable or 'sovereign'. In most of the other states of the world, there are limits to the legislature's powers, often prescribed in the nation's constitution. If the United Kingdom is peculiar in this respect, it would not be so from logical necessity, but only as a result of constitutional history. With history,[1] we had better start.

THE DEVELOPMENT OF LEGAL SUPREMACY

1652 Oliver Cromwell Lord Protector

The seventeenth century was a crucially formative period for the British constitution. The period of civil war in the 1640s, resulting in the success of the parliamentary forces, led to a succession of experiments in republican government, none entirely successful. After Cromwell's death, these novelties were repudiated. The restoration of the monarchy in 1660 was at the same time a deliberate return to the principles and practice of government under law. Unfortunately, the restored Stuart kings proved to be unworthy recipients of the authority this gave them, not least because they seemed to pervert principles of legality by their exercise of the powers of suspending or dispensing with laws. In 1688, James II of England and VII of Scotland fled into exile from a country which could tolerate no longer the abuse of his powers in furtherance of his fellow Catholics' cause.

So in 1688, after a long, unsettled period, there was a need for a new constitutional settlement. A monarchy was thought desirable, but it had to be a Protestant monarchy. It had also to be a limited monarchy, subordinate

---

1 Only a potted version. See further F W Maitland *The Constitutional History of England* (1908); T P Taswell-Langmead *English Constitutional History* (11th edn, 1960).

in its powers to Parliament. These points were taken for granted when an informal group of peers, past members of the Commons (which had not been summoned since 1685), and authorities of the City of London invited William, Prince of Orange, to summon a Convention. This irregular assembly met, declared the throne vacant, and offered it to William and Mary jointly. The gift was not absolute, but conditional, the terms being set out in a Declaration of Right. When the offer was accepted, the Convention passed an Act, the Crown and Parliament Act 1689, declaring itself to be a duly constituted Parliament, then enacted the Bill of Rights, incorporating the Declaration of Right. The principle implicit in the Bill of Rights is the supremacy of Parliament in the law. Parliament was to be its own master and free from interference, for by Article IX 'the freedom of speech and debates or proceedings in Parliament ought not to be impeached or questioned in any court or place out of Parliament'. Parliaments were to be held frequently, and the election of their members was to be free. The Crown's power to levy taxes was made subject to parliamentary consent, its power to keep a standing army made subject to statute, and the powers of suspending or dispensing with laws, as exercised by the Stuart kings, were declared illegal. The Scottish Crown too was offered to William and Mary, upon similar terms, as incorporated by the Scottish Parliament in the Claim of Right in 1689. The constitutional settlement was completed by the Triennial Act of 1694, requiring that Parliament be summoned at least every three years, and by the Act of Settlement in 1700, which ensured a Protestant succession to the throne and protected judicial tenure against the Crown.

Earlier in the seventeenth century, parliamentary legislation had not been obviously pre-eminent among the sources of law.[2] According to Coke CJ in *Dr Bonham's Case*, 'when an Act of Parliament is against common right and reason, or repugnant, or impossible to be performed, the common law will control it, and adjudge such act to be void'.[3] A few years later Hobart CJ observed in *Day v Savadge* that 'even an Act of Parliament, made against natural equity, as to make a man judge in his own case, is void in itself'.[4] How much weight should be attached to these obiter dicta, reported by the judges themselves, is debatable, but the courts' decisions in such cases as *R v Hampden, Ship Money Case*[5] and *Godden v Hales*[6] are more significant. In the former, royal taxation for navy building, without parliamentary consent, was held by a majority of the common law judges to be lawful when justified by necessity. Although the Petitition of Right in 1628 and other statutes purported to require parliamentary consent to taxation, their view was that

2 See J W Gough *Fundamental Law in English Constitutional History* (1955).
3 (1610) 8 Co Rep 114 at 118.
4 (1615) Hob 85 at 97.
5 (1637) 3 St Tr 825.
6 (1686) 11 St Tr 1165.

the king had an inseparable prerogative to defend the realm, and any statute which attempted to deprive him of it was void. Similarly, in *Godden v Hales* the king's prerogative to dispense with statutes was viewed by Lord Chief Justice Herbert and ten of the other eleven judges as an inseparable prerogative which could not be taken away.

These cases are only of historical interest, for the Glorious Revolution of 1688 brought an end to the dramatic struggles between monarchs and Houses of Parliament. That is not to say that skirmishing was over. William and Mary and their successors would seek to exercise to the full what authority they had, and the leaders of the House of Commons would make further attacks on prerogative powers. But the boundaries had been marked out. After 1688 it could not be claimed that any of the king's prerogatives were untouchable or denied that any which came into conflict with a statute must give way. The reasons for this are to be found in the alliance formed between parliamentarians and the common lawyers, fostered in part by the recognition that Parliament was itself a court of law.[7] In alliance, they subordinated the powers of the king, and the means of defeating the Crown's attempts to rule by prerogative was the judge's insistence that the limits of prerogative powers, as part of the common law, are determinable by the courts: 'the King hath no prerogative, but that which the law of the land allows him'.[8] The principle had been propounded in 1611, but its consequences were not fully apparent until 1688. For the common lawyers, there was a price to pay, and that was the abandonment of the claim they had sometimes advanced, that Parliament could not legislate in derogation of the principles of the common law. As Lord Reid commented in a case in 1974:

> In earlier times many learned lawyers seem to have believed that an Act of Parliament could be disregarded in so far as it was contrary to the law of God or the law of nature or natural justice, but since the supremacy of Parliament was finally demonstrated by the Revolution of 1688 any such idea has become obsolete.[9]

Thus, from the Revolution settlement Parliament emerged as the supreme law-maker in the state, while two other competing sources of legal rules were put firmly in their place.

DICEY ON PARLIAMENTARY SOVEREIGNTY

The events of the seventeenth century ensured that Parliament enjoyed a legal supremacy amongst the institutions of the state. One undoubted consequence of this was that Acts of Parliament were recognised by the

---

7 See C H McIlwain *The High Court of Parliament and its Supremacy* (1910).
8 *Case of Proclamations* (1611) 12 Co Rep 74. On the history of the prerogative, see further ch 8.
9 *British Railways Board v Pickin* [1974] AC 765 at 782, [1974] 1 All ER 609 at 614.

courts as being at the top of the hierarchy of legal rules. In the event of a clash between an Act of Parliament and principles of common law, or the body of law comprising the royal prerogative, the courts, after 1688, unhesitatingly allowed the statute law to prevail.

This was naturally regarded as an important feature of the legal system, and both Coke and Blackstone commented on it. However, it was A V Dicey who provided the classic exposition of it in his *Introduction to the Study of the Law of the Constitution*, first published in 1885, and it is Dicey's account which is still the starting-point for discussion today.

In his search for the guiding principles of the British constitution, Dicey discovered three, and the first of these in importance, 'the very keystone of the law of the constitution',[10] was what he called the sovereignty of Parliament. The nature of parliamentary sovereignty, he said, was: 'that Parliament . . . has . . . the right to make or unmake any law whatever; and further, that no person or body is recognised by the law of England as having a right to override or set aside the legislation of Parliament',[11] and these two aspects he called 'the positive side' and 'the negative side'.[12]

The negative aspect, more fully expounded, is that 'there is no person or body of persons who can, under the English constitution, make rules which override or derogate from an Act of Parliament, or which (to express the same thing in other words) will be enforced by the courts in contravention of an Act of Parliament'.[13] We may notice that this is no more than a recognition that Acts of Parliament are supreme within the hierarchy of laws and a fortiori prevail over any principles or rules which are not laws. Dicey demonstrates the point by reference to the absence of any legislative power able to compete with Parliament:[14] the Crown's authority to legislate had, since the *Case of Proclamations*[15] in 1611, been restricted; judge-made law was recognisably subordinate to statute; one of the Houses of Parliament acting alone, even the House of Commons, could not make law, as *Stockdale v Hansard*[16] showed; the electorate, which chose the members of the Commons, had no other role in the legislative process. All of these points were uncontroversial, for they were already well established.

The positive aspect of sovereignty, however, is made to carry much more weight.[17] It means not only that Parliament may legislate upon any topic, but also that any parliamentary enactment must be obeyed by the courts. In a further reworking, sovereignty is said to involve first, that there is no law

---

10 *Law of the Constitution* (10th edn) p 70 (hereafter, *Dicey*).
11 Dicey pp 39–40.
12 Dicey pp 40–41.
13 Dicey p 40.
14 Dicey pp 50–61.
15 (1611) 12 Co Rep 74.
16 (1839) 9 Ad & El 1.
17 Dicey pp 87–91 and ch 2.

which Parliament cannot change, so that even constitutional laws of great importance may be changed in the same manner as other laws; secondly, the absence of any legal distinction between constitutional and other laws; and thirdly, that there exists no person or body, executive, legislative or judicial, which can pronounce void any enactment of Parliament on the ground of its being opposed to the constitution or any other ground.

Dicey's treatment of all these points as attributes of a sovereign legislature, and his referring to the positive and negative 'sides' of sovereignty, imply that we have here a number of corollaries flowing from the same proposition. Such an inference, however, would be wrong. That statute law is superior to other forms of law in the hierarchy does not necessarily entail that Parliament may legislate upon any topic or repeal any law; for example, it would be possible to maintain (and some do)[18] that some parts of the Acts of Union between England and Scotland are unalterable, without doubting that Acts of Parliament prevail over other kinds of law. Again, the absence of a judicial power to hold Acts of Parliament void does not of itself mean that the legislature is unlimited, for in some countries excess of legislative authority may be left as a matter between the legislature and the electors, or may be dealt with by a non-judicial process. Dicey did recognise this last point,[19] but the general impression left by his account is that the different attributes he ascribes to Parliament are all of a piece. This is not so, and it is instructive to unpack Dicey's doctrine. When we do, we see that, while the 'negative side' of sovereignty was uncontroversial, the other propositions advanced by Dicey were more wide-reaching and not so obviously justified.

In purporting to show that Parliament's legislative authority was unlimited, Dicey offered evidence of a different sort.[20] He cited the opinions of Coke, Blackstone, and De Lolme. He exhibited historical instances of the width of Parliament's powers: it could alter the succession to the throne, as it did in the Act of Settlement; it could prolong its own life, as with the Septennial Act of 1716; it could make legal past illegalities by Acts of Indemnity. He argued that some supposed limitations on Parliament's capacity were not real: the existence of inalienable prerogative powers could no longer be maintained; that doctrines of morality or the rules of international law could prevail against Acts of Parliament found no support in case law. Finally, Dicey denied that earlier Acts had ever limited what a Parliament could do. The language of certain enactments, such as the Acts of Union, suggested an intention to restrict later Parliaments, but their subsequent history demonstrated the futility of the attempts. Therefore, Parliament's authority was not only unlimited, but illimitable, for attempts to bind succeeding Parliaments would be ineffective.

18 See ch 4.
19 Dicey pp 131–137.
20 Dicey pp 41–50, 61–70.

These matters, informative as they are, scarcely compel us to accept Dicey's case. One does not establish that Parliament can do anything merely by pointing to a number of things that it has done, however impressive, any more than one proves that Parliament is limited in some respect by pointing to an area in which it has not legislated. So Dicey does not really establish that Parliament is unlimited, still less that it is illimitable. But if his propositions are not verifiable, they are falsifiable by appropriate evidence. No evidence to that effect existed at Dicey's time. We may see whether it has been thrown up in the hundred years since. First, however, it is necessary to examine the nature of parliamentary sovereignty a little more closely.

A MERELY LEGAL CONCEPTION

In order to prevent misunderstanding, one point needs to be emphasised before embarking on any discussion of whether Dicey was right or wrong. It is that the principle of the sovereignty of Parliament only expresses certain legal rules. Students of the constitution sometimes fail to grasp this point, and some of Dicey's critics have displayed a similar lack of appreciation of it.

Some confusion is perhaps understandable. In its teaching and its exposition, the topic is often clothed with a mystique which suggests that something much grander and more arcane is involved than a set of associated legal rules. Maybe Dicey kindles false expectations when he treats it as one of the guiding first principles which will lead us through the maze of the British constitution. If we pause to consider his other guiding principles, the rule of law and the dependence of the conventions of the constitution upon the law, it is evident that they are not composed of legal rules, but are rather extrapolations from the legal and other features of the constitution, which he puts forward as higher order principles.

However, a careful reading of Dicey suggests that, even if he has inadvertently misled his readers, his own understanding of the point was clear enough. Parliamentary sovereignty was, he said, the dominant characteristic of our political institutions 'from a legal point of view'.[1] Later he criticises Austin for blurring the distinction between different uses of the term 'sovereignty', as follows:

> It should, however, be carefully noted that the term 'sovereignty', as long as it is accurately employed in the sense in which Austin sometimes uses it, is a merely legal conception, and means simply the power of law-making unrestricted by any legal limit.[2]

[handwritten margin note: PS only certain legal rules]

1 Dicey p 39.
2 Dicey p 72.

Thus employed, and it is in this sense that constitutional lawy
the concept of parliamentary sovereignty is only indicative
relationship between the legislature and the courts, nothing less b
more.

The use of the term 'sovereignty' to express this relationship is pe.
be regretted, for the word had a past history of usage in political writings,[3]
and besides bears other meanings in constitutional law (where the monarch
may be referred to as the Sovereign) and in international law (where
sovereignty is an attribute of states). However, Dicey not only did his best to
make clear the sense in which he was employing the term, but additionally
sought to dispose of one of the most obvious sources of possible confusion:

> The word 'sovereignty' is sometimes employed in a political rather than in a
> strictly legal sense. That body is 'politically' sovereign or supreme in a state the
> will of which is ultimately obeyed . . . In this sense of the word the electors of
> Great Britain may be said to be . . . the body in which sovereign power is vested
> . . . But this is a political, not a legal fact . . . The political sense of the word
> 'sovereignty' is, it is true, fully as important as the legal sense or more so. But the
> two significations . . . are essentially different . . . [4]

This, it is submitted, is a perfectly clear and sensible distinction. Even if in
more sophisticated times sociologists or political scientists might dispute
that political power is to be so easily located in 'the electors', this does not
affect the central point. However, Dicey's clarity has not saved him from
being misunderstood. Sir Ivor Jennings said with regard to Dicey's
distinction that 'if this is so, legal sovereignty is not sovereignty at all. It is
not supreme power.'[5] But this is a criticism which depends upon the
assumption that sovereignty may mean only one thing, which is unfounded.
Jennings cited Harold Laski in support, but Laski was hardly an exemplar in
this respect, as has been observed:

> Sometimes the target that Laski called 'sovereignty' was the immunity of the
> Crown: sometimes it seemed to be unjust legislation or unqualified allegiance.
> Sometimes again it appeared as absolute power and at other times it became the
> 'Austinian' theory of unlimited legal authority.[6]

Even an editor of Dicey, E C S Wade, was occasionally subject to confusion,
as where he suggested that the sovereignty of Parliament was difficult to
reconcile with the state of affairs in which governments were dominant
within Parliament.[7]

The drawing of a distinction between legal and political sovereignty has

---

3 See F H Hinsley *Sovereignty* (1966).
4 Dicey pp 73–74.
5 *The Law and the Constitution* (5th edn, 1959), p 149.
6 Geoffrey Marshall *Constitutional Theory* (1971) p 40.
7 In his Introduction to *Law of the Constitution* (10th edn, 1959) p xxi.

been criticised by C H McIlwain[8] as well as Jennings, but it seems obvious that if confusion is to be avoided, just such a distinction has to be made. Parliamentary sovereignty, as lawyers use the phrase, is only concerned with the effect to be given by the courts to Acts of Parliament. It is not concerned with the politics of the making of legislation, or with political dominance in the state.

Another feature of discussions of the sovereignty of Parliament since Dicey's time may be traced to the same confusion between legal authority and political realities. If Parliament can do anything, why does it not command that all blue-eyed babies be killed, asked Dicey's contemporary, Leslie Stephen.[9] 'There are many things . . . which Parliament cannot do,' says Jennings, who suggested that 'it never passes any laws which any substantial section of the population violently dislikes'.[10] However, a non sequitur is present in discussions of this sort. Parliamentary sovereignty denotes only the absence of legal limitations, not the absence of *all* limitations or, a more appropriate word, inhibitions on Parliament's actions.

It is perfectly obvious that utterly abhorrent legislation is unlikely to be enacted by the United Kingdom Parliament; that governments are influenced by political considerations in deciding what legislation to propose; that international law and international obligations and relations are factors which affect the making of legislation; and that certain conventions are customarily observed by Parliament, so that, to give one example, it does not normally seek to legislate for the Channel Islands in domestic affairs. But these are not legal limitations, and there should be no need to mention them in a discussion of this sort, provided again that it is understood that sovereignty is only a legal conception. Dicey felt compelled to deal with the difficulty, and divided 'actual limitations' into the 'internal limit' (what the sovereign cannot bring himself to do) and the 'external limit' (what the subjects would not tolerate without resistance).[11] No doubt this is an imperfect analysis, which does not exhaust the different kinds of inhibition to which Parliament is subject, but his heart cannot have been in a task which he rightly perceived as peripheral to the matter in hand.

There is another matter often mentioned in discussions of sovereignty which falls to be treated in the same way as Dicey's 'actual limitations'. It is evident that if every succeeding Parliament is to enjoy the same degree of legislative authority as its predecessors, then attempts to bind subsequent Parliaments do not succeed. Dicey expressed this by numbering preceding Acts amongst the things which had been alleged to be, but were not, limitations on Parliament's legislative authority.[12] However, another way of

8 'Sovereignty' in *Constitutionalism and the Changing World* (1969).
9 Leslie Stephen *The Science of Ethics* (1882).
10 *The Law and the Constitution* (5th edn, 1959) p 148.
11 Dicey pp 76–85.
12 Dicey p 64.

presenting the matter would be by saying that 'there is one thing which Parliament cannot do' (that is, to pass a law which would bind its successors), or viewing it as a limitation upon or exception to Parliament's sovereignty.[13] This perplexed Dicey, or so at least it is alleged.[14] Again, however, the answer is simple enough when the distinction between law and fact is remembered. To say that Parliament 'cannot' bind its successors is like saying that Parliament cannot require good weather over England or cannot turn a woman into a man: 'cannot' in these contexts means 'is not able effectively to in fact'. But when we say that Parliament 'can' make any law, we mean only that anything enacted by Parliament will be treated as valid by the courts.[15] In this sense, Parliament can make a woman into a man, and in fact frequently does.[16] Acts which purport to bind later Parliaments, assuming Dicey was correct in his view, are not invalid, but merely ineffective (like, in varying degrees, many other provisions) and, like all other enactments, liable to repeal.

THE CASE LAW

It used to be said that Dicey's doctrine of sovereignty had not been deduced from, and was not much supported by, case law, for there was little to which he could point. There was some truth in this, although the interpretation to be put on it was problematical. It could be said that the principle of sovereignty was so well established that litigants would not attempt to question it, and so judicial pronouncements were scarce. Or it could be implied that, since there were few dicta in support of Dicey's views, the views were not well founded, and indeed, on the appropriate occasion, would be judicially controverted.

It is no longer true that there is a shortage of judicial authority concerning parliamentary sovereignty. The reports of the last hundred years or so provide much relevant material, and in the last few years one challenge to the validity of an Act has reached the House of Lords, and another the Court of Appeal.[17]

We may begin by considering the case which reached the House of Lords

13 Even Dicey's most distinguished defender refers to this at one point as being a 'limit to Parliament's legal power': H W R Wade 'The Basis of Legal Sovereignty' [1955] CLJ 155 at 174.

14 R F V Heuston *Essays in Constitutional Law* (2nd edn, 1964) p 4.

15 The ambiguity of 'can', which is the cause of confusion here, is a parallel to the ambiguities of words like 'sovereignty', 'supremacy' or 'power', already noted.

16 By the Interpretation Act 1978, s 6, in statutes, 'unless the contrary intention appears . . . words importing the masculine gender include the feminine'.

17 The Court of Appeal decision was *Manuel v A-G* [1983] 1 Ch 77, [1982] 3 All ER 822; affirming the Vice-Chancellor, [1983] 1 Ch 77, [1982] 3 All ER 786. See Munro 'Dicey Two, Jennings Nil' (1983) 34 NILQ 162.

in 1974, *British Railways Board v Pickin*.[18] Pickin, a railway enthusiast, had bought for ten shillings in 1969 the reversionary interest in a few yards of a disused railway line, but the Board subsequently claimed that it owned the land by virtue of a private Act of Parliament, the British Railways Act 1968. Pickin asked the court to declare the Act ineffective on the ground that the Board had obtained its enactment by misleading Parliament and that the standing orders of each House, which required individual notice to be given to owners affected by private legislation, had not been complied with.

An inquiry into the matter would have required the court to examine what happened during the proceedings at Bill stage. Their Lordships were unanimous that the courts had no power to disregard an Act of Parliament, whether private or public, and no jurisdiction to inquire into the procedures in Parliament. Lord Reid observed that 'the idea that a court is entitled to disregard a provision in an Act of Parliament on any ground must seem strange and startling to anyone with any knowledge of the history and law of our constitution'.[19] Lord Simon of Glaisdale said that the sovereignty of Parliament involved 'that, contrary to what was sometimes asserted before the 18th century, and in contradistinction to some other democratic systems, the courts in this country have no power to declare enacted law to be invalid'.[20] Lord Morris of Borth-y-Gest said: 'When an enactment is passed there is finality unless and until it is amended or repealed by Parliament'.[1]

These are strong and unqualified statements in support of the view that an Act of Parliament may not be invalid. There was agreement that no distinction was to be drawn between private Acts and public Acts, and that the examination of proceedings in Parliament was not open to the courts. Lord Simon pointed out that the privileges of Parliament were a concomitant of its sovereignty, and that Article IX of the Bill of Rights forbade the questioning of proceedings in Parliament by outside bodies.

The *Pickin* case affirms what is sometimes called 'the enrolled bill rule'. In an appeal to the House of Lords in *Edinburgh and Dalkeith Rly Co v Wauchope*,[2] a rather similar case also involving alleged lack of notice to landowners by a railway company which had obtained a private Act, Lord Campbell had declared:

> All that a Court of Justice can do is to look to the Parliamentary Roll: if from that it should appear that a Bill has passed both Houses and received the Royal Assent, no Court of Justice can inquire into the mode in which it was introduced into Parliament, nor into what was done previous to its introduction, or what passed in Parliament during its progress in its various stages through Parliament.[3]

18 [1974] AC 765, [1974] 1 All ER 609, HL.
19 [1974] AC 765 at 782, [1974] 1 All ER 609 at 614, HL.
20 [1974] AC 765 at 798, [1974] 1 All ER 609 at 627, HL.
1 [1974] AC 765 at 789, [1974] 1 All ER 609 at 619, HL.
2 (1842) 8 Cl & Fin 710.
3 Ibid at 725.

Similarly, in another case involving a private Act, *Lee v Bud..*
Junction Rly Co,[4] Willes J had said: 'If an Act of Parliament has ..
improperly, it is for the legislature to correct it by repealing it; b..
exists as law, the courts are bound to obey it'.[5]

From these dicta, the 'enrolled bill rule' had been inferred. Tha..
Act bearing the signs of a duly enacted Act of Parliament must be t.. .. .ace
value: the courts may not question it. More recently, there have been attempts
to cast doubt on the rule. It was pointed out that the Parliament roll which
Lord Campbell mentioned no longer exists; but this is a red herring, for the
judge was speaking metaphorically, and other means of authentication exist
for cases of doubt. Sometimes it was stressed that Lord Campbell's words were
obiter dicta. Sometimes it was suggested that different considerations might
apply to private and to public Acts. But in *Pickin* Lord Reid said that 'the law is
correctly stated by Lord Campbell'[6] and Lord Simon described the dictum in the
case as 'particularly apposite and authoritative',[7] so the enrolled bill rule was
explicitly approved.

So far, we have seen that challenges to the validity of Acts on the ground that
Parliament has not acted properly will not be countenanced by the courts. In a
few cases litigants have actually tried to persuade a court that the body
regarded as Parliament lacked authority to legislate. Thus, in *Hall v Hall*,[8] a
case involving title to a house, one party sought to defeat the other's claim
under the Probate Act 1857 on the ground that it (and all other legislation
since 1688) had not received the royal assent, since the Stuart line had been
illegally deprived of the throne. As we have seen, there is a sense in which this
argument is tenable, but as the courts had long ago bowed to the political fact
of the 1688 Revolution, there is another sense in which it was wrong and
hopeless to maintain. You may safely guess how the Hereford County Court
judge treated it! In *Martin v O'Sullivan*,[9] a self-employed person in default of
National Insurance contributions argued that the Social Security Act 1975
was invalid. His argument was that a change in the status of MPs for tax
purposes, from self-employed to employed persons, rendered them holders of
an office of profit under the Crown, and so disqualified them from membership
of the House, as the number of holders of Crown offices who might sit in the
House of Commons was limited by statute. The High Court judge found that
his argument was flawed, and besides observed that all that a court could do
was to look at the 'parliamentary roll'. In *Sillars v Smith*,[10] the appellant, a

4 (1871) LR 6 CP 576.
5 Ibid at 582.
6 [1974] AC 765 at 786, [1974] 1 All ER 609 at 617, HL.
7 [1974] AC 765 at 799, [1974] 1 All ER 609 at 628, HL.
8 (1944) 88 Sol Jo 383. A counterpart is *Heath v Pryn* (1670) 1 Vent 14, where the validity of
   Acts of the Restoration Parliament was unsuccessfully challenged.
9 [1984] STC 258, CA.
10 1982 SLT 539.

mer MP who had been convicted of vandalism under the Criminal Justice (Scotland) Act 1980, argued that the Act was invalid. He maintained that Parliament had lost its authority to legislate on Scottish matters because it had acted unlawfully in repealing the Scotland Act 1978 (so that its provisions for legislative devolution never came into force), when a majority of those who voted in Scotland in the referendum had wanted the provisions to come into force. The High Court of Justiciary relied on Lord Campbell's dictum in *Wauchope* as precluding any inquiry into an Act of Parliament.

Dicey denied that any higher law or other body of rules could restrict the power of Parliament to make law, and there has been nothing to contradict this view. In *British Railways Board v Pickin*, as was noted earlier, Lord Reid described as obsolete the belief that 'the law of God or the law of nature or natural justice' might override an Act of Parliament. [11] In *R v Jordan*, [12] Colin Jordan, the leader of the British Movement, having been convicted of incitement to racial hatred, tried to justify an application for legal aid on the basis that the relevant provisions of the Race Relations Act 1965 were invalid because they curtailed a fundamental constitutional right of free speech. The Divisional Court held that Parliament was supreme, and the courts had no power to question the validity of an Act of Parliament. It is clear that in the eyes of the courts Parliament's legislative competence is unrestricted by constitutional conventions:

> In the British constitution though sometimes the phrase 'unconstitutional' is used to describe a statute, which though within the legal powers of the legislature to enact, is contrary to the tone and spirit of our institutions, and to condemn the statesmanship which has advised the enactment of such a law, still notwithstanding such condemnation, the statute in question is the law and must be obeyed. [13]

Dicey was confident that inconsistency with international law did not affect the validity of Acts of Parliament, although he cited no cases in support of his view. Time has supplied the omission, for a large number of decisions and dicta may be cited to that effect. 'Legislation of . . . Parliament, even in contravention of generally acknowledged principles of international law, is binding upon and must be enforced by the courts of this country', affirmed Lord Macmillan, giving the opinion of the Privy Council in *Croft v Dunphy*. [14] When it was contended that assessments of tax made under a Finance Act were directed partly to an unlawful purpose, because the manufacture of nuclear weapons for possible use was contrary to international law, Ungoed-Thomas J held that even if such a purpose were contrary to international law, What the statute itself enacts cannot be unlawful, because [it] is the highest

11 [1974] AC 765 at 782, [1974] 1 All ER 609 at 614, HL.
12 [1967] Crim LR 483.
13 *Webb v Outrim* [1907] AC 81 at 89, PC, per the Earl of Halsbury.
14 [1933] AC 156 at 164.

form of law that is known to this country . . . and it is not for the court to say that a parliamentary enactment . . . is illegal'.[15]

The Acts of Union were for Dicey evidence of a Parliament's inability to fetter its successors, even when that is intended. He referred to the Irish Church Act 1869 (which legislated contrary to supposedly unchangeable provisions in the Act of Union with Ireland) and did not even bother to cite the case in which the validity of the Act had been challenged. That was *Ex p Canon Selwyn*[16] in which the Court of Appeal denied it had jurisdiction to deal with such a matter. 'There is no judicial body in the country by which the validity of an Act of Parliament could be questioned', said Cockburn CJ.

If any particular enactments were, because of their constitutional status, impossible to repeal, the Acts of Union would have been obvious contenders. A more general question is whether any piece of legislation may, by some appropriate form of words, be protected against repeal. Dicey's view, that this was impossible because the British Parliament's sovereignty was of a continuing nature, was strongly supported by the courts in *Vauxhall Estates Ltd v Liverpool Corpn*[17] and *Ellen Street Estates Ltd v Minister of Health*.[18] These cases concerned a provision in the Acquisition of Land (Assessment of Compensation) Act 1919 which, in regulating the compensation to be paid when land was compulsorily acquired, said that if land was acquired under the terms of any other statute, then 'so far as inconsistent with this Act those provisions shall cease to have or shall not have effect'. These words could be read as an attempt to preclude repeal, and since the compensation allowed for under the later Housing Act 1925 was less generous, it was in the interests of the companies involved in the two cases to plead the invalidity of the 1925 Act on that ground. However, neither was successful, for the Divisional Court in the earlier case and the Court of Appeal in the second roundly condemned the argument. In the *Vauxhall Estates* case, Avory J said:

> It must be admitted that such a suggestion as that is inconsistent with the principle of the constitution of this country. Speaking for myself, I should certainly hold, until the contrary were decided, that no Act of Parliament can effectively provide that no future Act shall interfere with its provisions.[19]

In the *Ellen St Estates* case, Maugham LJ said:

> The legislature cannot, according to our constitution, bind itself as to the form of subsequent legislation, and it is impossible for Parliament to enact that in a subsequent statute dealing with the same subject-matter there can be no implied

15 *Cheney v Conn* [1968] 1 All ER 779 at 782, [1968] 1 WLR 242 at 247. See also *Mortensen v Peters* 1906 14 SLT 227; *R v Secretary of State for Home Department. ex p Thakrar* [1974] QB 684, [1974] 2 All ER 261, CA.
16 (1872) 36 JP 54.
17 [1932] 1 KB 733.
18 [1934] 1 KB 590, CA.
19 [1932] 1 KB 733 at 743.

repeal. If in a subsequent Act Parliament chooses to make it plain that the earlier statute is being to some extent repealed, effect must be given to that intention just because it is the will of the legislature.[20]

It may readily be seen, therefore, that the case law of the last hundred years offers support for, rather than denial of, Dicey's views, even for the proposition that it is impossible to bind future Parliaments.

There have, however, been a few dicta which must be placed in the other scale of the balance. The case of *A-G for New South Wales v Trethowan*[1] concerned the powers of the New South Wales legislature but Dixon J in the Australian High Court indulged in some speculation concerning the United Kingdom Parliament:

> An Act of the British Parliament which contained a provision that no Bill repealing any part of the Act including the part so restraining its own repeal should be presented for the royal assent unless the Bill were first approved by the electors, would have the force of law until the Sovereign actually did assent to a Bill for its repeal. In strictness it would be an unlawful proceeding to present such a Bill for the royal assent before it had been approved by the electors. If, before the Bill received the assent of the Crown, it was found possible . . . to raise for judicial decision the question whether it was lawful to present the Bill for that assent, the courts would be bound to pronounce it unlawful to do so. Moreover, if it happened that, notwithstanding the statutory inhibition, the Bill did receive the royal assent although it was not submitted to the electors, the courts might be called upon to consider whether the supreme legislative power in respect of the matter had in truth been exercised in the manner required for its authentic expression and by the elements in which it had come to reside. But the answer to this question, whether evident or obscure, would be deduced from the principle of parliamentary supremacy over the law.[2]

In a later Australian case, however, Dixon CJ (as he had become) doubted whether *Trethowan* had been correctly decided, and said that an injunction ought not to issue to interfere with the legislative process.[3] So far as the position of the United Kingdom Parliament is concerned, that is almost certainly the case, in view of the dicta in *Pickin*.

In *MacCormick v Lord Advocate*,[4] judges in the Scottish Court of Session doubted Parliament's authority to legislate contrary to some of the terms of the Anglo-Scottish union legislation. However, no actual inconsistency had arisen in that instance, and the judges carefully stopped short of claiming jurisdiction to determine the validity of any purported legislation.

In a case concerning proposed British membership of the European

---

20 [1934] 1 KB 590 at 597.
1 (1931) 44 CLR 394. The case went on appeal to the Privy Council: [1932] AC 526, see below.
2 (1931) 44 CLR 394 at 426.
3 *Hughes and Vale Pty Ltd v Gair* (1954) 90 CLR 203. See Zelman Cowen 'The Injunction and Parliamentary Process' (1955) 71 LQR 336.
4 1953 SC 396. See ch 4.

Communities, *Blackburn v A-G*,[5] Lord Denning MR said abo[...] hypothetical situation of a later British withdrawal from membership, [...] will consider that event when it happens. We will then say whether Parliament can lawfully do it or not'. This was a typically teasing remark, and it is difficult to attach much importance to it. More significant is the Court of Appeal's decision in *Pickin v British Railways Board*,[6] to which Lord Denning was a party. There the court did at least consider it to be an arguable proposition that courts might impugn the validity of Acts which had not been properly passed. In the end the position agreed by the court was a modified and more cautious one, that is, that alleged defects might be judicially investigated and, if found proven, 'it might well be the duty of the court to report that finding to Parliament, so that Parliament could take cognisance of it'.[7] Of course, even this intermediate judicial reviewing power was denied by the House of Lords, and flatly and unequivocally denied; but it is interesting, nonetheless, that a court of the Court of Appeal's standing felt able to go that far.

Thus, a few dicta may be found with which to oppose the Diceyan view. They are substantially outweighed, however, by the authority and observations in its favour. What is more, it remains true that no British court since 1688 has claimed, let alone exercised, the right to treat the provisions of a duly enacted Act of Parliament as ultra vires or void.

On any view, this absence of any disposition on the part of the courts to question the binding nature of parliamentary enactments must be regarded as a striking feature of the British constitution. If explanations are needed, it is worth remembering that there has traditionally been some coincidence of membership between the legal and legislative professions in this country,[8] and that, in the absence of a written constitution specifying other arrangements, our institutions of government reflect the primacy of Parliament which was inherent in the 1688 settlement. The point is well put by Hood Phillips:

> British courts are not established as co-ordinate bodies with the legislature by a written constitution. The present system of courts and their jurisdictions are based on Acts of Parliament, and judges of the Supreme Court and Lords of Appeal are dismissible on an address from both Houses of Parliament. The House of Lords as the court of final appeal is technically part of Parliament, and its president is the Lord Chancellor who presides over the Upper House. As a minister and a member of the cabinet the Lord Chancellor would *ex hypothesi* be identified with the policy of any bills introduced into Parliament by the government of the day. These

5 [1971] 2 All ER 1380 at 1383, [1971] 1 WLR 1037 at 1040, CA.
6 [1973] QB 219, [1972] 3 All ER 923. See J W Bridge 'Judicial Review of Private Legislation in the United Kingdom' 1973 JR 135.
7 [1973] QB 219 at 230, [1972] 3 All ER 923 at 928.
8 See W S Holdsworth 'The Influence of the Legal Profession on the Growth of the English Constitution' in *Essays in Law and History* (ed by A L Goodhart and H G Hanbury, 1966).

...ld not affect the courts in their *interpretation* of Acts of ...ey might well be relevant if any litigant challenged the *validity*

...k that questions of parliamentary sovereignty should be ...in view of the predominance of authority in favour of Dicey's ...ar from settled. For thirty or forty years past, there has been a swe... ...us of dissent, and we must examine some of the opposing arguments.

HAS SOVEREIGNTY SHRUNK?

Some of Dicey's critics have found it hard to reconcile the view of an illimitable sovereign with the fact that Parliament seems to legislate for an ever-shrinking geographical area. At the height of British imperial power, when the surface of the globe was strewn with pink patches, the Parliament at Westminster legislated for a quarter of the people of the world, for it was the Imperial Parliament. Today Parliament rarely legislates for areas outside the United Kingdom. The explanation of this change lies principally in the transition of former colonies and dependent territories to independent status, and the member states of today's Commonwealth come to mind. However, the same point might be made with regard to the Republic of Ireland, or Heligoland (ceded to Germany in 1890), or the United States. So in a large number of areas it appears that the powers of the Westminster Parliament have been lost. Sometimes Parliament has acquiesced in the surrender, as when a statute is passed to complete the peaceful transition of a former colony to independence; sometimes, as with the American colonies where there was a successful rebellion, Parliament has simply lost its powers. In either event, it may be doubted whether Parliament can turn back the clock. The traditional doctrine has it that what one Parliament can do, another can undo. But events such as the cession of territory or the conferment of independence are naturally regarded as irreversible.

In spite of appearances, however, it is not clear that Dicey was wrong. The question used to be much discussed in relation to an Act of Parliament passed in 1931, the Statute of Westminster.[10] Under this, some of the countries of the Empire, such as Australia, New Zealand, Canada and South Africa, were given the status of 'Dominion'. These lands already enjoyed virtual

9 O Hood Phillips 'Self-Limitation by the United Kingdom Parliament' (1975) 2 Hastings Constitutional Law Quarterly 443 at 448.
10 See Geoffrey Marshall *Parliamentary Sovereignty and the Commonwealth* (1957) for a detailed account of developments in legislative relations, with special reference to South Africa and six Commonwealth countries, up to the 1950s.

legislative autonomy by convention, and section 4 of the Act appeared to enshrine the established position in legislation. It provides that:

> No Act of Parliament of the United Kingdom passed after the commencement of this Act shall extend, or be deemed to extend, to a Dominion as part of the law of that Dominion, unless it is expressly declared in that Act that that Dominion has requested, and consented to, the enactment thereof.

Ostensibly this provision precluded Parliament from legislating for the Dominions without their consent, or, more accurately, without a declaration of their consent. Was this a limitation, or could Parliament legislate for Canada or South Africa regardless of the section? The question was soon canvassed, in *British Coal Corpn v R*,[11] where it was suggested in argument that the power of Parliament to legislate as it thought fit for Canada remained unrestricted. Lord Sankey LC, delivering the opinion of the Judicial Committee of the Privy Council, stated:

> It is doubtless true that the power of the Imperial Parliament to pass on its own initiative any legislation it thought fit extending to Canada remains in theory unimpaired: indeed the Imperial Parliament could, as a matter of abstract law, repeal or disregard section 4 of the Statute. But that is theory and has no relation to realities.[12]

What this means is that the United Kingdom Parliament, for political reasons, was in fact most unlikely to legislate in disregard of the Statute of Westminster, but that, if it were to do so, British courts would be bound to obey the resulting law. The remark about theory and realities is often quoted, but the choice of words was unhappy. The term 'theory' is an unfortunate one for describing what is the legal position. That the possibility under consideration was not so fanciful was later to be proved by events. Southern Rhodesia had in practice enjoyed self-government and legislative autonomy for many years when, in 1965, Mr Ian Smith's government made a unilateral declaration of independence. The British Parliament immediately enacted the Southern Rhodesia Act 1965 which reasserted its right to legislate and deprived the Rhodesian legislature of power. When a case concerning the legality of emergency regulations made by the rebel Smith regime came to the Privy Council, it was held that the regulations were void and that the provisions of legislation passed by Parliament still had full legal effect in Rhodesia.[13] With reference to the relevant convention, Lord Reid said:

> It is often said that it would be unconstitutional for the United Kingdom Parliament to do certain things, meaning that the moral, political and other reasons against doing them are so strong that most people would regard it as highly

11 [1935] AC 500.
12 [1935] AC 500 at 520.
13 *Madzimbamuto v Lardner-Burke* [1969] 1 AC 645, [1968] 3 All ER 561, PC.

improper if Parliament did these things. But that does not mean that it is beyond the power of Parliament to do such things. If Parliament chose to do any of them the courts could not hold the Act of Parliament invalid. [14]

This seems to be an endorsement of Dicey's views.

In order to complete the picture, however, a distinction has to be drawn between the British and the local courts, and in this lies the answer to the puzzle. The courts in Rhodesia, following the declaration of independence, denied that decisions of the Privy Council would be effective there. [15] Mr Smith's government, although regarded as illegal here, was able to, and continued to, govern Rhodesia effectively, and the British Parliament did not in fact attempt to legislate on a regular basis for Rhodesia. In *R v Ndhlovu*, [16] the Appellate Division of the Rhodesian High Court ruled that the revolutionary constitution of 1965 had become the only lawful constitution of Rhodesia. Thus, while Parliament might make any law and British courts could not but obey it, it had lost the ability to legislate effectively so as to be able to change the law applied in Rhodesian courts.

A similar analysis may be applied to the other cases. Parliament may legislate concerning affairs in Heligoland or the Republic of Ireland or the United States, and while our courts will accept the legislation as valid, it may safely be predicted that the local courts in those places will not, because their judges no longer owe obedience to the United Kingdom Parliament. Where judges who previously acknowledged the authority of Parliament do so no longer, there has been, if you like, a judicial revolution. [17] Whether there has been, outside the courtrooms, a bloody rebellion or a peaceful transition to complete independence from Westminster, the judges, recognising a changed political situation, have altered the rules of judicial obedience.

When things are seen in this light, no special problem is caused by the Statute of Westminster, or later Acts which have been more explicit in their terms. The Nigeria Independence Act of 1960, for example, said plainly that no Act of Parliament of the United Kingdom passed thereafter should extend or be deemed to extend to Nigeria as part of the law of Nigeria. In the highly improbable eventuality of Parliament ever seeking to alter Nigerian law, we may concede that the Nigerian courts would deny the validity of the attempt and, like a South African judge in 1937, hold that 'Freedom once conferred

---

14   Ibid at 723.

15   In *Dhlamini v Carter* 1968 (2) SA 464. There are many accounts of legal aspects of the events in Rhodesia, mostly written from the standpoint of legal theory and in the light of Kelsen's theory of law. See Geoffrey Marshall *Constitutional Theory* (1971) pp 64–72, and the works cited there.

16   1968 (4) SA 515.

17   This is the analysis offered by H W R Wade: 'The Basis of Legal Sovereignty' [1955] CLJ 172, and *Constitutional Fundamentals* (1980) ch 3.

cannot be revoked'.[18] But what does this prove? In reality the situation is the same as in Sir Ivor Jennings's well-known hypothesis of Parliament legislating so as to make smoking in the streets of Paris an offence;[19] French courts would ignore it, English courts, if a guilty Frenchman could be apprehended while visiting Folkestone, would enforce it. In both cases, Nigeria and France, what the 'limitation' on Parliament amounts to is simply that courts not subject to the United Kingdom Parliament will not enforce its laws. This is no doubt a practical limitation on what Parliament may effectively do, but it needs to be restated that parliamentary sovereignty is not a political concept, but a legal one. In *Manuel v A-G*,[20] Sir Robert Megarry V-C discussed the argument 'that Parliament may surrender its sovereign power over some territory . . . to another person or body . . . [and] after such a surrender, any legislation which Parliament purports to enact for that territory is not merely ineffective there, but is totally void, in this country as elsewhere, since Parliament has surrendered the power to legislate'.[1] The argument was unfounded because, the Vice-Chancellor observed, 'legal validity is one thing, enforceability is another'.[2] Parliamentary sovereignty is a proposition about validity, and the criteria of validity applied by British courts have not changed in the least, even if the courts in the United States or South Africa or Nigeria may no longer be counted as British courts.

What is hardly ever acknowledged is that Dicey himself dealt clearly with the supposed problem.[3] He discussed not the Statute of Westminster but the Taxation of Colonies Act 1778, an Act which ostensibly limited Parliament's right to impose taxation on the American colonies, the independence of which the British Government had recognised in 1783. On the one hand, he said policy and prudence so militated against violating the spirit of the enactment that it might 'looked at in the light of history, claim a peculiar sanctity'; but, on the other hand, 'there is under our constitution no legal difficulty in the way of repealing or overriding this Act'. That said it all.

THE 'MANNER AND FORM' ARGUMENT

The most sustained attack on Dicey's views has come with the argument that a Parliament may limit its successors as to 'manner and form'.

The challenge was posed by Sir Ivor Jennings, who contrasted two kinds of authority:

---

18 *Ndlwana v Hofmeyr* 1937 AD 229 at 237, per Stratford ACJ. Reiterated by Lord Denning MR in *Blackburn v A-G* [1971] 2 All ER 1380 at 1382.

19 *The Law and the Constitution* (5th edn, 1959) p 171.

20 [1983] 1 Ch 77, [1982] 3 All ER 786; affd [1983] 1 Ch 77, [1982] 3 All ER 822, CA.

1 [1983] 1 Ch 77 at 85, [1982] 3 All ER 786 at 792.

2 [1983] 1 Ch 77 at 88, [1982] 3 All ER 786 at 794.

3 Dicey pp 66–67.

If a prince has supreme power, and continues to have supreme power, he can do anything, even to the extent of undoing the things which he had previously done. If he grants a constitution, binding himself not to make laws except with the consent of an elected legislature, he has power immediately afterwards to abolish the legislature without its consent and to continue legislating by his personal decree.

But if the prince has not supreme power, but the rule is that the courts accept as law that which is made in the proper legal form, the result is different. For when the prince enacts that henceforth no rule shall be law unless it is enacted by him with the consent of the legislature, the law has been altered, and the courts will not admit as law any rule which is not made in that form. Consequently a rule subsequently made by the prince alone abolishing the legislature is not law, for the legislature has not consented to it, and the rule has not been enacted according to the manner and form required by the law for the time being.[4]

It is, of course, correct as a matter of theory to say that either of these situations is possible. The question is, to which does the British constitution correspond? Dicey held the sovereignty of the United Kingdom Parliament to be of a continuing nature, but did not particularly consider whether any distinction should be drawn between the substance of legislation and the composition or procedures of the legislative body. Jennings says that it is unclear whether our Parliament corresponds to his first prince or his second because there is a dearth of judicial authority, but it is evident that he prefers the proposition that 'the law is that Parliament may make any law in the manner and form provided by the law'. Some other writers were less equivocal in their support for it, and by 1961 Professor Heuston felt able to claim that the 'new view' of sovereignty, as he called it, had made considerable headway.[5] With more support from writers such as Geoffrey Marshall,[6] J D B Mitchell[7] and S A de Smith,[8] the view could justifiably be said to be favoured by 'the great majority of modern constitutional lawyers'.[9]

Such a popular view deserves to be examined. In Heuston's formulation, it is this:

(1) Sovereignty is a legal concept: the rules which identify the sovereign and prescribe its composition and functions are logically prior to it.

(2) There is a distinction between rules which govern, on the one hand, (a) the composition, and (b) the procedure, and, on the other hand, (c) the area of power, of a sovereign legislature.

---

4 *The Law and the Constitution* (5th edn, 1959), p 152. Jennings was not above employing tricks of argument, and we may note that his example predisposes all good democrats to prefer the second hypothesis.

5 *Essays in Constitutional Law* (1st edn, 1961, 2nd edn, 1964) ch 1.

6 *Parliamentary Sovereignty and the Commonwealth* (1957); *Constitutional Theory* (1971) ch 3.

7 *Constitutional Law* (2nd edn, 1968) ch 4.

8 *Constitutional and Administrative Law* (2nd edn, 1973) ch 4.

9 George Winterton 'The British Grundnorm: Parliamentary Supremacy Re-examined' (1976) 92 LQR 591 at 606.

(3) The courts have jurisdiction to question the validity of an alleged Act of Parliament on grounds 2(a) and 2(b), but not on ground 2(c).

(4) This jurisdiction is exercisable either before or after the Royal Assent has been signified – in the former case by way of injunction, in the latter by way of declaratory judgment.[10]

The practical consequences of such a view, if it is correct, are spelt out by Marshall:

> Parliament as at present constituted might conceivably bind the future or circumscribe the freedom of future legislators, not by laying down blanket prohibitions or attempting to enact a fundamental Bill of Rights, but by using their authority to provide different forms and procedures for legislation. A referendum or a joint sitting, for example, might be prescribed before certain things could be done. Or a two-thirds majority. Or a seventy-five per cent or eighty per cent majority. If it is also provided that any repeal of such provisions should not be by simple majority, the courts may be able to protect the arrangements laid down by declaring in suitable proceedings that any purported repeal by simple majority of a protected provision is ultra vires as being not, in the sense required by law, an 'Act of Parliament'. In this finding they would not be in any way derogating from parliamentary sovereignty but protecting Parliament's authority from usurpation by those not entitled for the purpose in hand to exercise it.[11]

Thus, if this is correct, provisions in a Bill of Rights, or any other provisions which it was desired especially to safeguard, might be protected by requirements of special procedures or majorities. They might be 'entrenched', as it is often described.

But is it correct? To take the first of Heuston's points, it is obviously true that there must be rules applied by the courts so as to identify what is an expression of the Sovereign's will in the form of an enactment. Thus, the meaning of Parliament (or, more correctly, the Queen in Parliament or the King in Parliament) and the meaning of an Act of Parliament are the subjects of rules of common law. So in *The Prince's Case*,[12] it is said:

> If an Act be penned that the King with the assent of the Lords, or with the assent of the Commons, it is no Act of Parliament, for three ought to assent to it *scilicet* the King, the Lords and the Commons, or otherwise it is not an Act of Parliament.

Cases such as *Stockdale v Hansard*[13] and *Bowles v Bank of England*[14] are instructive, for they show the courts distinguishing between what are Acts of Parliament and what, being merely resolutions of the House of Commons,

---

10 *Essays in Constitutional Law* (2nd edn, 1964) pp 6–7.
11 *Constitutional Theory* (1971) p 42.
12 (1606) 8 Co Rep 1a.
13 (1839) 9 Ad & El 1.
14 [1913] 1 Ch 57.

are not. In the earlier case, Lord Denman dealt with the claim that a resolution of the Commons had to be obeyed by the courts by answering that

> the supremacy of Parliament, the foundation on which the claim is made to rest, appears to me completely to overturn it, because the House of Commons is not the Parliament, but only a co-ordinate and component part of the Parliament. That sovereign power can make and unmake the laws; but the concurrence of the three legislative estates is necessary. [15]

It is undeniable that the courts decide what is or is not an Act of Parliament, but as has been said, 'this is not a matter of limiting Parliament, but of identifying its enactments'. [16] Once something is identified as an Act of Parliament, the 'enrolled bill rule' comes into operation, which, as we have seen, means that the courts have no choice but to accept it.

So runs the Diceyan view. But the 'new view', while conceding that Parliament is unlimited with regard to the subject matter of legislation, maintains that it may be limited as to composition and procedure, or, as it is often put, 'manner and form'. What evidence is offered for this contention?

A case much relied on is *A-G for New South Wales v Trethowan*, [17] a decision of the Privy Council which concerned the New South Wales legislature. That legislature was subject to section 5 of the Colonial Laws Validity Act 1865, which provides:

> every Representative Legislature shall, in respect to the Colony under its jurisdiction, have, and be deemed at all times to have had, full power to make laws respecting the Constitution, Power and Procedure of such legislature; provided that such laws shall have been passed in such manner and form as may from time to time be required by any Act of Parliament, Letters Patent, Order in Council, or Colonial law for the time being in force in the said colony.

In 1929 the Parliament of New South Wales passed an Act which provided that no Bill for abolishing the upper house of the legislature (the Legislative Council) should be presented for the royal assent unless it had been approved at a referendum by a majority of the electors. It was further provided that this requirement of a referendum might not itself be repealed except by the same process. The government which sponsored the legislation was a right wing one, and its aim was to 'entrench' the position of the upper house, which the Labour Party had declared its intention of abolishing. In 1930, however, a new Parliament was elected in which the Labour Party held the majority of seats in the lower house. Two Bills were passed through both Houses, the first purporting to repeal the referendum requirement, and the second purporting to abolish the Legislative Council. Neither Bill was submitted to

---

15 (1839) 9 Ad & El 1 at 108.

16 O Hood Phillips *Constitutional and Administrative Law* (6th edn by O Hood Phillips and Paul Jackson, 1978) p 80.

17 [1932] AC 526, PC.

the electors, and accordingly two members of the threaten
Council sought an injunction to restrain the submission of the
royal assent. The Supreme Court of New South Wales
injunction, and appeals to the High Court of Australia and
Committee of the Privy Council were unsuccessful.

What does this case show? Two views are possible. The first is that there is
a general rule that legislation may be enacted only in such manner and form
as is laid down by law, and that the United Kingdom Parliament is just as
subject to that rule as was the New South Wales legislature. However, the
opposing view is that the decision has no relevance at all. The Privy Council
said that the case depended 'entirely upon a consideration of the meaning and
effect of section 5 of the Act of 1865',[18] and it is hard to see how this can tell
us anything about the United Kingdom Parliament, whose powers are not
defined in or derived from any statute. Dicey had had no difficulty in classing
the New South Wales legislature as a non-sovereign law-making body,[19] and
the *Trethowan* decision merely emphasises that it was indeed subordinate to a
higher law (the 1865 Act passed by the Imperial Parliament) and that its
purported legislation could be ultra vires.

What the *Trethowan* case shows is merely that some legislatures are
limited with respect to the procedure by which they may legislate. But
Dicey, who devoted two chapters of his book to non-sovereign legislatures
and legislatures in federal countries, would certainly not have denied this. Of
course, it is a logical possibility that any particular legislature may be of that
sort, but what we wish to know is whether the British Parliament *is*, and
Trethowan seems to advance us no further than Jennings's tale of the two
princes.

Other cases are open to the same objection. In *Harris v Minister of the
Interior*,[20] the Appellate Division of the Supreme Court of South Africa held
that a measure passed by the South African Parliament in 1951 (depriving
Cape coloured voters of electoral rights) was not a valid Act, because the
matter was subject to an entrenched clause in the constitution, contained in
the South Africa Act 1909. The 'manner and form' required for alteration,
namely a two-thirds majority of both Houses of Parliament sitting together,
had not been complied with. This merely shows that the South African
legislature, even if unlimited as to the area of its power, was procedurally
subject to a higher law, the Act which established it and was logically and
historically prior to it. Heuston cites an Irish case, *R (O'Brien) v Military
Governor, NDU Internment Camp*,[1] where the Irish Court of Appeal held that a
measure rushed through the Parliament was invalid because procedural

---

18 Ibid at 539.
19 Dicey ch 2.
20 1952 (2) SA 428, sub nom *Harris v Donges* [1952] 1 TLR 1245.
 1 [1924] 1 IR 32.

requirements had not been followed. But these requirements were specified in Article 47 of the Constitution: again the legislature was subject to a higher law.

In *Bribery Comr v Ranasinghe*,[2] the Privy Council held that the Bribery Tribunal by which the respondent had been convicted was not lawfully appointed, because it had been set up by an ordinary Act of the Parliament of Ceylon whereas, since it was inconsistent with provisions in the Constitution concerning judicial appointments, a special majority was required under the Constitution. An argument that the Parliament of Ceylon was sovereign and that the courts must regard official copies of its Acts as conclusive of their validity was rejected. Much has been made of one of the remarks of Lord Pearce, who delivered the opinion:

> The proposition which is not acceptable is that a legislature, once established, has some inherent power derived from the mere fact of its establishment to make a valid law by the resolution of a bare majority which its own constituent instrument has said shall not be a valid law unless made by a different type of majority or by a different legislative process.[3]

Geoffrey Marshall says of this that Lord Pearce 'seemed to imply . . . that both non-sovereign and sovereign legislatures may be made subject to procedural rules entrenching parts of the law from simple majority repeal'.[4] However, this perhaps does not take sufficient account of the possibility that the United Kingdom Parliament is sovereign precisely because it is not subject to any 'constituent instrument' such as Lord Pearce describes. Earlier in his speech, Lord Pearce had said exactly that: 'In the United Kingdom there is no governing instrument which prescribes the law-making powers and the forms which are essential to those powers'.[5]

The cases cited by the 'manner and form' school do not, in the end, seem very helpful. The powers and forms of law-making by the United Kingdom Parliament, as Lord Pearce observed, are not prescribed by any higher law. As to whether Parliament may alter these so as to restrict future Parliaments, the suggestion has not been supported in British cases, and was denied in *Vauxhall Estates Ltd v Liverpool Corpn*[6] and *Ellen St Estates Ltd v Minister of Health*.[7] It should, however, be said that the dicta in those Housing Act cases hardly settle the question finally with regard to all possible circumstances. It is at best doubtful whether in that instance Parliament had intended to prevent repeal, and it was scarcely an issue which would tempt judges to break new ground.

---

2 [1965] AC 172, [1964] 2 All ER 785, PC.
3 Ibid at 198.
4 *Constitutional Theory* (1971) p 55.
5 [1965] AC 172 at 195.
6 [1932] 1 KB 733.
7 [1934] 1 KB 590.

A MATTER IN THE KEEPING OF THE COURTS

If case law provides little encouragement to Dicey's opponents, might there nonetheless be an argument on principle which could come to their aid? Something of the sort was attempted by Sir Ivor Jennings.

We have seen that the sovereignty of Parliament is a legal principle, expressing the relationship between Parliament and the courts. This principle, being recognised and acted upon by the courts, may be counted as a principle of the common law. There is, after all, no Act of Parliament which says that the courts must act in that way, nor would one be appropriate, for as Salmond observed: 'No Statute can confer this power upon Parliament, for this would be to assume and act on the very power that is to be conferred'.[8] If the powers do not come from statute, then they must be part of the common law, for our legal system knows no sources of law other than those two.

This proposition appears to be right, and Sir Ivor Jennings employed it in order to construct an ingenious challenge to Dicey's views.[9] The essence of Jennings's argument may be put in syllogistic form, as follows:

(a) The authority of Acts of Parliament depends on the common law;
(b) Parliament can change the common law in any way whatever, since Acts of Parliament override common law;
(c) Therefore Parliament can change the legal rules on which the authority of Acts of Parliament rests.

The premises seem incontestable, and lead inescapably to the conclusion. If the conclusion is right, it would be possible for Parliament to alter the present rules of judicial obedience, so that it might, for example, effectively entrench a charter of civil rights or any other legislation it was thought desirable to protect.

We need not accept that conclusion, however, because upon deeper reflection it appears that the premises are wrong. To establish this, we must think again about the seventeenth century background. There is an unbroken continuity between 1688 and the legitimacy of our present legal order. But what gave validity and legality to the legislation of 1689? The authority to legislate did not come from the existing law, for under the law James II was still the King of England and Parliament was not sitting. Only a sequence of irregular and illegal acts clothed William and Mary with their royal title and the Convention they summoned with the status of a Parliament. In short, it was, however glorious, a revolution, an overthrow of the existing legal order. However, the success of the revolution was reflected

8 J W Salmond *Jurisprudence* (11th edn by G Williams, 1957) p 137.
9 *The Law and the Constitution* (5th edn, 1959) pp 150–170.

in judicial acceptance of the validity of the Crown and Parliament Act 1689, and subsequent enactments.

The importance of this is that while the authority given to the legislature was reflected in judicial behaviour, and so is in that sense part of the common law, it was not derived from any legal principle, but rather had its source in a recognition of political events. This makes the principle of parliamentary sovereignty, which is the expression of this judicial recognition, unique, and in its uniqueness lies the answer to Jennings's argument. It was given definitively by H W R Wade:

> [T]he rule that the courts obey Acts of Parliament . . . is above and beyond the reach of statute . . . because it is itself the source of the authority of statute. This puts it into a class by itself among rules of common law, and the apparent paradox that it is unalterable by Parliament turns out to be a truism. The rule of judicial obedience is in one sense a rule of common law, but in another sense – which applies to no other rule of common law – it is the ultimate *political* fact upon which the whole system of legislation hangs. Legislation owes its authority to the rule: the rule does not owe its authority to legislation. To say that Parliament can change the rule, merely because it can change any other rule, is to put the cart before the horse . . .
>
> [It is] unique in being unchangeable by Parliament – it is changed by revolution, not by legislation; it lies in the keeping of the courts, and no act of Parliament can take it from them.[10]

This is a subtle and persuasive account. It is evident from the facts of history that law depends upon politics, and so it would appear that legal systems are ultimately based upon first principles which cannot be derived from within the legal order itself.[11]

Of course, these first principles may often result in obedience to a constitution or some other state of affairs under which the legislature is limited. What Professor Wade has done is to provide us with a rational explanation of how and why the United Kingdom Parliament might have unlimited legislative power of a continuing nature, such that it is unable to deprive future Parliaments of enjoyment of the same capacity. Thus, contrary to Jennings's argument, we need not accept that it is possible by suitably framed legislation to disable future Parliaments. The matter, as Wade says, lies in the keeping of the courts.

---

10 H W R Wade 'The Basis of Legal Sovereignty' [1955] CLJ 172 at 187. Lord Denning MR has said judicially that Wade's explanation is true: *Blackburn v A-G* [1971] 2 All ER 1380 at 1383.

11 There is, as Wade points out, a close correspondence between his account with regard to English law and the description of a legal system by theorists such as Salmond and Kelsen. To their names we might add H L A Hart, who employs Wade's thesis in *The Concept of Law* (1961).

SOVEREIGNTY AND CHANGE

There may, however, be cause to question whether Professor Wade has fully acknowledged that rules which are in the keeping of the courts are also rules at the mercy of the courts, and that this applies not only to dramatic political changes but also to the everyday handling of legal rules.

Certainly, one must admire the intellectual elegance of Wade's theory, which not only affords a plausible explanation for continuing sovereignty but aptly supplies the means by which changes in judicial behaviour, such as in Rhodesia or Nigeria, may be interpreted (as revolutions). Even changes in British judicial behaviour, should they take place, may be categorised in the same way. Not the least merit of such a theory is that it can never be wrong: parliamentary sovereignty is of a continuing kind, while it continues, but may be altered by a judicial revolution, and when it is shown to have altered, there has been a revolution. However, when a theory cannot be wrong, it may be suspected of circularity, and on reflection we may wonder whether it is entirely adequate.

Besides, the terms in which it is advanced are perhaps liable to mislead rather than to inform. The terminology of 'revolution' is obviously appropriate for the events of 1688 in England. When it is made clear that the revolution may be a bloodless, legal revolution only, it also seems reasonable to describe in this way the shift of judicial obedience which has happened in Commonwealth countries, for we may accept that 'when sovereignty is relinquished in an atmosphere of harmony, the naked fact of revolution is not so easy to discern beneath its elaborate legal dress'.[12] As Wade puts it in a later formulation of his theory, there has been in either event 'a break in legal continuity' which, he contends, 'seems to be lurking in any situation where there is a shift of the seat or the forms of sovereign legislative power'.[13]

May there not, however, be reform without revolution? In other words, are changes not possible without the necessity for anything so cataclysmic as to be classifiable as a 'revolution' or even a 'break in legal continuity'?

In the last few years, this question has been frequently asked. Advocates of a Bill of Rights for the United Kingdom have usually wished for such a law to be specially protected or entrenched. Of course, the same problem would arise if it were desired to entrench a complete written constitution or anything else. One approach to the problem is exemplified by Professor Hood Phillips. Accepting the implications of Wade's theory, he would seek to create the necessary break in continuity:

> The solution is to bring into being a 'New' Parliament which would owe its existence to a Constitution *not enacted by itself*, from which it would derive both its powers and its limitations . . . A Constitution limiting the powers of the 'New'

12 'The Basis of Legal Sovereignty' [1955] CLJ 172 at 191.
13 *Constitutional Fundamentals* (1980) p 37.

Parliament . . . would be adopted by the 'Old' Parliament, and then submitted for adoption by the people in a referendum. The Old (unlimited) Parliament would be abolished, and it would be superseded by the New (limited) Parliament.

Alternatively, it might be preferable for Parliament first to transfer its power to a *Constituent Assembly*, and at the same time to abolish itself.[14]

Professor Wade himself has come to the view that a simpler way exists, without the need for revolution or obvious discontinuity:

All that need be done in order to entrench any sort of fundamental law is to secure its recognition in the judicial oath of office. The only trouble at present is that the existing form of oath gives no assurance of obedience to statutes binding later Parliaments. But there is every assurance that if the judges undertake upon their oath to act in some particular way they will do so.[15]

Thus, even Dicey's most able defenders agree that change is possible, even if there is some difference over what would be a sufficient means.[16]

We may agree that a written constitution or Bill of Rights, if it were desired, could be entrenched, and probably the device suggested by Professor Wade would suffice. However, his submission that this is 'the one and only way'[17] in which there may be change without revolution or discontinuity is, it seems to me, quite wrong. To put it plainly, some of the rules making up 'parliamentary sovereignty' are subject to change in other ways, which can hardly be classed as revolutions. Indeed, they have changed.

An example that is often given of change in the rules is the Parliament Acts 1911 and 1949. These Acts allow Bills to become law notwithstanding the dissent of the House of Lords, and so many have seen in them a 'redefinition' of Parliament. In fact, the example is not a good one. The tripartite Parliament which existed in 1910 still existed in 1912, and anything that the 1910 Parliament could do, the 1912 Parliament could still do. The Acts only created an additional, and permissive, means of legislating. So there is a fallacy in the contention that 'if Parliament can make it easier to legislate, as by passing the Parliament Acts . . ., it can also make it harder to legislate'.[18] That obviously does not follow, since in the one case there is no question of limitation, while in the other there is.

However, one area in which there obviously has been change, and by a process better described as evolution rather than revolution, is in the composition of Parliament. Parliament is composed of three parts, as it was in 1688, but statutes have altered how these parts are composed. The

---

14 *Reform of the Constitution* (1970) pp 156–157.

15 *Constitutional Fundamentals* (1980) p 37.

16 Although Dicey is sometimes said to have portrayed sovereignty as 'perpetual', this is misleading, for he foresaw that sovereignty could be surrendered: see Dicey pp 68–69.

17 *Constitutional Fundamentals* (1980) p 39.

18 S A de Smith *Constitutional and Administrative Law* (5th edn by Harry Street and Rodney Brazier, 1985) p 103.

succession to the Crown as laid down in the Bill of Rights was further regulated by the Act of Settlement in 1700 and amended by His Majesty's Declaration of Abdication Act 1936. The Great Reform Act of 1832 and other Acts concerning constituency distribution have changed the face of the House of Commons. The House of Lords has been altered by the statutory introduction of new elements, Lords of Appeal from 1876 (Appellate Jurisdiction Act 1876) and holders of life peerages since 1958 (Life Peerages Act 1958). [19]

These changes have to be regarded as 'binding future Parliaments'. Parliament in these instances was able to 'redefine itself' or alter the 'manner and form' required for legislation. This may be demonstrated by comparing the Parliament sitting in 1831 with that sitting in 1833. The Great Reform Act was not only accepted as valid, it was effective. So what the 1832 Parliament had succeeded in doing was in altering the composition of the legislative body. In 1833, the manner and form required for the enactment of valid legislation included their passing through the House of Commons as composed under the statute law then in force, but that was a quite different House of Commons from the one which sat in 1831 with its members for Old Sarum, Castle Rising and the other rotten boroughs. The body which had sat in 1831 had lost the authority to legislate in 1833 as a result of an Act which it had passed, and if that is not a limitation, what is?

Where the 'manner and form' school go wrong is in appearing to suggest that *any* change in composition or procedure is possible, if made in the proper form of the time. But not all would be effective. It is hardly surprising that the courts are prepared to accept as Parliament a body which has only been altered by the addition of a few Law Lords to the House of Lords, and to give equal obedience to the redefined legislature. It does not follow from that, however, that an attempt to make the repeal of legislation on labour law subject to the consent of the Trades Union Congress or the Confederation of British Industry would be regarded by the courts as effective to prevent a later Parliament, on its own, doing as it pleased. To take a real example, the Northern Ireland Constitution Act 1973 provides that Northern Ireland will not cease to be part of the United Kingdom without the consent of the majority of the people of Northern Ireland voting in a border poll. But it is unlikely that the courts would regard that as a redefinition of Parliament for this purpose or a limitation in law on Parliament's actions, however strong its political force. A corresponding provision in the Ireland Act 1949, with the difference that it was the consent of the Northern Ireland Parliament that was referred to, was simply repealed in the ordinary way in 1973.

Professor Wade deals with changes in the composition of Parliament in this way:

19 Indeed, the House of Lords could be abolished under the Parliament Acts procedure: see G Winterton 'Is the House of Lords Immortal?' (1979) 95 LQR 386; cf P Mirfield 'Can the House of Lords Lawfully be Abolished?' (1979) 95 LQR 37.

The crucial question is simply one of fact, will the courts recognise the new legislature or not? There is no reason why the withdrawal of Irish members should have any greater effect on the authority of Parliament than did the exclusion of the bishops from 1642–1661.[20]

That may be right, but let us then acknowledge its implications. First, if the rules about composition or procedures can effectively be changed, then Parliament cannot at the same time be regarded as illimitable. Secondly, if the rules may be changed in minor respects, then talk of revolutions or even breaks in legal continuity seems misplaced. Thirdly, a theory which merely says on the question of the courts' recognition that it is 'simply one of fact', gives no guidance as to *when* attempts to change the rules will be effective or not. Of course, the answer to that might be that no guidance can usefully be provided, only guesswork.

As students of law, we may yearn for certainty. However, in areas such as these, that certainty may be most lacking. That is simply because of the nature of the questions at stake, not because the concept of 'parliamentary sovereignty' is itself especially difficult or mysterious. In discussions of the British constitution, that concept has been used to embody a number of different propositions concerning relations between the legislature and the courts. Dicey saw some aspects of the subject very clearly, while other writers have muddied the waters. But Dicey obscured the fact that the concept was comprising a number of propositions which need not stand or fall together, and so later discussion has also proceeded too often on an all-or-nothing basis. The way forward lies in a more careful analysis, in which the concept has to be unpacked. So, for example, the demonstration that the body which is 'Parliament' may be redefined effectively in certain respects, does not require us to accept that it may be redefined in any way whatever, and does not affect the proposition that Parliament is unrestricted with regard to the subject matter of legislation. Similarly, the fact that there may be qualifications upon the doctrine of implied repeal, as we shall see in the next chapter, need not imply that an earlier Act can ever be proof against express repeal.

By breaking 'sovereignty' down into a number of more limited propositions, which have to be separately and carefully assessed, there will be a less dramatic, but maybe more accurate, tale to tell.

20 'The Basis of Legal Sovereignty' [1955] CLJ 172 at 197.

6 The European Community and the British Constitution

On 1 January 1973, the United Kingdom became a member of the European Communities. It was an action which had profound implications for our legal systems. A substantial body of law became automatically part of the law to be applied in this country, and to the existing sources of law were added some new, extraterritorial sources.

The effects of these changes have been especially noticeable in such fields as the law of trade competition, company law and employment law, for in these the substantive law of the European Communities figures quite prominently. Law students may encounter this body of law in another way, since sometimes the substantive law, as well as the law concerning the institutions of the Communities, may be studied as a separate subject in a law school's curriculum.

This is not the place for an extensive study of the law and institutions of the European Communities, to which a vast literature is already devoted. However, the student of constitutional law should certainly be interested in aspects of that study. Remember that constitutional law concerns the institutions of government and the relations between them. Since 1973 the government of this country has been affected by other legislative, executive and judicial organs beyond those in this country with which we are more familiar. In particular, legislative power over certain matters has effectively been transferred to Brussels, and with regard to these laws a court in Luxembourg, and not the House of Lords, has final authority. We should be interested in the composition, functions and powers of these unfamiliar institutions, and in their control, and in their relations with each other and with the Parliament and government and courts of this country. In fact, constitutional lawyers have been especially interested in one question involved in these relations, that is, whether the sovereignty of Parliament has been affected by the United Kingdom's membership of the Communities. They have probably been over-concerned with that question, and insufficiently concerned with some others, but time may make good these omissions.

In this chapter, it will be best to say something first of the Community, and its institutions and law. After that, we may consider the means and the constitutional implications of the United Kingdom's membership.

THE EUROPEAN COMMUNITY

The origins of the Communities and some other European organisations lie in the devastation suffered by the continent in the 1939–45 war. After the war, the United States and the Soviet Union seemed to be on the verge of world domination, while the countries of Europe were struggling to emerge from the ruins. To those countries, the consequences of unbridled nationalism were only too obvious. The time was ripe for a new and more effective form of internationalism, when Mr Winston Churchill, in a speech at Zurich in 1946, suggested that the remedy was 'to recreate the European family, or as much of it as we can, and provide it with a structure under which it can dwell in peace, in safety and in freedom . . . we must build a kind of United States of Europe'. In this, he added, a partnership between France and Germany was essential.

Churchill's vision of European unity struck a chord amongst those nations yearning for security, harmony and recovery. One result was the formation of the Council of Europe, inaugurated in 1949 at Strasbourg.[1] On the economic front, the Organisation for European Economic Co-operation was created in 1948 to administer the Marshall Plan, under which American aid was offered to assist in the economic reconstruction of Europe by means of a common programme. In the same year, the Benelux countries (Belgium, the Netherlands, Luxembourg) established a free trade area as a step on the way to a full customs union.

Then, under the inspiration of Jean Monnet and Robert Schuman, the French government in 1950 proposed 'to place the whole Franco-German coal and steel production under one joint High Authority, in an organisation open to the participation of the other countries of Europe'. According to Schuman, this would constitute the 'first stage of the European Federation.' The French plan was accepted in principle by Germany, the Netherlands, Belgium, Luxembourg and Italy, but the United Kingdom declined to join in. In 1951 those six countries concluded a treaty at Paris, establishing the European Coal and Steel Community (ECSC), which became operative in 1952 upon ratification by the national legislatures.

The Treaty of Paris[2] created four principal institutions: the High Authority (an appointed executive which would have powers to take decisions in the common interest of the member states); the Special Council (composed of ministers representing each state); the Assembly (which would

1 See F E Dowrick 'Juristic Activity in the Council of Europe – 25th Year' (1974) ICLQ 610. As a political federation, the Council of Europe has remained in embryonic form. Its principal achievements lie in the protection of human rights, through the European Convention of Human Rights and Fundamental Freedoms and its associated enforcement machinery.

2 Cmnd 5189. The more important Treaties are also collected in B Rudden and D Wyatt (eds) *Basic Community Laws* (2nd edn, 1986).

give opinions, but would lack legislative powers); and a Court of Justice, to settle disputes arising out of the Treaty or actions under it. The institutional structure was novel, as was the 'supranational' character of the creation. The signatories had not merely accepted mutual obligations in international law. They had invested institutions outside the state with continuing powers to act and to alter their laws, without the intervention of national legislatures or governments, in ways which would bind them and could affect their subjects. They had created a new legal system, the law of the Community.

This model, and the experience of it, were to be influential when the member states involved, the 'Six', entered into further co-operation. Two proposals brought forward in the following two years, for a European Defence Community and a European Political Community, were failures, being peremptorily rejected by the French National Assembly. However, in 1955 the Benelux countries suggested to their partners in the Coal and Steel Community that further steps be taken towards economic integration. The Spaak Report, from a committee chaired by that Belgian statesman, led to negotiations for treaties which would provide for a common market and for the common development of nuclear energy. These were successfully concluded, and the two Treaties of Rome were signed in 1957.[3] In 1958 the European Economic Community (EEC), often known as the Common Market, and the European Atomic Energy Community (Euratom) came into being.

. Thus, from 1958 there were three Communities, with the same six member states participating in each. A single Court of Justice and a single Assembly served all the Communities, as a result of arrangements made in 1957,[4] but the Treaties of Rome provided for Commissions and Councils of Ministers on a different pattern from the ECSC's High Authority and Special Council. In practice, this separation of institutions was found to be unsatisfactory in view of the overlapping interests of the three Communities, and in 1965 a treaty[5] (the 'Merger Treaty') was concluded which established a single Council and Commission. From 1967, when it became effective, there was one Council, one European Commission, one Court of Justice, and one European Parliament or Assembly. As a consequence of the institutional merger, the three Communities are increasingly referred to in the singular as 'the European Community'.[6] That represents the political reality, although in strictly juristic terms there are still three Communities and their fusion would require the negotiation of a new treaty.

Unlike the ECSC and Euratom, which are limited to particular sectors of

3 Cmnd 5179 – II.
4 Convention on Certain Institutions Common to the European Communities.
5 Cmnd 5179 – II.
6 A resolution of the European Parliament on 16 February 1978 was to the effect that they should be so designated.

the economy, the EEC is general in its scope. Its basic objectives are economic development and the improvement of standards of living.[7] To these ends, its policies include the establishment of a customs union between the member states and common commercial policy towards other countries; free movement of persons, services and capital within the Community; a common agriculture policy; a common transport policy; and fair competition.

Through the 1950s, United Kingdom governments remained aloof from the infant Communities. Politically, the special relationship with the United States was thought more important than links with the European countries. In economic and cultural matters, the closest ties were with the countries of the British Empire and Commonwealth. Besides, the supranational character of the Communities' structure was regarded as unacceptable, or at least viewed with some suspicion.

Attitudes began to change when the success of the Common Market was demonstrated by the six countries' economic performance and rising standards of living. In 1959 the government entered into the European Free Trade Association (EFTA) with six other countries which were outside the EEC, in an attempt to obtain similar benefits. The arrangement was not very successful, and in 1961 Mr Macmillan's government despatched Mr Edward Heath to enter into negotiations with the Six. These were at an advanced stage when the French President, General de Gaulle, concerned that British entry to the Community would diminish his country's influence, exercised a veto. He did the same in 1967, when the Labour government applied for membership.

De Gaulle's resignation cleared the way, and in 1969 the Six agreed to commence negotiations with the states which had applied to join. The successful culmination of these was in the Treaty of Brussels,[8] signed in January 1972, which allowed for the accession of the United Kingdom, Ireland, Norway and Denmark to the three Communities. In fact, it became a Community of nine, for Norway, as a result of a referendum on entry, did not ratify the Treaty. Greece became the tenth member state in 1981, and Spain and Portugal, restored to democracy, joined in 1986.[9]

The Community's nature is sui generis. In some respects, it has the features of an ordinary international organisation, but its legal order is unique, and in other respects it resembles an embryonic federation. The reasons for this may be found in the different hopes and expectations it has aroused. The founding fathers intended it to develop into a political union, a

---

7   EEC Treaty, arts 2 and 3.
8   Cmnd 5179 – I.
9   However, in 1982 the territory of the Community was more than halved when Greenland, which was part of Denmark having self-government, left the Community following a referendum.

United States of Europe. Others have nurtured no such ambitions, but have merely found it expedient to participate to the extent necessary. The history of the Community offers frequent reminders that the national interests of members are not readily forgone, as does the shape of the Community's institutions.

COMMUNITY INSTITUTIONS

Two or three other bodies have been set up in the Community, such as the European Investment Bank, set up under the EEC Treaty, and the Court of Auditors, set up under a Treaty of 22 July 1975. We are most interested in the four principal institutions, since 1967 common to the three Communities.

The Council

The Council of the European Communities, often called the Council of Ministers, is the principal decision-making and legislative body. It is the Council which enacts most of the important legislation, adopts the budget, and concludes international agreements on behalf of the Community. It is the body charged under the EEC Treaty with ensuring 'that the objectives set out in this treaty are attained'.[10]

The Council usually meets in Brussels, where its staff are based. The Council is composed of one representative from each member state, who is normally a government minister. Foreign ministers most often constitute the Council, when general or political questions are on the agenda. When the meeting is concerned with agriculture or transport or some other specialised subject, however, then the ministers appropriate to that subject would represent their countries. There are some 80 or so meetings a year of this sort, and the Presidency of the Council, for all its meetings, is held in rotation amongst the member states for terms of six months. So the United Kingdom, which held the Presidency in the second semester of 1986, will not have that responsibility again until 1992.

Meetings of the Council are normally attended by members of the Commission, although they do not have the right to vote. The Council spends much of its time on considering legislative proposals from the Commission. Normally these proposals will have been sent first to the European Parliament for its opinion, and sometimes also to the Community's Economic and Social Committee, a consultative body representing trade unions, employers, consumers and other interest groups. Then the proposals would be studied by a working party, under the

10 EEC Treaty, art 145.

supervision of the Committee of Permanent Representatives ('COREPER'). That body, consisting of the officials who are ambassadors to the Community from its member states, is responsible, in the words of the Merger Treaty, for 'preparing the work of the Council and for carrying out the tasks assigned to it by the Council'.[11] In fact, with its permanent presence on site and its diplomatic skills, Coreper has come to play a distinctive and important role in Community affairs.

There is a subtle balance of power between Council and Commission. The Council appears to have the ascendancy, and, unlike the Commission, is not constitutionally responsible to the European Parliament (or to anyone else, for that matter, although its members may be responsible for their actions in their own countries). However, it is the Commission which has the right of initiative as to legislation, and moreover the Council may only amend a Commission proposal by unanimous vote, and otherwise must accept it, reject it, or return it for reconsideration. The Council's ability to act of its own accord is limited, although it may do so to an extent in the co-ordination of economic policy, and through a provision which empowers it to request appropriate proposals from the Commission for the attainment of the Treaty's objectives.[12]

The interplay between Commission and Council is often interesting, for the Council, as a forum for the views of national governments, is obviously the least supranational of the institutions. A supranational philosophy may be detected in the Treaties' provisions allowing for majority voting on many decisions. However, a constitutional convention developed to limit majority voting. In 1966, after France had adopted its 'empty chair' policy of boycotting Community institutions for some months, it was agreed in the 'Luxembourg Accords' that unanimity must be sought (and reached, according to the French view) before taking decisions where 'very important interests of one or more partners' were at stake. That this was no more than a convention was shown in 1982 when the United Kingdom's opposition to a decision on agricultural prices did not avail against the majority view. Besides, in 1986 the member states agreed to extend majority voting so as to expedite decision-making.[13] But it remains to be seen whether governments will swallow their national interests more easily.

Since 1975 the heads of government of the member states, with their foreign ministers, have held regular meetings three times a year. These are referred to, perhaps confusingly, as meetings of the European Council. In fact, some of the business has been Community business, as when some

---

11 Merger Treaty, art 4.
12 EEC Treaty, art 152.
13 In the Single European Act: Cmnd 9758. It provides for the extension of majority voting to other decisions, particularly in relation to the completion of the European internal market, research and technology, regional policy, and improvement of the working environment.

understanding was reached on the introduction of the European Monetary System. At other times, the matters discussed have been general issues of world politics, and then the meetings are really summit conferences. So it would seem that the European Council has a hybrid nature, but may be regarded as a meeting of the Council of the Communities when it is acting appropriately.

The Commission

The Commission has 17 members. They are appointed 'by common accord of the governments of the member states',[14] and must be nationals of a member state, although no more than two must be nationals of the same state. In practice, two Commissioners have been appointed from the larger states (France, Germany, Italy, the United Kingdom, and Spain) and one from each of the smaller states. The appointees have usually had a background in national politics, and the nominations have been influenced by domestic political considerations. For example, the United Kingdom Commissioners have been drawn equally from the Labour Party and the Conservative Party.

The Commissioners hold office for renewable terms of four years, and from their number the member states' governments appoint in the same way a President and Vice-Presidents for renewable terms of two years.[15] A Commissioner cannot be removed from office by a national government or by the Council. Only the Court of Justice has the power to compel a Commissioner's retirement on grounds of incapacity or misconduct, while the entire Commission may be removed upon a vote of censure passed by the necessary majority in the Parliament.

Once appointed, Commissioners may not seek or accept instructions from any government, and the member states in turn are bound not to try to influence Commissioners in their work. The requirement that the Commission's members act independently makes it the most genuinely supranational of the political institutions. The Commission represents and expresses the Community's interests, and its impartiality is its greatest asset. Moreover, it decides and acts as a collective body, on the basis of a simple majority vote if required.

The Commission's headquarters is in Brussels, where most of its employees,[16] numbering upwards of 11,000, are based. They are divided into about twenty Directorates-General, corresponding to the Community's functions (agriculture, competition, transport, and so on) and some auxiliary service units. The members of the Commission are customarily assigned to

---

14 Merger Treaty, art 11.
15 Mr Roy Jenkins, formerly a Deputy Leader of the Labour Party, held the Presidency from 1977 to 1981.
16 About one third of whom are employed on linguistic work.

one or more portfolios, and the Directors-General of those are always of different nationality from the Commissioners they serve.

The Commission is really the motive force of the Community, with a variety of political and executive functions. First, as we have already seen, it is the initiator of policy, and since the merger of the institutions it is the co-ordinator of the Communities' policies. It has the power, and in some instances the obligation, to propose to the Council measures likely to advance the development of Community aims. For example, in 1985 it sent 694 proposals to the Council. These proposals are the product of wide consultation, involving national civil servants, relevant interest groups, and staff of the Council, and may also take account of views expressed in the Parliament. The Commission tries to anticipate and meet possible objections from the Council, sometimes successfully, sometimes not. Often the end result, after a process of dialogue, is something of a compromise between the Commission's Community-centred view and the national interests involved. In limited fields, or where powers are delegated to it by the Council, the Commission itself may legislate.

As the guardian of the Treaties, the Commission acts to ensure that Community law is obeyed. For this purpose, it has investigative powers, and can impose fines on individuals or companies, notably those who are found to be in breach of competition rules.[17] The Commission deals with requests from member states to invoke the provisions which allow for temporary waivers or derogations from Community obligations. It also instigates infringement proceedings when member states seem not to be complying with Community law, at the rate of two or three hundred per year. If it remains dissatisfied with the state's response, it can issue a reasoned opinion to that effect, and if necessary it will bring proceedings against the state before the Court of Justice.

The Commission has a number of other executive roles. It is responsible for maintaining relations with international organisations such as the United Nations. It acts sometimes as the agent or delegate of the Council, for example in the negotiation of trade agreements with other countries, and in the management of agricultural markets. In the coal and steel sector, the Commission has especially wide powers of its own, and it also has important powers of decision over the functioning of the common market in matters such as the customs union and the competition rules. It also prepares the draft budgets of the Communities, and administers and implements them after their adoption.

The Parliament

Article 137 of the EEC Treaty refers to the Assembly, which 'shall consist of representatives of the peoples of the States'. But since 1962 the Assembly has

17 Appeals against these decisions are heard by the Court of Justice

called itself 'The European Parliament', and this term is used by the other institutions and in Community law.

The Parliament was until 1979 composed of delegates nominated by the member states' legislatures from amongst their own members. However, article 138, as later amended, required direct elections under a uniform procedure. In 1976 the Council agreed to institute direct elections, and provided for some aspects of these, including the numbers of seats allocated to each member state.[18] The influence of national interests is evident in the arrangements made, for the numbers do not fully reflect the differences in population. The United Kingdom, in common with the other larger states, has 81 seats, whereas Luxembourg has 6. But the United Kingdom population is more than 150 times that of Luxembourg. In the absence of agreement on some other aspects of the elections, national legislatures were able to make their own arrangements for the 1979 election, and that was still the position in 1989.[19] The procedures adopted here were similar to those for parliamentary elections, and the same 'first past the post' voting system was employed for the British constituencies,[20] while different systems obtained in the other countries.

The European Parliament meets in plenary session for one week in the month, and sometimes for shorter periods. It usually sits at the Palais de L'Europe in Strasbourg, but sometimes in Luxembourg; its committees normally meet in Brussels, and its secretariat is based in Luxembourg. In the chamber the 518 members[1] (MEPs) do not sit in national groupings. They sit in the party groupings within which, a few independents apart, they also operate politically. Amongst these are the European Right, the European Democrats (which includes the British Conservative MEPs), the Socialists (including Labour MEPs), and the Rainbow Group.

The title of 'Parliament' which has been assumed could possibly mislead. The European Parliament lacks the power to legislate; it cannot raise taxes; and the executive government of the Community is not drawn from it in the way that the United Kingdom government is formed from the United Kingdom Parliament.

The functions which the Parliament does have, according to article 137 of the EEC Treaty, are 'advisory and supervisory'. The advisory aspect is most obviously its role with regard to legislation. In this respect, the Parliament works mainly through its standing committees, which meet during another two weeks of the month. There are committees specialising in all the main areas of Community activity, such as the Transport, Social and

---

18 Act concerning the election of representatives of the Assembly by direct universal suffrage: OJ 1976, L 278/1.

19 For this country, see European Assembly Elections Acts 1978 and 1981.

20 However, the three MEPs for Northern Ireland have been elected under the single transferable vote system.

1 60 members from Spain and 24 from Portugal have been added to the previous total of 434.

Employment, and Agriculture, Fisheries and Food Committees. Often members of the Parliament are able to influence the content of proposed legislation before it is drafted, either at sessions of the committees, which are attended by members of the Commission too, or in the plenary sessions, at which they are also present. Moreover, there are many provisions in the Treaties requiring that the Parliament be consulted on proposed legislation before its adoption by the Council, and a failure to observe this requirement may lead to the annulment of the legislation. That is what happened in the isoglucose case: when a Council regulation, introducing rules for isoglucose similar to those for sugar, was challenged in the Court of Justice, the Court annulled it because the Parliament had not been given a reasonable opportunity to prepare its opinion.[2]

The supervisory function of the Parliament is gradually developing. Under the Treaty, 'the Commission shall reply orally or in writing to questions put to it by the Assembly or by its members'.[3] Partly as a result of British prompting, the Parliament amended its rules in 1973 so as to institute a 'question time' for this purpose, rather along the lines of practice in the House of Commons. Since then the time set aside for this has been increased, and the Council has voluntarily accepted similar obligations, so that it replies to written questions and its President appears before the Parliament to answer oral questions. The Parliament asked 4,599 questions of the two other institutions in 1985.[4] Council Presidents also make a statement to the Parliament at the beginning of their term of office, and the Commission is required to submit an annual general report to it.

So the Parliament has the ability to seek information from the Council and the Commission, and some opportunity to influence them. It has besides a power which implies that the Commission is responsible to it, albeit only in a general way. That is its ability to pass a motion of censure on the Commission. If such a motion is carried, by a 'two thirds majority of the votes cast, representing a majority of the members',[5] then the Commissioners in their entirety are obliged to resign. It has not happened so far. Like many drastic powers, it is of limited utility. Another option arises if, in violation of the EEC Treaty, either the Commission or the Council has failed to take such action as it should, for proceedings may then be brought against the institution at the Court of Justice. The right of the Parliament to bring proceedings was confirmed by the Court in 1985, when it upheld in part the Parliament's complaint that the Council had not introduced a common transport policy as required by the Treaty.[6]

2 Case 138/79 *Roquette Frères SA v EC Council* [1980] ECR 3333.
3 EEC Treaty, art 140.
4 Commission of the European Communities, *Nineteenth General Report on the Activities of the European Communities, 1985* (1986).
5 EEC Treaty, art 144.
6 Case 13/83 *European Parliament v EC Council* [1986] 1 CMLR 138.

In one respect, the Parliament has acquired powers which are more than merely advisory or supervisory. As a result of amendments to the original Treaties signed in 1970 and 1975,[7] the Parliament has joint control of the Community's budget with the Council. The Council has ultimate control of 'compulsory' expenditure (broadly, that required by existing legislation), but the Parliament has the last word on the 'non-compulsory' expenditure. The Parliament also has formally to adopt the budget. Acting 'by a majority of its members and two-thirds of the votes cast', it may reject the draft budget, as it did in 1979 and in 1984 because it disagreed with the Council's spending priorities.

The Court of Justice[8]

The Court of Justice of the European Communities sits in Luxembourg. Since the accession of Spain and Portugal to the Community, it has consisted of 13 judges. Judges must possess the qualifications required for appointment to the highest judicial office in their own country or be 'jurisconsults of recognised competence'.[9] They are appointed by common accord of the member states' governments. That formulation is intended to underline the Court's supranational character, as is the difference between the numbers of judges and member states. But the invariable practice has been to appoint a judge from every member state, although the Treaties do not require this, and the 'extra' judge has been selected from the larger states in rotation. Judges are appointed for terms of six years, which are renewable, and elect a President from amongst themselves, for a renewable term of three years.[10] A judge may only be removed for incompetence or misbehaviour on the unanimous wish of the other judges and the advocates-general.

The advocates-general, now six in number, are appointed to assist the Court. After the parties in proceedings before the Court have completed their submissions, an advocate-general considers the issues impartially and presents the Court with a reasoned submission. His submission is not binding on the Court, and he does not participate in the Court's composition of a judgment; but the Court frequently accepts his conclusions and generally refers to his submissions in its judgment. The office has no British counterpart, but is similar to that of *Commissaire du Gouvernement*, a public interest attorney in the French *Conseil d'Etat*. In other respects too, the

7 Budgetary Treaty of 22 April 1970 (effective from 1 January 1971), Budgetary Treaty of 22 July 1975 (effective from 1 June 1977).
8 See L Neville Brown and F G Jacobs *The Court of Justice of the European Communities* (2nd edn, 1983).
9 EEC Treaty, art 167. This enables legal academics or practitioners to be appointed, and even non-lawyers. Judges of the ECSC Court included an economist and a social scientist.
10 Lord Mackenzie Stuart, formerly a judge of the Court of Session in Scotland, was the first to be appointed from the United Kingdom, and was elected President of the Court in 1984.

Court's procedures are more like those of continental courts, and written submissions are more important than oral argument. The Court deliberates in secret, and decides by majority vote if necessary, but delivers a single judgment in open court without dissenting opinions. The Full Court hears the most important cases, but many are decided by a Chamber of three, four or five judges.

Each of the Treaties establishing the Communities uses the same broad terms to define the Court's responsibilities, which are to 'ensure that in the interpretation and application of this Treaty the law is observed'.[11] In fact, the kinds of proceeding which may come before the Court are quite varied, extending to such matters as the Community's contractual and non-contractual liability, and disputes between the Communities and their staff (which occupy a disproportionate share of the Court's time).

There are three types of proceeding which are especially important. First, there are actions against member states for failure to fulfil a Community obligation. Such actions may be brought by the Commission or, provided the matter has been brought before the Commission first, by another member state. If the state is held by the Court to be in breach of its obligations, then, according to article 171 of the EEC Treaty, it 'shall be required to take the necessary measures to comply with the judgment of the Court of Justice'. However, the Court has no coercive powers to enforce that. The Court's ruling in 1979, that French regulations which prevented the free importing of British lamb were illegal, was defied by the French government for some months, simply as a tactical manoeuvre.[12]

Another kind of proceeding is that which is brought against a Community institution in order to review the legality of its act. This corresponds to the jurisdiction of the British courts in controlling the actions of the government and other public authorities, although the grounds of challenge are modelled on those found in French administrative law. Actions of this sort may be brought by a member state or by a Community institution, or in some circumstances by affected persons. The defendant is normally the Council or the Commission, but in 1981 the Grand Duchy of Luxembourg brought proceedings for the annulment of a resolution of the Parliament concerning its place of sitting, and the application was held admissible, although it failed on the merits.[13] Proceedings may also be brought against a Community institution for its failing to act when a Treaty imposes a duty to act.

Aside from its contentious jurisdiction, the Court has an important

---

11 Eg EEC Treaty, art 164.
12 **Case 232/78** *EC Commission v France* [1979] ECR 2729, [1980] 1 CMLR 418. Later proceedings: Cases 24, 97/80R [1980] ECR 1319, [1981] 3 CMLR 25.
13 **Case 230/81** *Grand Duchy of Luxembourg v Parliament* [1983] ECR 255, [1983] 2 CMLR 726.

interpretative jurisdiction. Under article 177 of the EEC Treaty, it gives preliminary rulings on the interpretation of the Treaties and on the validity and interpretation of Community legislation, when a national court refers a question to it because its interpretation or ruling is necessary for the decision in a case. The Court only rules on Community law: the case has to be remitted to the national court for disposal by the application of that law (and national law, if it is relevant) to the facts. But, as to Community law, the national court is bound to follow the Court's preliminary ruling.

A treaty signed in 1986, the Single European Act, provides for a new Court of First Instance, as a subsidiary part of the Court of Justice. The intention is to divert some of the less important cases, so as to ease the Court's workload.

COMMUNITY LAW

Community law is unusual, if not unique. Like other kinds of international law, it is derived from treaties. But they are exceptional treaties, providing as they do for legislative, executive and judicial institutions, and for legal rights and obligations applicable through national courts. However, Community law, although interwoven with it, is also distinct from national law. It might be regarded as an autonomous legal system. Community law cannot be altered by national legislatures, and imposes rights and obligations which are binding without the member states' intervention. The view of the Community as a different and autonomous legal order has been consistently promoted by the Court of Justice, since promulgated in the *Van Gend en Loos* case in 1963:

> The Community constitutes a new legal order of international law for the benefit of which the States have limited their sovereign rights, albeit within limited fields, and the subjects of which comprise not only Member States but also their nationals. Independently of the legislation of Member States, Community law therefore not only imposes obligations on individuals but is also intended to confer upon them rights which become part of their legal heritage. These rights arise not only where they are expressly granted by the Treaty, but also by reason of obligations which the Treaty imposes in a clearly defined way upon individuals as well as upon the Member States and upon the institutions of the Community.[14]

The first of the sources of Community law is the Communities' treaties. In these we include the foundation treaties establishing the three Communities, and others which have amended them, such as the Treaty and Act of Accession enabling the United Kingdom's entry. As we have seen, the objectives of the Communities, the composition and powers of the

14 **Case** 26/62 [1963] ECR 1 at 12.

institutions, and the rights and obligations of member states are provided for there. They may be regarded as the constitution of the Communities.

If the treaties are the Community's primary law, then that which emanates from the Community institutions is secondary legislation. In fact, the Treaties do not use the term 'legislation', but refer to official 'acts'. Under article 189 of the EEC Treaty, these are classified in five forms: the Council and the Commission may 'make regulations, issue directives, take decisions, make recommendations or deliver opinions'.[15] Recommendations and opinions, however, have no binding force, so are not very significant.

Regulations are of 'general application . . . binding in [their] entirety and directly applicable in all member states'. These are instruments used in order to secure the uniform application of Community policy throughout the member countries, and which take effect without any adoption process. A directive is 'binding, as to the result to be achieved, upon each member state to which it is addressed, but [leaves] to the national authorities the choice of form and methods'. Normally a time limit will be set for the implementation of directives, which will often require legislation, but may sometimes be achieved by administrative action. A decision is 'binding in its entirety upon those to whom it is addressed', who may be member states or natural or legal persons. These are usually applications of law, executive rather than legislative acts. Regulations, directives and decisions must be 'reasoned', that is, they should indicate the authority by which they are made, the reasons for which they are made, and compliance with any required consultation procedures.[16]

Incidentally, the Council and other bodies sometimes issue 'declarations', or 'resolutions' or 'programmes' or something else. However important these may be as expressions of policy, they are not official acts done under the procedural requirements of the Treaties, and they are not subject to review by the Court.

There are two or three other sources of law. Treaties entered into by the Community with others become part of Community law, as in some circumstances do treaties concluded by all or some of the member states. The rulings and decisions of the Court may also be regarded as a source of law. The Court has developed the doctrine that rules of Community law may be derived not only from treaties and secondary legislation but also from 'general principles of law' found in the legal systems of member states or even in international law. In one case, for example, the English law concept of

---

15 Articles 161–163 of the Euratom Treaty employ the same terminology. However, article 14 of the ECSC Treaty provides for 'decisions' and 'recommendations'. Decisions are 'binding in their entirety', so that general decisions correspond to regulations under the EEC and Euratom Treaties, and individual decisions correspond to decisions under those Treaties. Recommendations correspond to directives under the other two Treaties, and are similarly binding.

16 EEC Treaty, art 190.

natural justice was influential,[17] and in several a concept of fundamental human rights has been adumbrated.[18]

Two concepts used in describing Community law are sometimes confused. 'Direct applicability' is the quality which regulations have, in order to ensure uniformity throughout the Community. It means that a regulation becomes binding in the absence of any national implementation and also that national authorities cannot prevent its being applied. A provision is described as having 'direct effect'; when it confers upon individuals or entities rights which they may invoke in the national courts.[19] But that quality may be produced by treaty provisions or by measures of Community law of any type. In Case 26/62 *Van Gend en Loos*, a company was able to resist the Dutch authorities' increase in the import duty for ureaformaldehyde because the European Court decided that article 12 of the EEC Treaty was directly effective.[20] In Case 41/74 *Van Duyn v Home Office*, the British government's entry ban on Scientologists had to be tested against a directly effective directive limiting the public policy exception to free movement of workers to cases 'based exclusively on the personal conduct of the individual concerned'.[1] Regulations will normally be directly effective. For other kinds of Community law, the question is whether the terms are appropriate to confer rights on individuals, but the Court of Justice has moved towards treating direct effect as the norm rather than the exception.

Community law and national law

It was soon appreciated that the proper functioning of the Community depended on the simultaneous and uniform application of its rules throughout the Community's territory. The direct application of regulations was one method of facilitating this; the doctrine of direct effect which was developed was another; and they both pointed to another quality which Community law ideally should possess: primacy over national law. For both direct application and direct effects could lead to rules of Community law directly governing situations to which national laws also applied, and the underlying premise was that the national law would have to give way to the Community law. To take the *Van Gend en Loos* case as an example, it would have been pointless for the Court to find that the Treaty provision could be relied on by the Company, if the inconsistent national legislation was going to prevail.

17 Case 17/74 *Transocean Marine Paint Association v EC Commission* [1974] ECR 1063, [1974] 2 CMLR 459.
18 Eg Case 4/73 *Nold v EC Commission* [1974] ECR 491, [1974] 2 CMLR 338; Case 149/77 *Defrenne v Sabena* [1978] ECR 1365, [1978] 3 CMLR 312.
19 See A Dashwood 'The Principle of Direct Effect in European Community Law' (1978) 16 Journal of Common Market Studies 229.
20 [1963] ECR 1.
 1 [1974] ECR 1337, [1975] Ch 358, [1974] 3 All ER 178.

In fact, the primacy of Community law has been consistently proclaimed and promoted by the Court of Justice, although it is not expressed in terms anywhere in the Treaties. In Case 6/64 *Costa v ENEL*, which arose out of the nationalisation of the electricity industry in Italy, the European Court had to deal with an argument that Community law was irrelevant because there was an applicable Italian law. The Court said:

> The executive force of the Community law cannot vary from one state to another in deference to subsequent domestic laws, without jeopardizing the attainment of the objectives of the Treaty . . .
>
> The obligations undertaken under the Treaty establishing the Community would not be unconditional, but merely contingent, if they could be called in question by subsequent legislative acts of the signatories . . .
>
> The precedence of Community law is confirmed by Article 189, whereby a regulation 'shall be binding' and 'directly applicable in all Member States'. This provision, which is subject to no reservation, would be quite meaningless if a state could unilaterally nullify by means of a legislative measure which could prevail over Community law.
>
> It follows from all these observations that the law stemming from the Treaty, an independent source of law, could not, because of its special and original nature, be overridden by domestic legal provisions, however framed, without being deprived of its character as Community law and without the legal basis of the Community itself being called into question.
>
> The transfer by the states from their domestic legal system to the Community legal system of the rights and obligations arising under the Treaty carries with it a permanent limitation of their sovereign rights, against which a subsequent unilateral act incompatible with the concept of the Community cannot prevail.[2]

In the view of the Court of Justice, Community law always prevails over national law, irrespective of the form of the Community law or the source of the national law.[3] Nor is it significant whether any conflicting national law was made prior to or subsequent to the relevant Community law. This was emphasised most clearly in the *Simmenthal* case, which involved a conflict between two Community regulations on the market in beef and veal passed in 1964 and 1968, and an Italian law passed in 1970, under which a company had been required to pay a fee for a public health inspection when importing beef from France into Italy. The Court held that:

> . . . every national court must, in a case within its jurisdiction, apply Community law in its entirety and protect rights which the latter confers on individuals and must accordingly set aside any provision of national law which may conflict with it, whether prior or subsequent to the Community rule . . .

2 [1964] ECR 585 at 593.
3 Even when it is the constitution of the state, as in the Case 11/70 *Internationale Handelsgesell-schaft* [1970] ECR 1125, [1972] CMLR 255.

. . . and it is not necessary for the court to request or await the prior setting aside of such provisions by legislative or other constitutional means.[4]

So, according to Community law doctrine, Community law invariably prevails over national law to the extent of any inconsistency. Inconsistency arises, according to the Court, not only when the terms of legislation directly conflict, but also when 'national legislative measures . . . encroach upon the field within which the Community exercises its legislative power'.[5]

Of course, Community law doctrine is one thing, but the position in national law may be something else. Questions concerning the place of Community law within the laws of a particular jurisdiction are questions not of Community law but rather of constitutional law in that state. In the other countries of the Community, a variety of means have been used to allow for the reception of Community law, depending upon the terms of their constitutions and the extent to which treaty obligations formed part of their law. As for the supremacy which Community law lays claim to, some reservations have been expressed by the German Constitutional Court[6] and the Italian Constitutional Court,[7] with regard to any conflict with the fundamental rights provisions of their constitutions; and in France the Conseil d'Etat was defiant enough in *Minister of the Interior v Cohn-Bendit*[8] to deny direct effect to the same directive as had figured in *Van Duyn v Home Office*. Nonetheless, it is fair to say that in general the courts of the other member states have accepted the primacy of Community law. However, the practice of other member states, even if it is of interest, is of no authority in the United Kingdom, and the place of Community law in our legal systems is a matter for our constitutional law.

COMMUNITY LAW IN THE UNITED KINGDOM

In the United Kingdom, there was no documentary constitution providing for, or requiring amendment for, British entry to the Communities. Therefore, it had to be done by an Act of Parliament which, it may be recalled, is 'the highest form of law that is known to this country'.[9] An Act of Parliament was necessary because of the principle that prerogative acts do not alter the law of the land,[10] an application of which is that treaties entered into by the United Kingdom government do not affect the law applied in

4 Case 106/77 [1978] ECR 629 at 644.
5 Ibid at 643. See Case 83/78 *Pigs Marketing Board v Redmond* [1978] ECR 2347, [1978] 1 CMLR 177; and J A Usher *European Community Law and National Law* (1981), ch 3.
6 In the *Internationale Handelsgesellschaft* case [1974] 2 CMLR 540.
7 In the *Frontini* case [1974] 2 CMLR 372.
8 [1980] 1 CMLR 543.
9 *Cheney v Conn* [1968] 1 All ER 779 at 782, per Ungoed-Thomas J.
10 See ch 8.

United Kingdom courts. [11] A treaty is binding in international law, but will only have effect in the domestic legal systems if an Act of Parliament incorporates it. [12] In view of this, accession to the Community Treaties, with the consequent changes in domestic law which were to be involved, had to be implemented by statute, and so the European Communities Act 1972 was passed. It not only incorporated Community law, but enabled the United Kingdom to comply with all of the obligations of membership.

Today the same Act is still the foundation for the operation of Community law in this country, and it is worth considering some of its principal provisions. Section 1 of the Act defines the Community Treaties which were being incorporated into national law, and provides that the government by Order in Council may declare others to be Community Treaties for the purposes of the Act. Then section 2 provides for the Community Treaties, the secondary legislation and the case law of the Court of Justice to be applied in United Kingdom courts. By section 2(1):

> All such rights, powers, liabilities, obligations and restrictions from time to time created or arising by or under the Treaties, and all such remedies and procedures from time to time provided for by or under the Treaties, as in accordance with the Treaties are without further enactment to be given legal effect or used in the United Kingdom shall be recognised and available in law, and be enforced, allowed and followed accordingly; and the expression 'enforceable Community right' and similar expressions shall be read as referring to one to which this subsection applies.

Without using the terms, what that subsection does is to provide for the direct applicability and the direct effect of Community law, whenever either is appropriate, as determined by Community law. Future Community law was included, as well as that existing at the time, by the phrase 'from time to time created'.

Sections 2(2) and 2(4), with Schedule 2, of the Act give the government powers to make delegated legislation for the implementation of Community legislation, when action of that kind is necessary or desirable. However, such delegated legislation has to be approved by the Houses of Parliament, and there are four things which cannot be done by that means. If the implementation of Community law involves imposing or increasing taxation, enacting retrospective legislation, sub-delegating legislative power, or creating a new criminal offence with penalties in excess of a specified amount, then it may be effected only through an Act of Parliament.

---

11 *A–G for Canada v A–G for Ontario* [1937] AC 326, PC.
12 In contrast to Community law, the Council of Europe's European Convention on Human Rights and Fundamental Freedoms has not been incorporated by statute. Some, but not all, of the proposals for introducing a Bill of Rights into the law of this country, involve utilising the European Convention for that purpose. See further J Jaconelli *Enacting a Bill of Rights* (1980).

Community law is designed to be applied primarily in the national courts of member states. Section 3 of the Act provides that judicial notice will be taken of Community law, and that it will be treated as law in our courts (unlike foreign law, which has to be proved as fact). It is also provided, in furtherance of the aim of ensuring the uniform application of Community law, that any question as to the meaning or effect of the Treaties, or the meaning, effect or validity of Community legislation, if not referred to the Court of Justice, shall be decided by the courts in this country in accordance with any relevant principles laid down by that court. A statutory instrument made in 1972 under section 2(2) of the Act provided for the enforcement in this country of judgments of the Court of Justice and fines imposed by the Community institutions.[13]

With the entry into force of these provisions, and the continuing development of Community law, its application in the courts and tribunals of this country has become commonplace, even if there are also many areas of law which are unaffected by it. It is applied, usually, as a matter of course. The procedure of referring to the Court of Justice for a preliminary ruling[14] should, and in certain cases must, be employed by a national court or tribunal when it considers that 'a decision on the question is necessary'. But courts in the United Kingdom have not made as much use of the procedure as the courts of most of the other states. Guidelines for its use suggested by Lord Denning MR in *Bulmer v Bollinger*[15] were decidedly restrictive, and these have been influential.

Community primacy and parliamentary sovereignty

There is nothing revolutionary or alien to constitutional traditions in the techniques and provisions of the European Communities Act as described so far. Community law is a system of law created by treaty, and in some respects the Act is apt to remind us of other Acts which incorporate treaty obligations into domestic law.

In other respects the Act is reminiscent of those enabling Acts which confer powers to legislate on ministers, local authorities, or other bodies. The analogy between ordinary delegated legislation and Community law is usually rejected as inaccurate.[16] Admittedly, it would be inappropriate to regard Community law as an 'ordinary' form of it, for it is exceptional as

---

13 European Communities (Enforcement of Community Judgments) Order 1972, SI 1972/1590.

14 Under art 177 of the EEC Treaty, art 150 of the Euratom Treaty, or art 41 of the ECSC Treaty.

15 [1974] Ch 401, [1974] 2 All ER 1226, CA. See further L Collins *European Community Law in the United Kingdom* (3rd edn, 1984) ch 3; F G Jacobs 'When to Refer to the European Court' (1974) 90 LQR 486.

16 Eg S A de Smith *Constitutional and Administrative Law* (5th edn by Harry Street and Rodney Brazier, 1985) p 344.

regards the width of powers conferred, the volume of legislation which results, and in its being made outside the United Kingdom. But a form of delegated legislation it certainly is. Community lawyers would dispute this on the ground that Community law is autonomous and its institutions do not owe what powers they have to a grant of power by the United Kingdom Parliament. However, as has been observed, the status of Community law in this country is a matter of constitutional law, not Community law, and here it does owe its force entirely to an Act of Parliament. As Sir Leslie Scarman put it, 'Community law has the force of law because Parliament says so'. [17] As with other delegated legislation, the validity of Community law is judicially reviewable, even if the court is different and the grounds of review slightly different. It is not common for subordinate legislation to come directly into force when made, without some form of parliamentary approval, as much Community law does under section 2(1) of the Act. But it is not unknown: prerogative legislation does not require parliamentary approval, and statutory instruments do not invariably have to be laid before Parliament. [18] It is not common for subordinate legislation to amend or repeal Acts of Parliament, as directly applicable or directly effective Community law can, and the delegated legislation made under section 2(2) can. [19] But again it is not unknown. The so-called 'Henry VIII clauses', under which ministers are given powers to modify an enabling Act so far as necessary for bringing it into operation, are of a similar character, and there are other examples. [20]

Another characteristic which of course distinguishes subordinate or delegated legislation is that it is repealable by Parliament. It should first be emphasised that the European Communities Act contains no provision purporting to exclude or limit the power of Parliament to repeal or amend the Act itself. But, as you will recall, a characteristic of Community law is its claim to primacy, and this was well understood by the time of the United Kingdom's entry, as is evidenced by reliance on it in argument in proceedings aimed at preventing entry. [1] Once the government had decided to join the Communities, if it were to comply with the rules of the club, it would have to ensure that Community law would prevail over national law. Rather than national legislatures being able to repeal Community law, what was necessary was for national provisions to be overridden or set aside.

The means adopted by the government's draftsmen[2] for compliance with

---

17　Sir Leslie Scarman 'The Law of Establishment in the European Economic Community' (1973) 24 NILQ 61, 70.

18　See eg British Nationality Act 1948.

19　By virtue of the empowering words in section 2(4): '. . . any such provision (of any such extent) as might be made by Act of Parliament'.

20　See eg Health and Safety at Work etc Act 1974, s 15; Sex Discrimination Act 1975, s 80.

1　See *Blackburn v A—G* [1971] 2 All ER 1380, [1971] 1 WLR 1037, CA; *McWhirter v A—G* [1972] CMLR 882, CA.

2　The minister responsible for the Bill was Sir Geoffrey Howe.

its obligations was the unspectacular provision in section 2(4) declaring that 'any enactment passed or to be passed, other than one contained in this Part of this Act, shall be construed and have effect subject to the foregoing provisions of this section'. This seems to require that national legislation, including Acts of Parliament, will not have effect when it is inconsistent with Community law. Besides, the requirement is strengthened by section 3 which, as explained above, directs courts to follow the principles laid down by the European Court of Justice, for the principle of primacy is derived from the judgments of that court.

There is no difficulty in accepting that the 1972 Act achieves what was intended with regard to indigenous legislation passed before the Act.[3] In providing for the modification of earlier law by a specified body of law and by future Community law, the Act was not breaking any new ground.

The more problematic situation arises when there is a conflict between Community law and an Act of Parliament passed after the European Communities Act. Section 2(4) seems designed to ensure the priority of Community law. But the sovereignty of Parliament is generally understood as involving the principle that no Parliament can bind its successors, from which it would follow that section 2(4) would be ineffective in so far as it purports to limit the capacity of Parliament to legislate on any matter or repeal any law.

Yet somehow the courts in this country seem to have felt their way towards an accommodation which damages neither the primacy of Community law nor the sovereignty of Parliament. It is something of a conjuring trick, which has been achieved with modifications of existing principles.

First, a rule of construction has been employed to the effect that, if a provision in an Act of Parliament is ambiguous, it should be given that interpretation which is consistent with international obligations rather than one which conflicts. That rule, already established,[4] has been usefully applied to Community obligations.[5]

When there is an unambiguous inconsistency, something else is needed to meet the problem, and what the courts have done is to refine the rules concerning implied repeal. It is normally the case that subsequent Acts of Parliament repeal earlier ones to the extent of any inconsistency, even when repeal is not express.[6] However, that is not an invariable rule. For example, on the maxim *generalia specialibus non derogant*, local Acts and others which make particular provision for circumstances will not easily be impliedly

3 As was accepted by the House of Lords in *Henn and Darby v DPP* [1981] AC 850, [1980] 2 All ER 166.
4 *Collco Dealings Ltd v IRC* [1962] AC 1, [1961] 1 All ER 762.
5 Eg *Snoxell and Davies v Vauxhall Motors Ltd* [1978] QB 11, [1977] 3 All ER 770.
6 *Vauxhall Estates Ltd v Liverpool Corpn* [1932] 1 KB 733; *Ellen St Estates Ltd v Minister of Health* [1934] 1 KB 590. See ch 5.

repealed by later Acts more general in their application or terms.[7] There is also some authority to the effect that constitutional principles may be protected from unintentional or implied repeal. For instance, in *Nairn v University of St Andrews*,[8] a statutory provision apparently giving the vote to all university graduates was held by the House of Lords not to repeal by implication the ordinary election legislation, under which women were disenfranchised.

In a similar but more systematic way, Community law has been treated as deserving protection from unintended repeal. Section 2(4) operates as a rule of construction which enables Community law to have effect notwithstanding a subsequent Act of Parliament which is inconsistent. To put it another way, Parliament is presumed by the courts not to intend, normally, to legislate contrary to Community law. So in two cases the National Insurance Commissioner has held that a Community regulation of 1971 on social security for migrant workers prevailed over the Social Security Act 1975.[9] Actual inconsistencies of that sort have been very rare, but in a number of other cases the courts have recognised the priority of Community law in such circumstances.[10]

There is a limit, however, to their acquiescence. The presumption of Parliament's willingness to play by the rules may be rebutted. The courts have indicated that if Parliament deliberately chose to legislate contrary to Community law, or to repeal or amend the European Communities Act, then they would be bound to give effect to the will of Parliament. The clearest statement of this approach was by the Master of the Rolls in *Macarthys Ltd v Smith*.[11] The Court of Appeal, in considering a woman's claim that her employer was acting illegally in paying her less than her male predecessor in the job, treated the case as involving a conflict between the Equal Pay Act 1970 and article 119 of the EEC Treaty. Lord Denning dealt with it in this way:

> In construing our statute, we are entitled to look to the Treaty as an aid to its construction: and even more, not only as an aid but as an overriding force. If on close investigation it should appear that our legislation is deficient – or is inconsistent with Community law – by some oversight of our draftsmen – then it is our bounden duty to give priority to Community law. Such is the result of section 2(1) and (4) of the European Communities Act 1972 . . .
>
> Thus far I have assumed that our Parliament, whenever it passes legislation, intends to fulfil its obligations under the Treaty. If the time should come when our

7   See eg *Bishop of Gloucester v Cunnington* [1943] KB 101, CA; *The Vera Cruz* (1884) 10 App Cas 59 at 68 per the Earl of Selborne LC.

8   [1909] AC 147. See also *Earl of Antrim's Petition* [1967] 1 AC 691 at 724 per Lord Wilberforce.

9   *Re an Absence in Ireland* [1977] 1 CMLR 5; *Re Medical Expenses Incurred in France* [1977] 2 CMLR 317.

10 Eg *Esso Petroleum Co Ltd v Kingswood Motors (Addlestone) Ltd* [1974] QB 142, [1973] 3 All ER 1057.

11 [1979] 3 All ER 325, [1979] 3 CMLR 44, CA; after reference: [1981] QB 180, [1981] 1 All ER 111, CA.

Parliament deliberately passes an Act – with the intention of repudiating the Treaty or any provision in it – or intentionally of acting inconsistently with it – and says so in express terms – then I should have thought that it would be the duty of our courts to follow the statute of our Parliament . . . Unless there is such an intentional and express repudiation of the Treaty, it is our duty to give priority to the Treaty.[12]

In the same case, Lawton LJ commented that 'Parliament's recognition of European Community law and of the jurisdiction of the European Court of Justice by one enactment can be withdrawn by another'.[13] Later, in a House of Lords case, Lord Diplock also may be taken as agreeing that an intentional repeal of Community law by Parliament would be effective when in his speech he raised (without answering) the question:

[whether] anything short of an express positive statement in an Act of Parliament passed after 1 January 1973 that a particular provision is intended to be made in breach of an obligation assumed by the United Kingdom under a Community treaty would justify an English court in construing that provision in a manner inconsistent with a Community treaty obligation of the United Kingdom however wide a departure from the prima facie meaning of the language of the provision might be needed in order to achieve consistency.[14]

As these dicta show, the courts in this country have solved the problem in a typically pragmatic and undramatic way. What we understand as the sovereignty of Parliament has been preserved. If Parliament were incapacitated from legislating in a particular way, it would have been lost. But these dicta deny its incapacity. The rules of implied repeal have been modified to take account of Community law, but that may be regarded as a matter of interpretation. As was argued in the last chapter, it is not necessary to regard this as involving 'sovereignty' at all, and there is judicial as well as academic support for that view.[15] What Parliament did in 1972 was merely to provide for an order of priority as between competing orders of law, to take effect unless or except when countermanded. But it did so on its own terms, and it did not incapacitate itself from changing its mind.[16]

What governments and Parliaments have done since is to refrain from

---

12 [1979] 3 All ER 325 at 329. Earlier dicta from Lord Denning had seemed to point in opposite directions: *Felixstowe Dock and Rly Co v British Transport Docks Board* [1976] 2 CMLR 655; cf *Shield v E Coomes (Holdings) Ltd* [1979] 1 All ER 456, [1978] 1 WLR 1408, CA.

13 [1979] 3 All ER 325 at 334.

14 *Garland v British Rail Engineering Ltd* [1983] 2 AC 751 at 771, [1982] 2 All ER 402 at 415, HL. See O Hood Phillips 'A Garland for the Lords: Parliament and Community Law Again' (1982) 98 LQR 524.

15 'I can see nothing in this case which infringes the sovereignty of Parliament.': *Macarthys Ltd v Smith* [1979] 3 All ER 325 at 334 per Lawton LJ. See also L Collins *European Community Law in the United Kingdom* (3rd edn, 1984,) ch 1; T R S Allan 'Parliamentary Sovereignty: Lord Denning's Dexterous Revolution' (1983) 3 Ox JLS 22.

16 The Referendum Act 1975, providing for a referendum on continuing membership after the Labour government's 're-negotiation' of entry terms, is indicative of the assumption that Parliament could legislate so as to take the United Kingdom out of the Community.

legislating in deliberate disregard of international obligations. They have adopted a self-denying ordinance. Of course, it is a matter of great importance for the British constitution if in some large areas of activity Parliament has chosen to accept an indefinite transfer of its traditional functions to other bodies. Undoubtedly, it constitutes a serious inhibition on Parliament, but that is not the same as a legal limitation.

Supervision

We have perhaps sufficiently considered the role of the courts in regard to Community law, and should think about the position of the United Kingdom Parliament and government as regards the Community's acts.

The government is most naturally seen as a participant in Community acts. Through its representation in the Council of Ministers, it is involved in all the more important political decisions, and has the opportunity to influence them at the time.

The view from Parliament is rather different. Seen from that perspective, membership of the Communities has meant a further delegation or transfer of powers, including its legislative responsibilities, into other hands. In terms of our constitution, it may be seen as a transfer of power to the executive, since persons who are government ministers in this country become policy-makers and legislators for the Community when they form part of its Council. Therefore, the supervision of Community acts and activities became an additional aspect of a traditional parliamentary function, the scrutiny of the executive; and traditional means have been employed or adapted for the supervision of Community activities, including those in which our government participates.[17]

So, in accordance with the usual notions of ministerial responsibility, the Foreign Secretary and other ministers when appropriate are obliged to keep Parliament informed about what is happening. This responsibility is discharged by the provision to the Houses of all documents published by the Commission for submission to the Council, by the making of ministerial statements following Council meetings, and by the compilation of twice-yearly reports on developments within the Communities. In the House of Commons, six days are set aside in each parliamentary session for debates on Community affairs, and there are slots allocated for ministers to answer on Community matters in the question time rota.

The more systematic supervision has been entrusted to committees, the House of Lords Select Committee on the European Communities and the House of Commons Select Committee on European Secondary Legislation. These committees consider draft Community legislation and other

17   See St J Bates 'The Scrutiny of European Secondary Legislation at Westminster' (1975–76) 1 European Law Review 22.

Commission proposals, and report on them to their respective Houses, making recommendations for something to be debated when they regard that as being desirable. To give some indication of the committees' activity, in the last six months of 1985, the Commons Select Committee considered 317 proposals, and recommended that 43 of those be debated further.[18] Those debates might take place in the chamber or in a Standing Committee. The House of Commons has resolved that when such a debate has been recommended, a minister may not consent to a legislative proposal in the Council before it has been held, except when there are special reasons to justify his doing so.[19] The House of Lords Select Committee is even more active than its Commons counterpart, and it has won respect for the expertise and thoroughness it has brought to the task.

On the whole, the committees direct their attention to the merits of the proposed legislation and the problems associated with its introduction in this country, rather than to the British government's part in it. That approach is no doubt the most sensible, but it does involve a recognition that it is difficult for Parliament to call ministers to account for Community acts in the same way as they are responsible for domestic administration. There are other reasons why ministerial responsibility is nebulous in this sphere, such as the fact that Community proposals often involve more than one ministry, and the government's declining to reveal to Parliament its negotiating position in the Council. More generally, there are obvious impediments to the ability of Parliament to supervise Community activities, such as the sheer volume of paper in circulation and the limited time available.

To put things in context, of course, the supervision exercised *within* the Community should also be taken into account. But, as we saw earlier, the powers in this regard of the Parliament, which is the democratically elected institution of the Community, are somewhat limited. The real task for constitutional lawyers in the years ahead should be to seek to strengthen the controls on Community powers, nationally and inside the Community.

18 Developments in the European Community, July-December 1985 (Cmnd 9761).
19 991 HC Official Report (5th series) col 843.

7 Parliamentary privilege

The Houses of Parliament, and particularly the House of Commons, had to fight hard for their independence. In the law of parliamentary privilege, we view some of the battlegrounds of these struggles, and their outcomes.

It would be a mistake, however, to regard this subject as being only of historical interest. Today the battle lines are differently drawn, but the same issues arise. Are members of Parliament suitably independent? Are the privileges which they enjoy necessary to that end? And, since privilege carries with it responsibilities, are they fairly and sensibly invoked? At the end of this chapter, some questions of topical importance will be raised. First, we have to examine the nature of this part of the law, and chart its scope.

THE NATURE OF PRIVILEGE

Parliamentary privileges had their origin in the insistence of monarchs that they would not be deprived of the services of their advisers and officials. Many of those advisers and officials sat in Parliament. If they could be harassed on their journey to the Parliament chamber or arrested by creditors, Crown and Parliament would have lost their services. To prevent this, a privilege of freedom from molestation and arrest was granted and enforced.

Enforcement was initially by the Crown, but during the reign of Henry VIII, the Houses of Parliament began to assume jurisdiction themselves, and took the opportunity that offered to lay claim to further rights, powers and immunities as customary. Some of these, repeatedly and successfully asserted, came to be legally recognised as privileges of Parliament. So, for example, the Houses began to require that their members should be able to speak freely in Parliament, without fear of repercussions in the courts, and began to insist that questions affecting their composition and membership should be settled by the Houses themselves and not outside.

What the privileges have in common, it may be seen, is that they are designed to protect the Houses against outside interference, so that they are able to perform their constitutional functions effectively and without hindrance. Their character is ancillary, but they are a necessary complement to the Houses' functions, or are at least presented as such: 'The sole justification for the present privileges of the House of Commons is that they are essential for the conduct of its business and maintenance of its authority,' according to one Clerk of the House of Commons.[1] If the constant general purpose has been the maintenance of Parliament's independence, the threats to that independence have come from various quarters: at times from the ordinary courts seeking to enforce the general law of the land, at times from the Crown, at times from other persons or bodies, including the mass media. Sometimes the enemy is within, and then privilege enables the House to deal with members who abuse their office or seek to obstruct its business.

The Houses are able to deal with offenders and enforce their privileges because they are the High Court of Parliament, and so have an inherent jurisdiction. As Coke said:[2] 'Every court of justice hath rules and customs for its direction . . . so the high court of parliament *suis propriis legibus et consuetudinibus subsistit*'. When any of the rights and immunities known as privileges are disregarded or attacked by anybody, the offence is called a breach of privilege, and is punishable under the law of Parliament. By virtue of the same jurisdiction, each House may punish offences against its authority or dignity, even if they do not involve breaches of specific privileges. Such offences are contempts of Parliament: the concept is analogous to contempt of court. The Houses' penal jurisdiction, or power to punish offenders, may be regarded as complementing their privileges, or as being itself an aspect of privilege.

Coke mentioned the *lex et consuetudo parliamenti*, and parliamentary privilege is regarded as part of the law and custom of Parliament. Its origin is customary; it is recognised as having the status of law; but it will be found, for the most part, not in statutes or cases, but in parliamentary proceedings. It has to be collected, said Coke,[3] 'out of the rolls of Parliament and other records, and by precedents and continued experience'. Since it is enforced primarily by the Houses themselves, it is defined principally in resolutions of the Houses and rulings by the Speakers.

Of course, like any other part of the law, parliamentary privilege is subject to the supremacy of Acts of Parliament. Acts have curtailed the scope of privilege, as for example when members' privilege of freedom from arrest was withdrawn from the servants of members, to whom it had previously extended (Parliamentary Privilege Act 1770). Again, Acts of Parliament may regulate the exercise of privilege. The determination of disputed elections for parliamentary constituencies, which lay within the Commons' privilege of regulating its own composition, has effectively been transferred by statute to judges of the ordinary courts. But it is also possible for statute to

1 Memorandum by Sir Barnett Cocks in Report of the Select Committee on Parliamentary Privilege, HC 34 (1966–67).
2 4 *Institutes* p 15.
3 Ibid.

maintain or extend the scope of privileges. The privileges of freedom of speech and exclusive cognisance of internal proceedings were given a statutory foundation when included as Article 9 of the Bill of Rights: 'That the freedom of speech, and debates or proceedings in Parliament, ought not to be impeached or questioned in any court or place out of Parliament.'

We have reached a point where a definition of parliamentary privilege may be offered. It is that part of our constitutional law which consists of special rules developed by the Houses of Parliament so as to augment their dignity and independence, and in order to protect themselves collectively and their members when acting for the benefit of their House, against interference, attack or obstruction.

There are several parallels with the royal prerogative[4] to be noticed. Both privilege and prerogative consist of special rules evolved to enable public bodies to perform their functions. These rules were customary in origin, and developed in special courts: as matters of state were decided in the Star Chamber or Privy Council, so matters concerning the Houses were decided in the High Court of Parliament. Both are recognised as part of the law of the land, and may be regarded as common law, in so far as they are not statutory. Both are residual. The Crown cannot enlarge its prerogatives; the two Houses recognise that they cannot by their own act create new privileges. When acts are done under prerogative powers, the courts have often been unwilling to review them, although it depends what question is involved. When acts are done by either House within what is acknowledged to be its privilege, the courts will not examine the propriety of those acts.

But the prerogative courts have been abolished, and the Crown cannot punish infringements of its prerogatives, whereas the two Houses have retained their penal jurisdiction, and so are able to punish breaches of privilege. Moreover, and for the same reason, the Crown has long since had to concede that the ambit of prerogative is determinable by the courts, and not by the Crown's claim. The Houses of Parliament, however, still claim that it is for them exclusively to determine the extent of their privileges. That claim is contested by the courts, and so, in matters of privilege, a potential conflict of jurisdictions is still a possibility.

The problem of that dualism will be examined after we survey the scope of parliamentary privilege as it exists today.

THE SCOPE OF THE PRIVILEGES

The Lords are regarded as having ever enjoyed their privileges. There is, however, a symbolic reminder that the Commons had to fight harder for theirs: some of their privileges are specifically claimed at the commencement

4 On which, see ch 8.

of each Parliament. The practice dates from the sixteenth century, although the wording of the claim has altered from time to time. In form, it is a petition to the Crown. The Speaker, on behalf of the Commons, claims

> their ancient and undoubted rights and privileges, particularly to freedom of speech in debate, freedom from arrest, freedom of access to Her Majesty whenever occasion shall require; and that the most favourable construction should be placed upon all their proceedings.

The Lord Chancellor replies that Her Majesty 'most readily confirms' them.

Nothing really turns upon the Speaker's petition, which does not even mention all the House's privileges. Of the privileges expressly claimed, two are not nowadays very important. Freedom of access to the monarch, and the demand for the most favourable construction, remind us of the days when the attitude of monarchs towards petitions by the Commons was unpredictable and sometimes intemperate. The privileges claimed were intended to ensure a hearing, and a fair hearing, for the Commons' views, and to prevent the imprisonment of their Speaker or others who had opposed royal policies. Another privilege which is no longer significant is the right of impeachment, by which the Commons brought judicial proceedings against persons accused of offences beyond the reach of the law, or which no other authority would prosecute. The last case of impeachment was in 1806.

As well as freedom of speech and freedom from arrest, amongst the matters which are generally classed as privileges are the right of the Houses to regulate their own composition, their exclusive cognisance of internal affairs, and their power to punish breaches of privilege and contempts. These last three belong primarily to each House as a collective body. Freedom of speech and freedom from arrest are privileges which are enjoyed by the members of each House as individuals, although they exist for the benefit of the House and not for their personal benefit. This will be seen when we examine these five privileges in detail. The two Houses may be treated together, as their privileges are substantially similar.

Freedom of speech

This may be considered the most important privilege. Parliament is a deliberative and legislative assembly, and it may be regarded as an essential characteristic of a free legislature that its members are able to perform their duties without fear of penalty.

That is what the privilege is designed to ensure. When Richard Strode, a Commons member, was imprisoned by the Stannary Court of Devon for having introduced a Bill to regulate the tin industry there, the Privilege of Parliament Act 1512 was passed to nullify the court's decision and to protect members against similar interference in future. In the seventeenth century the privilege was of the greatest importance in establishing the position of the Commons against the Crown. In 1629 three members were imprisoned and fined by the Court of King's Bench for seditious words spoken in the House, the court having decided that the 1512 Act did not apply.[5] But resolutions against the judgment were passed in 1641 and 1667, and it was reversed by the House of Lords in 1668, when the court accepted that words spoken in Parliament could not be dealt with out of Parliament.[6]

The privilege, claimed in the Speaker's petitions since 1541, was effectively secured at the Revolution. Its inclusion in the Bill of Rights gave it a statutory foundation. Article 9 of the Bill of Rights proclaimed: 'That the freedom of speech, and debates or proceedings in Parliament ought not to be impeached or questioned in any court or place out of Parliament'. This was primarily declaratory of the existing law, and Erskine May[7] is careful to note that 'it may prove to be the case that the law is wider than Article 9'. Be that as it may, it is plain that the interpretation and implications of Article 9 are of great importance.

Article 9 applies equally to both Houses, and its effect is that no action or prosecution can be brought against a member for anything said or done in the course of 'proceedings in Parliament'. The most important application of this is that it invests members with an immunity from the law of defamation, when they are speaking in Parliament and on some other occasions. So, when an action for defamation was brought against a member of the Commons for words spoken in the House, the court recognised that it had no jurisdiction in the matter, and ordered that the writ should be removed from the records.[8] In the same way, the courts would be unable to entertain prosecutions or actions of other kinds. In 1938, when Mr Duncan Sandys raised a matter of national security in a parliamentary question, and refused to reveal the sources of his information, a prosecution on an Official Secrets charge was threatened. The House asserted its privilege in order to avert the threat.[9] In 1977, at a trial on Official Secrets Act charges, a judge had allowed a witness, an officer in the Security Services, to be identified only as 'Colonel B'. When some organs of the press referred to the officer by his real name, in disregard of the judge's wishes, proceedings for contempt of court were brought against them. However, four members of the Commons, who named the officer during questions in the House, were, under the shelter of privilege, immune from such proceedings themselves. Article 9 also means that matters arising in the course of parliamentary proceedings cannot be relied on for the purpose of supporting an action or prosecution based on events occurring elsewhere. For example, the Church of Scientology,

5 *R v Eliot, Hollis and Valentine* (1629) 3 State Tr 294.
6 (1668) 3 St Tr 332.
7 (20th edn by Sir Charles Gordon, 1983) p 89. Thomas Erskine May's *Treatise on The Law, Privileges, Proceedings and Usage of Parliament*, first published in 1844, is 'the Bible' for the law and custom of Parliament.
8 *Dillon v Balfour* (1887) 20 LR Ir 600.
9 HC 146 (1937–38), HC 173 (1937–38).

bringing a libel suit against an MP for remarks made in a television interview, was unable to refer to his speeches in the House of Commons in seeking to prove his malice. [10]

How far the protection of parliamentary privilege extends is not entirely clear. Article 9 refers to 'speech' and 'debates', categories which obviously overlap. Together they would seem to cover all the oral business of the Houses and their committees, and protect not only members and officers but also, for example, members of the public giving evidence before a committee. [11] The difficulty really arises over what may be counted as 'proceedings in Parliament'. Something is not a 'proceeding in Parliament' merely because it happens there. A defendant's defamatory statements about his former wife, put in letters to MPs, were not protected by reason of having been posted within the Palace of Westminster. [12] Even a conversation between members, if on private affairs, would probably not be privileged. [13] Rather the phrase seems intended to cover what is the business of Parliament or its members. A committee once provided an explanation:

> It covers both the asking of a question and the giving written notice of such question, and includes everything said or done by a Member in the exercise of his functions as a Member in a committee of either House, as well as everything said or done in either House in the transaction of Parliamentary business. [14]

That is a helpful formulation, but still leaves some areas of uncertainty. The London Electricity Board case in 1958 was on the borderline. Mr George Strauss MP, in a letter written to a minister, described the Board's practices in selling scrap metal as 'a scandal which should be instantly rectified'. The letter was passed on to the Board, which threatened to sue Mr Strauss for libel. The House determined that the letter was not a 'proceeding in Parliament', although the Committee of Privileges had taken the opposite view. [15] However, it is difficult to infer much from this, for the vote was narrow and the decision is not binding on the House. It may too have been significant that the subject of the letter (being a matter of day-to-day administration of a nationalised industry) was not within ministerial answerability, and therefore could not have formed the basis of a parliamentary question. The Speaker ruled that if a member tabled a question, and a minister invited him to discuss it with him, the correspondence or discussions were covered by privilege. [16] Indeed, if the test is whether a matter is connected with, or a preliminary to, actual business of

10 *Church of Scientology of California v Johnson-Smith* [1972] 1 QB 522, [1972] 1 All ER 378.
11 *Goffin v Donnelly* (1881) 6 QBD 307.
12 *Rivlin v Bilainkin* [1953] 1 QB 485, [1953] 1 All ER 534.
13 HC 101 (1938–39).
14 Ibid, p v.
15 HC 305 (1956–57), HC 227 (1957–58), 591 HC Official Report (5th series) col 208.
16 591 HC Official Report (5th series) col 808.

the whole House or a committee, it is arguable that even unsolicited correspondence is covered, if it is immediately related to a question or motion already tabled or a pending debate. But, in most circumstances at least, letters from the public to MPs and letters from MPs to the public, would appear not to be 'proceedings in Parliament'.

Parliament's official reports and papers enjoy a corresponding privilege. Following *Stockdale v Hansard*,[17] the Parliamentary Papers Act 1840 was passed, which bars proceedings, criminal or civil, against persons for the publication of papers or reports printed by order of either House of Parliament, or copies of them.

The freedom of speech in Parliament has certain corollaries, which historically were designed to allow the avoidance of publicity. First, the Houses and their committees may exclude strangers, and go into private session. They may even, as happened in wartime, go into secret session, when even members would commit a contempt by disclosing what took place. Secondly, the Houses may treat unauthorised publication of their debates and proceedings as contemptuous. Resolutions were passed to that effect in the eighteenth century, but attempts to enforce them, frustrated by John Wilkes, proved unpopular and ineffective, and were abandoned. It was not, however, until 1971 that the House of Commons formally declared that reporting of proceedings of the House and its committees would not be contemptuous, except where the proceedings were held in private session or where publication is expressly forbidden.[18]

Something else which may be treated as a breach of privilege or contempt is the impeaching or questioning of privileged proceedings elsewhere. Article 9 implies as much. In the London Electricity Board case, it was taken for granted in parliamentary discussion that the commencement of proceedings in a court in respect of a 'proceeding in Parliament' was in itself a breach of privilege. That assumption may be criticised, and the assumption that a mere threat to institute proceedings amounts to a breach of privilege is even more doubtful.[19] It may be noted too that the Select Committee on Parliamentary Privilege recommended in 1967 that, save in exceptional circumstances, such matters should be left to the ordinary processes of the courts.[20] But it is by no means certain that the House might not take a similar view again.

There is another implication also to be drawn from Article 9. Members' freedom is only put beyond question 'out of Parliament'. Nothing prevents

---

17 (1839) 9 Ad & El 1.
18 821 HC Official Report (5th series) col 993. However, the publication of a Select Committee's work before it is reported to the House is still expressly forbidden, as explained below.
19 See S A de Smith 'Parliamentary Privilege and the Bill of Rights' (1958) 21 MLR 465; D Thompson 'Letters to Ministers and Parliamentary Privilege' [1959] PL 10.
20 HC 34 (1967–68).

the House from itself punishing a member on account of his words or actions, and if it were thought that a member was abusing his privilege by, for example, using it in order to make unjustified attacks on individuals, such a response would be possible. This is discussed further in the last section of this chapter.

When members of Parliament are not clothed by parliamentary privilege, they may benefit from some other privilege or defence. For example, under the Parliamentary Commissioner Act 1967, communications between MPs and the Parliamentary Commissioner for Administration are protected by absolute privilege (which is a defence to actions for defamation). Actions by members in pursuit of their parliamentary duties would seem generally to be protected by qualified privilege, which is a defence in the law of defamation unless lost by proof of malice. In *Beach v Freeson*,[1] an MP's letters to the Lord Chancellor and to the Law Society, reporting complaints about a solicitors' firm in his constituency, were held to be so protected. Had the London Electricity Board gone on to sue Mr Strauss, which they did not, he would have been protected as well. By statute, a similar defence applies to the publication of extracts from, or abstracts of, parliamentary papers, and by common law to the fair and accurate reporting of parliamentary proceedings.[2]

Freedom from arrest

Parliament claims the paramount right to the unimpeded attendance and uninterrupted services of its members, and this is the justification for the freedom from molestation and arrest which members individually enjoy. Physical molestation of members is a breach of privilege. So, in certain circumstances, is their arrest as part of legal process. The immunity from arrest was important in times when imprisonment was commonly the remedy for debt. Immunity was claimed for members, their goods, and their servants, but abuse of the privilege in the seventeenth century led to its curtailment, in the Parliamentary Privilege Acts 1700, 1703, 1737 and 1770. By the last of these, members' immunity from being impleaded was taken away: a claim of privilege would not prevent actions being brought against them. Privilege was confined to immunity from civil arrest, and that for members only.

Since imprisonment for debt was abolished in the later nineteenth century, the immunity has lost much of its importance. It may operate so as to prevent arrest or imprisonment for civil contempt and in a few other circumstances. Thus in *Stourton v Stourton*,[3] a peer who had not complied with

1 [1972] 1 QB 14, [1971] 2 All ER 854.
2 Parliamentary Papers Act 1840, s 3, Defamation Act 1952, s 9; *Wason v Walter* (1868) LR 4 QB 73.
3 [1963] P 302, [1963] 1 All ER 606.

the provisions of a maintenance order availed himself of the privilege. A peer's privilege is continuous and independent of the sitting of Parliament. Members of the Commons enjoy theirs only during the sitting of Parliament and for forty days before and after (the time deemed necessary for their coming and going in the days of the stagecoach).

The privilege does not extend to arrest in respect of criminal offences, so it did not protect John Wilkes when he was accused of sedition, nor in recent years Bernadette Devlin or John Stonehouse, who were arrested on criminal charges whilst they were MPs. In one nineteenth century case, a member convicted of conspiracy escaped custody and fled to the House of Commons. His arrest in the chamber, which was empty since the day's business had not begun, was held not to violate privilege.[4]

Related privileges, also based on the prior claim of the House to the service of its members, are the privileges of exemption from jury service and exemption from attending court as a witness. As to the former, the Juries Act 1974 now provides that members and officers of both Houses are entitled to excusal from jury service as of right. As to the latter, the House may ask that a member be excused and may even treat the service of a subpoena as a breach of privilege, but often the privilege is not insisted upon.

Regulating composition

Another privilege possessed by the Houses is the right to regulate their own composition. At one time, the most important aspect of this was the right of the Commons to determine the result of disputed parliamentary elections. Their right was established in the seventeenth century, as a result of *Goodwin v Fortescue*,[5] when the Crown had tried to deny Sir Francis Goodwin's election on the ground that he was an outlaw. From the seventeenth to the mid-nineteenth century, disputed elections were tried either by Select Committees or by the whole House, but decisions were often made on party lines. In 1868 the Parliamentary Elections Act handed jurisdiction over to the Court of Common Pleas, and since then it has remained with the ordinary courts. Two judges of the High Court, sitting as an Election Court, determine election petitions under the Representation of the People Act 1983. The court's finding is certified to the Speaker, for the House to take appropriate action. The form of privilege is thus preserved, although under the provisions of the Act the House is effectively bound to accept the court's decision.

Whether a candidate is elected is one thing, but whether a person is disqualified from membership of the House is another, and the Houses retain the power to determine the latter question. Thus when Mr Anthony

4 30 Official Report (1st series) cols 309, 336.
5 (1604) 2 St Tr 91.

Wedgwood Benn became Viscount Stansgate in succession to his father in 1960, his seat was declared vacant by the House of Commons and he was barred from the chamber (the law was subsequently changed to permit hereditary peerages to be disclaimed).[6] Similarly, it is for the House of Lords to determine whether a peerage entitles the holder to sit in that House. A life peerage had been created for the judge Sir James Parke in 1855, presumably so as to strengthen judicial expertise in the House of Lords without at the same time diluting its ranks for the future with the descendants of lawyers. But the House decided that a peerage of that sort did not entitle the holder to sit in Parliament.[7]

The House of Commons may also expel a member for grounds other than disqualification, if it considers him unfit to continue in that capacity. A sufficient cause would be conviction of a criminal offence involving turpitude. In 1922 that engaging Edwardian rogue, Horatio Bottomley, was finally expelled by the House upon a conviction for fraud, having been unjustly acquitted on two earlier occasions. In 1947 when Garry Allighan was expelled, it was his gross contempt of the House which caused it.[8] He had made unsubstantiated allegations that details of confidential party meetings, held within the precincts of Parliament, were being revealed by members to journalists for money or while under the influence of drink. He was himself receiving payments for doing just that, and had lied to the Committee of Privileges.

Indeed, if the government were to use its majority in the House to vote to expel all members who opposed it, no objection could be heard by the courts in this country. It is usually said in response to this that there is nothing to prevent expelled members, if not disqualified from standing, from being re-elected, as John Wilkes was by the electors of Middlesex in the eighteenth century. That is true, but the real protection against abuse lies in conventional self-restraint. The calling of an election is itself at the wish of a Commons majority, for another aspect of privilege is the House's right to determine when casual vacancies will be filled. When a vacancy arises through a member's death, expulsion or disqualification, it is for the House to resolve that a writ be issued for the holding of a by-election.

Exclusive cognisance of internal affairs

Each House collectively claims the right to control its own proceedings and to regulate its internal affairs and whatever takes place within its walls. The claim was partly protected by the provision in the Bill of Rights to the effect

6 Peerage Act 1963.
7 *Wensleydale Peerage Case* (1856) 5 HL Cas 958. The Appellate Jurisdiction Act 1876 authorised appointment of Lords of Appeal in Ordinary, and the Life Peerages Act 1958 allowed the creation of life peerages with a right to sit in the Lords.
8 HC 138 (1946–47).

that 'the freedom of speech and debates or proceedings in Parliament ought not to be impeached or questioned in any court or place out of Parliament', and so this aspect of privilege is linked to the freedom of speech. It is also linked to the privilege concerning composition, for the Houses regard their membership as their own affair.

The claim has been accepted by the courts, at least provided they can agree that 'internal concerns' are involved. 'Whatever is done within the walls of either assembly must pass without question in any other place', said Lord Denman in *Stockdale v Hansard*.[9] In *Bradlaugh v Gossett*,[10] Stephen J observed that 'the House of Commons is not a court of justice, but the effect of its privilege to regulate its own internal concerns practically invests it with a judicial character', and held that 'we must presume that it discharges this function properly and with due regard to the laws, in the making of which it has so great a share'. Indeed, the doctrines upon which claims to privilege are based, and upon which the jurisdiction of courts is denied or restricted have much in common with those which are expressed as the sovereignty of Parliament. When, for example, the validity of an Act of Parliament is challenged on the ground of alleged defects of parliamentary procedure, and the courts refuse to investigate, their refusal might be justified on grounds of sovereignty or privilege. In *British Railways Board v Pickin*,[11] described in chapter 5, the sovereignty aspect was emphasised, but privilege was also adduced as a justification in the speeches of Lord Simon of Glaisdale and Lord Morris of Borth-y-Gest. In the leading case of *Bradlaugh v Gossett*,[12] the question was whether Charles Bradlaugh, a militant atheist elected as member for Northampton, could properly take the oath required of members under the Parliamentary Oaths Act 1866, as he was willing to do. The House of Commons refused to allow him to do so (although on a proper construction of the Act he appeared to be entitled to take the oath if he chose), and resolved to exclude him. Bradlaugh's attempt to have the resolution declared unlawful and the Serjeant at Arms restrained from enforcing it was unsuccessful, because the court held it had no jurisdiction to interfere, even assuming that the Act had been misinterpreted.

However, if matters happen 'within the walls', but are unconnected with the business of Parliament, the ordinary courts may be entitled to assume jurisdiction without being in breach of privilege, or at least are allowed to. 'I know of no authority for the proposition that an ordinary crime committed in the House of Commons would be withdrawn from the ordinary course of criminal justice', said Stephen J in *Bradlaugh v Gossett*.[13] In practice it has

9 (1839) 9 Ad & El 1 at 114.
10 (1884) 12 QBD 271 at 285.
11 [1974] AC 765, [1974] 1 All ER 609, HL.
12 (1884) 12 QBD 271.
13 Ibid at 283.

been left to the ordinary authorities and courts to deal with incidents such as the killing of the Prime Minister by a madman in the lobby of the House of Commons (in 1812) and the projection of CS gas into the chamber by a protestor in the public gallery (in 1970). Sometimes there would be concurrent jurisdiction, as where one member assaults another in the course of proceedings.

The Divisional Court perhaps took a generous view of the scope of the House's internal affairs when in 1935 it upheld the Chief Metropolitan Magistrate's ruling that he lacked jurisdiction to deal with A P Herbert's complaint that drinks were being illegally sold in the House's bar, since it had no licence.[14]

Penal jurisdiction

We have already seen that the Houses, as the High Court of Parliament, possessed an inherent jurisdiction to deal with breaches of privilege or contempts, which they retain today.

Strictly speaking, the terms breach of privilege and contempt are to be distinguished. A breach of privilege is an infringement of or attack upon one of the specific privileges of the Houses already described. Contempt of Parliament is an inclusive term for any offence punishable by the Houses. Thus, while all breaches of privilege may be counted as contempts, there are many kinds of contempt besides those actions which are an infringement of privilege as such. As Erskine May says, each House may punish actions which, 'while not breaches of any specific privilege, are offences against its authority or dignity'.[15] More precisely:

> any act or omission which obstructs or impedes either House of Parliament in the performance of its functions, or which obstructs or impedes any Member or officer of such House in the discharge of his duty, or which has a tendency, directly or indirectly, to produce such results may be treated as a contempt even though there is no precedent of the offence.[16]

There is value in preserving the distinction. For one thing, it is accepted that the Houses cannot by resolution enlarge the scope of their own privileges, but, as the definition indicates, the categories of contempt are not closed, and the scope of contempt is a matter for each House alone to determine. Furthermore, while questions of the existence and extent of privilege may be brought before the ordinary courts, as we shall see, the causes of committal for contempt may be put outside their jurisdiction, so as not to be called in question.

However, the distinction between breaches of privilege and contempts is

14 *R v Graham-Campbell. ex p Herbert* [1935] 1 KB 594.
15 Erskine May p 71
16 Ibid, p 143.

frequently neglected. In parliamentary usage, even in reports of the Committee of Privileges, the terms are often used as if they were interchangeable. This blurring of the distinction may be regretted, but it is perhaps understandable, because the procedure for dealing with all kinds of contempts is the same, and the penalties available with which to punish all kinds of contempts are the same.

Since we know what the privileges of Parliament are, we know what sort of conduct would amount to a breach of privilege. Take, for example, the privilege of freedom from arrest. When in 1819 creditors of Mr Christie Burton, a member for Beverley, tried to have him kept in custody, they were declared guilty of a breach of privilege.[17] Similarly, an interference or attempted interference with a member's freedom of speech could be a breach of privilege.

But what kinds of conduct would amount to contempt, although not involving, or not necessarily involving, a breach of privilege? The answer depends not upon rules, but upon the discretion of the House, and what offends against the authority or dignity of the House is a rather subjective question. There are, however, some fairly well established categories of contemptuous conduct, which include the following: interruption or disruption of proceedings; serious misconduct by a member in the House; disobedience to rules or orders of the House; a refusal to give evidence to a committee of the House, or the giving of false evidence; bribery or attempted bribery of members, or corruption on the part of members; intimidation or molestation of members; obstruction of officers of either House, or of witnesses before a House or its committees; and publication of material which is derogatory of the House or its members.

It was a contempt of the last category, sometimes called 'constructive contempts', which was involved in Allighan's case, already described. The freedom of expression of newspapers and other media is limited to the extent that pejorative comment may be counted as a contempt. In the Sunday Graphic case,[18] in 1956, a newspaper committed contempt of another kind, by encouraging the molestation of a member. In an article it expressed disapproval of the attitude of a Labour member, Mr Arthur Lewis, to the Suez invasion, and encouraged its readers, if they felt likewise, to telephone him and so inform him, revealing his private telephone number for the purpose. The consequence was that Mr Lewis was inundated with calls and hampered in his normal parliamentary duties. The House found the newspaper editor guilty of contempt.

A notorious occasion of a member's contempt occurred in 1963. Rumours were circulating that Mr John Profumo, the Secretary of State for War, had been socialising with persons of dubious repute, so possibly constituting a

17 Commons Journals (1818–19) 44, (1819–20) 286.
18 HC 27 (1956–57).

security risk. Mr Profumo made a personal statement to the House of Commons in which he denied the association. However, he was later obliged to admit that his statement had been untrue. Although his resignation rendered further action unnecessary, his deliberate lie was regarded by the House as a grave contempt.[19]

There was an example of disruption amounting to contempt in 1969, when a sub-committee of the Select Committee on Education and Science, inquiring into relations between students and their colleges, decided to hold some meetings on location. At the University of Essex, the members of the committee soon gained first hand experience. Their first session was disrupted, the tables at which they were sitting overturned, and they were physically assaulted by being clasped around the legs. This was a disruption of parliamentary proceedings, although it took place outside the precincts of Parliament. The contempt was condemned, but the House resolved to take no action against the contemnors.[20]

As these examples perhaps show, the Houses are discriminating in their use of the various penalties at their disposal for dealing with offenders. It would be as well to describe what these penalties are.

So far as members are concerned, we have already seen that a member of the Commons may be expelled for a contempt, as for any other matter which, in the view of the House, renders him unfit to serve. A member of either House might be suspended for a period of time, in less serious cases. There are also specific provisions in Standing Orders[1] for requiring the withdrawal or enabling the suspension of members guilty of grossly disorderly conduct, disregard of the authority of the chair, or other serious misconduct. The Speaker has had to name members under these provisions more frequently in recent years.

Other penalties may be imposed upon members or strangers, as non-members are called. The most serious is imprisonment, in the Clock Tower (for members) or one of Her Majesty's Prisons (for strangers). Imprisonment by the Commons is during the pleasure of the House, but a prisoner is automatically released upon prorogation at the end of the session. The House of Lords has the power to commit offenders to prison for a definite period, extending beyond prorogation. Imprisonment has not been employed by either House since 1880, when it was used to punish one Grissell's refusal to attend as a witness. The House of Lords, as a court of record, has the power to impose fines on offenders. The Commons used in the sixteenth and seventeenth centuries to impose fines, but have not since 1666, and it has been denied that the House possesses such a power.[2]

19 679 HC Official Report (5th series) col 655.

20 HC 308 (1968–69).

 1 HC Standing Orders 24–26.

 2 By Lord Mansfield in *R v Pitt and Mead* (1762) 3 Burr 1335.

Further down the scale of penalties are reprimand and (a milder version) admonition, for which offenders are brought to the bar of the House to be duly rebuked by the Speaker (or, in the House of Lords, the Lord Chancellor). In many cases, of course, the House may decide that, even although a contempt has been committed, no action should be taken. A sufficiently humble apology seems to make this more likely. The fit punishment in any particular case is determined by the House as a whole, which usually, but not invariably, accepts the recommendation of the Committee of Privileges in this regard. The Committee of Privileges, a Select Committee nominated for the duration of a Parliament in proportion to party strengths, is the body to which questions of privilege may be referred for consideration and recommendations.

PRIVILEGE AND THE COURTS

As we have seen, the Houses, because they form the High Court of Parliament, have an inherent jurisdiction to deal with breaches of privilege and contempts. Moreover, since the privileges are enforced primarily by the Houses themselves, the law concerning them is principally found in the Houses' proceedings. However, issues of privilege have sometimes been raised in the ordinary courts, and in this way a second body of law on privilege could, and did, emerge, with no means of harmonising the two systems. What is more, since the Houses claim to be the sole judges of their own privileges, and do not concede that the courts have jurisdiction, there is the possibility of an untidy and unseemly conflict whenever the ordinary courts become involved, and particularly where their view of the matter differs.

Such a conflict occurred in the case of the men of Aylesbury. When a citizen, prevented from voting in a parliamentary election, sued the returning officer, the ordinary courts assumed jurisdiction and the House of Lords (in its judicial capacity) held in favour of the plaintiff.[3] As the election result was not in dispute, privilege was arguably not involved at all. But the Commons passed a resolution to the effect that their exclusive right to determine upon privileges had been infringed; and when further actions were brought arising from the same events, had the plaintiffs committed to prison and later, when an appeal against unsuccessful habeas corpus proceedings[4] seemed probable, their counsel.

A rather similar controversy recurred in the nineteenth century, when the printer Hansard was sued for libel by Stockdale, the publisher of a book which had been described as being 'of the most disgusting nature' by the

3 *Ashby v White* (1703) 2 Ld Raym 938, (1704) 3 Ld Raym 320.
4 *R v Paty* (1704) 2 Ld Raym 1105.

Inspectors of Prisons, who had found it circulating in Newgate gaol. The Inspectors' Report had been published by order of the House of Commons, who regarded it as privileged. A court first gave judgment for Hansard on another ground, but denied that privilege extended to the Report.[5] The Commons by resolution reiterated its view of the scope of privilege. It further resolved:

> That by the law and privilege of Parliament, this House has the sole and exclusive jurisdiction to determine upon the existence and extent of its privileges; and that the institution or prosecution of any action, suit or other proceedings, for the purpose of bringing them into discussion or decision before any court or tribunal elsewhere than in Parliament, is a high breach of such privilege, and renders all parties concerned therein amenable to its just displeasure, and to the punishment consequent thereon . . .[6]

Its threat had to be carried out. When Stockdale brought a second action, the Court of Queen's Bench held that the Report was not privileged, and that the resolution of one House did not change the law.[7] No other defence having been pleaded, Stockdale won, as he did in a third action where no plea was entered. But when the Sheriff of Middlesex took steps to enforce the judgment, the House of Commons imprisoned them (the office was held by two men); and an application for habeas corpus was unsuccessful, because the court held, out of deference to the House in its capacity as a superior court, that it could not go behind the Speaker's warrant, which merely stated that the men were 'guilty of a contempt and breach of the privileges of this House'.[8] That was a remarkable judgment, since the court knew the House's reasons perfectly well, and would have regarded them as unsound. It is attributable to the reticence of the Speaker's return, which had been formulated advisedly; for, if the Speaker had specified what constituted the breach of privilege, the court might have found the cause to be insufficient in law.[9]

The men were eventually freed by the Commons on their undertaking not to execute any court orders against Hansard, and, in an almost farcical turn of events, were then imprisoned for contempt of court as a result. The impasse was ended by the passing of the Parliamentary Papers Act 1840. What for the Commons was already the law became law which the courts would accept by virtue of their obedience to Acts of Parliament. But, of course, the Act only resolved the difference over the extent of freedom of speech, and not

---

5 *Stockdale v Hansard* (1837) 2 Mood & R 9.
6 Commons Journals (1837) 418.
7 *Stockdale v Hansard* (1839) 9 Ad & El 1.
8 *Case of the Sheriff of Middlesex* (1840) 11 Ad & El 273.
9 This was the view of Holt CJ in *R v Paty* (1704) 2 Ld Raym 1105, seconded by Lord Ellenborough in *Burdett v Abbot* (1811) 14 East 1, and it was approved in the *Case of the Sheriff of Middlesex* (1840) 11 Ad & El 273.

the competition over jurisdiction. As to that, as Erskine May puts it, 'the old dualism remains unresolved'.[10]

Certainly the Houses continue to assert their jurisdiction, and the Commons has not abandoned the claim to treat as a breach of privilege the assumption of jurisdiction elsewhere. It is also true that, in the last resort, the Houses can impose their own view by committing to prison persons held to have violated their privileges and by declining to specify what the breach is. But, by its participation in the enactment of the 1840 Act, the House of Commons perhaps began to acknowledge that the law of privilege is not finally determined by its resolutions, and the absence of serious clashes since may be read as further evidence of that recognition. For their part, the courts may accept that matters dealt with by the Houses within their recognised privileges are non-justiciable, but regard privilege, like royal prerogative, as simply part of the ordinary law determinable by the ordinary courts. This view was confidently expressed by Scarman J in a modern case:

> I do not think, however, that I, sitting in the High Court of Justice, must necessarily take the law that I have to apply from what would be the practice of the House. I think I have to look to the common law as deduced in judicial decisions in order to determine in the particular case whether the privilege arises and, if so, its scope and effect . . .[11]

REFORM PROPOSALS

Is the law relating to parliamentary privilege in need of reform? Certainly its antiquity and some anomalies have been revealed by our survey, but quaintness and irrationality are no strangers in the British constitution. There are uncertainties, for example over the meaning of 'proceedings in Parliament'. But many parts of the law are afflicted by uncertainty. In 1966, when the House of Commons appointed a Select Committee to consider the law and practice of privilege, it was motivated not so much by those reasons as by concern that complaints of breaches were being too frequently made, and that the procedures for dealing with them required review.

To outside critics, the principal defect of the procedures is that the House acts as judge in its own cause, which goes against natural justice. As Professor Harry Street put it, 'No Englishman should be imprisoned without having had the right to defend himself, to be legally represented, to call and cross-examine witnesses, and to be tried by an impartial body, not by his accusers'.[12] Imprisonment is perhaps unlikely today, but the safeguards mentioned are regularly denied to those who are accused of a breach. In the

---

10 Erskine May p 203.
11 *Stourton v Stourton* [1963] P 302 at 306.
12 *Freedom, the Individual and the Law* (5th edn, 1982) p 175.

Strauss case, for example, the Committee of Privileges condemned the members of the area board without hearing them. When 'defendants' are allowed or required to appear before the Committee, the practice has been not to permit them to be represented.

The Select Committee reported in 1967,[13] and recommended that persons against whom a complaint is made should be entitled to attend the hearings on the complaint, to make submissions and call witnesses, and to apply for representation and legal aid. The central criticism, of course, would only be met if the contempt jurisdiction were transferred to another body such as the ordinary courts, but the Committee rejected that as inappropriate and the House of Commons is unlikely to do it.

So far the reforms mentioned have not been implemented, and scarcely any of the others suggested in 1967 had been ten years after, when the Committee of Privileges itself reviewed the recommendations at the request of the House.[14] That Committee agreed with the earlier one that the phrase 'proceedings in Parliament' should be defined in legislation; that the privilege of freedom from arrest should be ended, and the power of impeachment formally abolished. Each recommended that the House of Commons be given the power to impose fines, being coupled in the later report with removal of the power to imprison. But, a further ten years later, there has been no legislation on any of these matters.

The Select Committee in 1967 had hoped that recourse to the House's penal jurisdiction would be confined to serious cases. The Committee in 1977 was able to report that the 'number of frivolous or unnecessary complaints has recently given less cause for anxiety', and in 1978 the House accepted guidelines to the effect that its powers of punishment should be resorted to as sparingly as possible.[15] The Select Committee had recommended that, in cases where a member had a remedy in the courts, he should not be permitted to invoke the penal jurisdiction of the House, but the House would not go that far. Some changes in the procedures for members' raising of privilege complaints were also made in 1978, which enable trivial complaints to receive less publicity.[16]

SOME CURRENT ISSUES

Aspects of parliamentary privilege are more relevant than one might suppose to a consideration of Parliament's functions in the present day. Indeed, items involving privilege figure quite frequently in the news, although not all are

---

13 HC 34 (1967–68).
14 HC 417 (1976–77).
15 943 HC Official Report (5th series) col 1155.
16 For details, see Erskine May pp 169–170.

of equal importance. Three matters of some topical interest will be briefly discussed here.

Committees and leaks

As explained, it was only in 1971 that the House of Commons formally accepted that the ordinary reporting of its proceedings would not be contemptuous. However, another restriction was left unaffected by this. In 1837 the Commons resolved:

> That the evidence taken by any select committee of this House, and the documents presented to such committee, and which have not been reported to the House, ought not to be published by any member of such committee or by any other person.[17]

The prohibition has been modified since, with regard to evidence given at public sittings and evidence published with a committee's consent, but not otherwise, so unauthorised or premature disclosure is still contemptuous. On a number of occasions, when newspapers have published accounts of evidence given behind closed doors or have revealed the contents of draft reports, not intended for publication, members of the House have bayed for blood. But there has been embarrassment too. Journalists normally have access to such information only because a member of the committee has chosen to 'leak' it. The leaker is in contempt too, and more culpable, but, because of the journalistic ethic which forbids disclosure of sources, is frequently not identified.

Mr Tam Dalyell MP, who admitted leaking evidence given to the Select Committee on Science and Technology on their visit to Porton Down, was reprimanded by the House in 1968.[18] The Observer's editor and the journalist who received the information were found guilty of contempt, but not penalised. Articles were published on the basis of draft reports by the Daily Mail in 1971 (the Select Committee on the Civil List)[19] and The Economist in 1975 (the Select Committee on a Wealth Tax).[20] In both cases the journalists and their editors were found to be in contempt, aggravated by refusal to identify their sources. They suffered no penalty, although it was a narrow escape for the men from The Economist, whose exclusion from the precincts had been recommended by the Committee of Privileges. The Guardian and the Daily Mail were in contempt in 1978 over another leaked draft report, and The Times in 1985, but no action was taken in these instances. After the last, the Committee of Privileges considered the whole

17 Commons Journals (1837) 282.
18 HC 357 (1967–68).
19 HC 180 (1971–72).
20 HC 22 (1975–76).

issue. It acknowledged that there were difficulties in enforcing the rule, but nonetheless recommended by twelve votes to two that it should be retained.[1]

In 1986 The Times was in trouble again, when the Select Committee on the Environment's conclusions on the disposal of nuclear waste were anticipated in an article by their lobby reporter.[2] The Committee of Privileges recommended his exclusion from the precincts for six months, so earning this rebuke from Bernard Levin:

> The judgment of the Committee of Privileges is based partly on their own pique (The Times had earlier published a leak from the Privileges Committee itself), partly on a vicarious sense of *amour propre* on behalf of their colleagues on the select committee, partly on the frustration caused by their failure to find which MP had leaked the information, partly on their guilty knowledge that every constituent part of our political life is leakier than any colander in any kitchen and that the most comprehensively perforated is the Cabinet, and most of all on their underestimate of the lack of regard for them among the public and their misunderstanding of the causes of that lack.[3]

The House decided to take no action.

It is difficult to resist the conclusion that the more sensitive members of the House are fighting a losing battle, and making themselves look ridiculous in the process. Moreover, it is a battle which they deserve to lose. Select committees, in examining the work of government, are rightly able to lift the veil of secrecy in Whitehall. It ill befits them to seek to preserve secrecy themselves, with punitive measures against journalists, when it is insufficiently respected by their own members.

The misuse of freedom of speech

As we have seen, the privilege of freedom of speech clothes members with immunity from civil or criminal proceedings when they are engaged in 'proceedings in Parliament'. Historically, the justification for this immunity was the need for members to speak freely, without fear of sanction, when discussing the affairs of the nation. That consideration may still have force, but some members' use of privilege to say with impunity in Parliament what they decline to say outside it, has caused some critics to call for a curtailment of this privilege, or at least means to prevent or correct what they see as its abuse.

Of course, opinions may vary as to what is abuse or (less emotively) misuse and what is proper use. It was under the protection of privilege that a member in 1955 named Kim Philby as a Soviet spy, an allegation which proved to be true, although it was denied at the time. In the 1960s the

1 HC 555 (1984–85).
2 HC 376 (1985–86).
3 The Times, 12 May 1986.

ill-advised social connections of Mr John Profumo, the Secretary of State for War, were brought to light in the Commons, as were the methods of the infamous property racketeer Peter Rachman. In these instances, freed from the inhibitions of the law of defamation, members were enabled to bring matters of importance to national attention, and further publicity and inquiries followed, until the matters were resolved. Cases like these attest to the beneficial effects of the privilege.

However, other instances are more controversial. Was it, for example, a proper use of privilege when four members named 'Colonel B' at a time when contempt of court proceedings had been instituted against others for doing just that?[4] In 1980 Mr Jeffrey Rooker MP made allegations against Rolls-Royce and one of its managers, whom he named, of commercial espionage and bribery.[5] A few weeks later, in a statement to the House, he withdrew the allegations against the individual. That individual, who had immediately protested his innocence, no doubt suffered damage to his reputation and an invasion of his privacy, but could have no recourse to the courts. Persons affected in this way might regard a subsequent retraction, if and when it happens, as a less than satisfactory resolution.

In 1985 and 1986 Mr Brian Sedgemore MP made a number of accusations in the House, against government ministers and others, in connection with the collapse of Johnson Matthey Bankers and some other City affairs, many of which were not repeated outside the House. Mr Geoffrey Dickens MP, a campaigner on child abuse, used a parliamentary question to name an Essex doctor whom he alleged to be guilty of raping a child. Some newspapers then published the man's name and photograph. The tactic was going to be repeated in order to name a Hull vicar allegedly guilty of sexual offences, but the Speaker disallowed the question.[6] Mr Dickens was angered by the authorities' failure (up to that time) to bring prosecutions in these cases. In fact, in the case of the doctor, the Director of Public Prosecutions had reviewed the results of police investigations and decided that there was insufficiently good evidence to justify a prosecution. Given that, we might doubt whether it is proper for such allegations, which may or may not be true, to be made and reported. There is force in the complaints of such individuals that they are suffering 'trial by newspaper' and are no longer regarded as 'innocent until proved guilty'. That is presumably why another member described Mr Dickens's actions as 'an irresponsible abuse of parliamentary privilege',[7] and commentators were moved to question whether members should enjoy privileges to the extent that they do.

In fact, within a few weeks of these matters being raised, a private

4 948 HC Official Report (5th series) col 671.
5 986 HC Official Report (5th series) col 1682, 987 HC Official Report (5th series) col 1776.
6 94 HC Official Report (6th series) col 23.
7 Mr Robin Corbett MP, reported in the Sunday Times, 16 March 1986.

prosecution was brought against the doctor, the costs of which were borne by The Sun, the vicar was charged with 28 offences, and there were calls for reforms in the law of evidence with regard to child witnesses. These developments might or might not be thought to justify Mr Dickens's actions, but it is at least arguable that he was carrying out the traditional functions of a member in the public interest, even if it is a more robust view than is currently fashionable.

In any event, a member's freedom is not absolute. It is only 'out of Parliament' that there is immunity. Within the House, there exist various rules and resolutions imposing restrictions.[8] Members may not, for example, comment on matters which are sub judice, use treasonable or seditious language, or refer disrespectfully to the Queen. More generally, the House is capable of treating an abuse of privileges by a member as a contempt. There are precedents for that, although it has not happened in any of the cases discussed.

Pressures and interests

The underlying purpose of privilege is the protection of Parliament's independence. The danger today is not of an overt attack on it, but is of its being insidiously undermined, by the pressures to which members are subject and the connections which many choose to accept.

Of course, it is very difficult to say where legitimate pressures end and where improper or unacceptable pressures begin. The most serious pressures on MPs come from their own parties, within and outside Parliament. Inside Parliament, party managers, by the use of the whip system and other means, seek to control and influence their members, and, outside it, the constituency parties. These, however, are justifiably regarded as legitimate pressures.

Then, too, it is not only proper, but desirable, in a democracy for the pressures of public opinion to be brought to bear on members in traditional ways. For example, it is not improper for groups to campaign vigorously about proposed legislation, even if members are deluged with their propaganda. The line seems to be crossed when, to borrow a phrase from the criminal law, someone does not employ a proper means of reinforcing the demand. In the Sunday Graphic case, described earlier, the Committee of Privileges agreed that: 'Whether communications to Members of Parliament by constituents or others amount to an improper interference . . . depends on the nature and manner of the communications.'[9] So anything which constitutes or might constitute obstruction, intimidation or blackmail would be on the wrong side of the line. That explains the House's objection

8 For a comprehensive account, see Erskine May ch 19.
9 HC 27 (1956–57).

to letters sent by the League for the Prohibition of Cruel Sports to MPs which said 'If we do not hear from you, we shall feel justified in letting your constituents know that you have no objection to cruel sports'.[10] There was a similar reaction in 1946 to a threat by a group to publish the names of members who voted in favour of bread rationing in a forthcoming debate as being 'public enemies and dictators'.[11]

The difficulties of drawing a line are greatest when the pressures, or the risks of influence, come from outside connections which members themselves have embraced. Until 1911 MPs did not receive a salary, so it is not surprising that there have always been many members with other sources of income. Cynics might even conclude that Parliament's peculiar hours of sitting are not unconnected with members' legal practices and company directorships. Nowadays, besides these more traditional activities, there are members who are trade union sponsored; there are some who are being rewarded directly or indirectly by foreign governments; and there are many acting as consultants or advisers to pressure groups or commercial concerns. In the last few years the problem has dramatically increased in scale, and has been aggravated by the growth of firms of specialised parliamentary lobbyists, in some of which members or sometimes their research assistants have been acting in a dual capacity.

It is not easy to say when these arrangements should or would become improper. In 1695 the House of Commons resolved that 'the offer of money, or other advantage, to a member of Parliament for the promoting of any matter whatsoever depending on or to be transacted in Parliament is a high crime and misdemeanour'.[12] A member who accepted rewards given for such purposes would also be in contempt. But these rules have been interpreted narrowly as referring only to specific payments for specific purposes.

Apart from that, the Brown case offers some guidance. In 1947, the Civil Service Clerical Association, becoming displeased with the behaviour of Mr W J Brown, an Independent MP to whom it had been making substantial payments as its 'Parliamentary General Secretary', proposed to terminate the appointment. To Brown's suggestion that the termination might be a breach of privilege, the Committee of Privileges replied that the agreement in this instance, which expressly preserved his freedom of action, was not improper, and that a member entering into such an agreement must be taken to have accepted its possible termination as a matter which would not influence him in his parliamentary duties.[13] The House accepted that, but resolved that it would be improper for a member:

10   301 HC Official Report (5th series) col 1545.
11   HC 181 (1945–46).
12   Commons Journals (1693–97) 331.
13   HC 118 (1946–47).

to enter into any contractual agreement with an outside body, controlling or limiting the member's complete independence and freedom of action in Parliament or stipulating that he shall act in any way as the representative of such outside body in regard to any matters to be transacted in Parliament.[14]

Consistently with that approach, the House has regarded it as contemptuous when trade unions have overtly tried to restrict the freedom of their sponsored MPs. So, when the Yorkshire Area Council of the National Union of Mineworkers threatened to withdraw sponsorship from members not complying with union policy, it was considered a serious contempt (although the House took no action, in view of the repudiation of the threats by the union's National Executive Committee).[15]

But incidents brought to the House's attention have been few and far between, and the House's approach may fairly be criticised as legalistic, not to say hypocritical. Content if the outward forms are observed, it is turning a blind eye to the realities. One wonders why so many members would be rewarded by outside organisations, if the paymasters did not feel that their interests were being promoted and represented. But when Mr Joe Ashton MP in a radio interview implied that there were members who were willing to sell their freedom of action, it was regarded as a serious contempt, for which he was obliged to apologise.[16]

In recent years the House has preferred to tackle the problem by publicity rather than prevention. First, the duty upon members to disclose their private interests when relevant was clarified and extended when, in 1974, the House resolved:

> That in any debate or proceedings of the House or its Committees or transactions or communications which a member may have with other members or with Ministers or servants of the Crown, he shall disclose any relevant pecuniary interest or benefit of whatever nature, whether direct or indirect, that he may have had, may have or may be expecting to have.[17]

Secondly, in 1975 the House resolved to establish a register of members' interests, that is, those rewards or benefits 'which a member may receive which might be thought to affect his conduct as a member or influence his actions, speeches or vote in Parliament'.[18] Members are required to provide information about nine categories of possible interest, and compulsorily, in as much as a refusal might be treated as a contempt (although it has not been in the case of Mr Enoch Powell MP, who has declined on constitutional grounds to comply). However, it is perhaps a weakness that members are not required to declare the amounts of their rewards, but only their existence.

14 440 HC Official Report (5th series) col 284.
15 HC 634 (1974–75).
16 HC 228 (1974).
17 874 HC Official Report (5th series) col 391.
18 HC 102 (1974–75), 893 HC Official Report (5th series) col 735.

Nonetheless, the systematic and public disclosure of interests is certainly to be welcomed, even if it is only a partial solution to the problem. In 1985 the Commons went a little further, when it decided to set up new registers covering sources of fees for journalists, researchers and secretaries, to be placed in the library, but not publicly available.[19] Whether these measures will be sufficient to dispel suspicions of venality remains to be seen. One wonders whether, in a matter such as this, the interests of the public need to be represented by somebody other than the members of the House of Commons.

19 89 HC Official Report (6th series) col 216.

8   The royal prerogative

The royal prerogative may be defined as comprising those attributes peculiar to the Crown which are derived from common law, not statute, and which still survive.

Some of these points need to be amplified, so that we may see what sort of creature we are dealing with. First, notice that the prerogative consists of legal attributes, not matters merely of convention or practice. The courts will recognise, in appropriate cases, that these attributes exist, and, when necessary, enforce them. So, when a university archaeological team excavated a treasure hoard from St Ninian's Isle in the Shetlands, an action was brought to establish that the treasure belonged to the Crown.[1] The courts will rule, in other cases, that a prerogative which has been claimed does not exist or that government action falls outside the scope of the prerogative. In 1964, a court had to decide whether the Crown's monopoly over the printing of Bibles applied to the new translation, the New English Bible, and held that it did not.[2]

Strictly speaking, the prerogatives are recognised, rather than created, by the common law, for their source is in custom. By origin, royal prerogatives were attributes which of necessity inhered in kings as the governors of the realm. It is natural to think of the prerogative as composed of powers, for it is in the exercise of the Crown's discretionary powers, and the control of that exercise, that our chief interest lies. But rules affected the Crown in a variety of ways. Some gave rights to the Crown, such as the right to treasure trove. Some gave immunities, such as the Crown's immunity from being sued. Some even imposed duties, such as the Crown's duty to protect subjects within the realm.[3]

It is with rules peculiar to the Crown that we are concerned. In owning property or entering into contracts, the Crown is doing nothing which an ordinary person might not do. The word 'prerogative', however, aptly describes only something over and above the ordinary, as Blackstone emphasised:

1 *Lord Advocate v University of Aberdeen* 1963 SC 533.
2 *Universities of Oxford and Cambridge v Eyre and Spottiswoode Ltd* [1964] Ch 736, [1963] 3 All ER 289.
3 *Glasbrook Bros Ltd v Glamorgan County Council* [1925] AC 270, HL.

It signifies, in its etymology (from *prae* and *rogo*) something that is required or demanded before, or in preference to, all others. And hence it follows, that it must be in its nature singular and eccentrical; that it can only be applied to those rights and capacities which the king enjoys alone, in contradistinction to others, and not to those which he enjoys in common with any of his subjects; for if once any one prerogative of the Crown could be held in common with the subject, it would cease to be prerogative any longer.[4]

Properly, then, the prerogative is confined to matters, such as the power to declare war or the power of creating peerages, which are peculiar to the Crown.[5] That is the best usage, but unfortunately not the only one. Dicey rather carelessly wrote that 'every act which the executive government can lawfully do without the authority of the Act of Parliament is done in virtue of the prerogative',[6] and this looser use of the term has caught on. Thus, courts have described the Criminal Injuries Compensation Board scheme as established 'under the prerogative'.[7] The scheme was set up by government action, without statutory authority, in order to distribute ex gratia payments to victims of crime. But anyone might have done the same. There was no employment of 'rights and capacities which the King enjoys alone'. It is the special legal attributes of the Crown which deserve our attention.

These special legal attributes are a residue, a remnant of what was possessed by medieval kings and queens. What remains is left to the executive by the grace of Parliament, for Parliament can abrogate or diminish the prerogative, like any other part of the common law. Enlargement, unlike diminution, is not possible. The Crown cannot claim that a new prerogative power has come into existence or that an existing prerogative has been extended. It is 'three hundred and fifty years and a civil war too late', as Diplock LJ put it.[8] Of course, new rights or powers may be given to the Crown or ministers of the Crown by statute, but these would then be not prerogative, but statutory, powers.

The prerogatives that remain are relics. But they are not unimportant relics. The conduct of foreign affairs is carried on mainly by reliance on the prerogative, as are the control, organisation and disposition of the armed forces. It is by virtue of the prerogative that Parliament is summoned, prorogued and dissolved, and under the prerogative that the royal assent is given to Bills. A prerogative immunity has the consequence that the Crown is not bound by statutes, unless by their terms it is evident that Parliament intended it to be. Appointments of the Prime Minister and other ministers, of judges, Privy Councillors, Archbishops and Bishops, and conferments of

4 *Commentaries*, I, p 239.
5 See further H W R Wade *Administrative Law* (5th edn, 1982) p 214.
6 *Law of the Constitution* (10th edn) p 425.
7 Eg *R v Criminal Injuries Compensation Board, ex p Lain* [1967] 2 QB 864, [1967] 2 All ER 770, DC.
8 *BBC v Johns* [1965] Ch 32 at 79, [1964] 1 All ER 923 at 941, CA.

peerages and honours, take place under prerogative powers. There are prerogative powers which may affect the administration of justice, such as the *nolle prosequi*, by which criminal proceedings may be stopped, and the powers to remit or reduce sentences, or pardon offenders. Appointments to the Civil Service, and the regulation of the terms of employment of civil servants, are done under the prerogative, and so this area of law was involved when in 1984 the government decided to withdraw from employees at Government Communications Headquarters (GCHQ) at Cheltenham the right to be a member of a trade union.[9]

Clearly, the place of these special attributes in our constitution merits our attention, and we shall want to know whether the manner of exercise of executive powers is sufficiently controlled, when these powers are derived from ancient prerogatives. But it is a long road to Cheltenham. We shall be better equipped for travelling it, if we start our survey some centuries back when the prerogative was at its height, and follow its fluctuating fortunes since.

A BRIEF HISTORY

Doctrines of royal absolutism never took root on this island's soil. Bracton, who wrote the first great treatise on English law in the middle of the thirteenth century, said that: 'the king must not be under man but under God and under the law, because law makes the king'.[10] The medieval kings of England and Scotland were feudal landlords and heads of their kingdoms. They enjoyed ordinary rights of property and some extraordinary rights, they had advantages and immunities in litigation, and they had some undefined powers to act for the protection of the realm and for the public good. But there were traditional modifications and limitations upon the powers of kingship. The rights which kings had to respect were spelt out in coronation oaths, and the Great Charter (or Magna Carta) of 1215 was itself an enumeration of the king's promises. A practical limitation was that the wealth and power of other barons often surpassed the king's. In the circumstances, it was hardly surprising that kings came to accept 'the necessity of taking the nation into partnership'.[11] By the fourteenth century in England, convention, or at least prudence, required that taxes should be levied only with consent and that general laws of the land should be made only by statute, with the consent of prelates and barons.

9 *Council of Civil Service Unions v Minister for the Civil Service* [1985] AC 374, [1984] 3 All ER 935, HL: discussed below.
10 *Bracton on the Laws and Customs of England* (translated and edited by S E Thorne, 1968), II, p 33.
11 C H McIlwain 'Medieval Estates', in *The Cambridge Medieval History* (1932) VII, p 712.

Under these doctrines, a king who would not rule according to law might forfeit his right to be obeyed. The removal of Richard II from the throne of England in 1399 is instructive. The charge laid against him was not incompetence or unworthiness. It was that he had broken the law, by claiming that the lives, liberties and property of his subjects lay at his disposal, and acted accordingly. Henry of Lancaster, who became Henry IV, raised a rebellion in the north, and Richard, finding himself bereft of support, was induced to execute a deed of abdication. A Parliament, summoned by Richard, accepted his abdication and, for good measure, formally deposed him. Henry claimed the Crown and secured parliamentary confirmation of his claim a few years later.

In these events, there are facts of great constitutional significance, especially the conception of the king as limited by law, and the emerging role of Parliament. 'Continuity', it has been suggested, 'has been the dominant characteristic in the development of English government',[12] and even during the turbulent Wars of the Roses this is evident. It would be wrong to represent as a contest of principles what was essentially a dynastic struggle for power and wealth, but the House of Lancaster, which had been put on the throne to replace an absolute monarch, was naturally identified with a tradition of parliamentary government.

The culmination of those struggles in the victory of Henry Tudor at Bosworth Field in 1485 may be compared with the events of 1399. At Bosworth the victor immediately assumed the Crown. He was entitled to it neither by hereditary right nor under the existing law, but he was quick to summon a Parliament so as to convert the fact of possession into legal title, and by an Act Henry VII and his heirs were acknowledged as Kings of England. Parliament was farther on the way to becoming the king-maker, and not merely a body through which the king governed. Obliged to prefer a statutory foundation to any claim based on heredity, Henry could not but be aware that 'law makes the king'.

We are apt to forget some of these circumstances in our recollection of the greatness of the Tudor dynasty, but the Tudors themselves did not. Under their rule, the monarchy enlarged the sphere of its activities and increased the effectiveness of its control. The feudal aristocracy had lost much of its wealth and power during the civil wars. With commercial prosperity, new groups of successful merchants, minor landowners and country knights and squires assumed importance, who in return for protection of their interests were happy to allow the Crown full control over national affairs and to assist its control over local administration. With the English Reformation, Henry VIII not only broke the power of the Catholic church to interfere in national affairs, and massively increased royal revenues, but added a practical gain to kingship and an additional motive for obedience to the Crown. Past

12 D L Keir *The Constitutional History of Modern Britain Since 1485* (8th edn, 1966) p 1.

insecurity, religious difficulties and external threats, produced in the nation a desire for peace and strong government. By governing efficiently and to the satisfaction of the greater part of the realm, the Tudors discharged the first obligation of kingship. Absolute obedience and the co-operation of Parliaments were natural consequences in what was anyway an essentially monarchical age.

But, if the Tudor period may fairly be regarded as the zenith of royal authority, yet it would be wrong to regard it as a period of absolutism, either in practice or in constitutional theory. Bracton's principle had been restated by Chief Justice Fortescue in the fifteenth century. In *The Governance of England*, he contrasted the constitutional monarchy (*dominium politicum et regale*) of England with the absolute monarchy (*dominium regale*) of France.[13] Sir Thomas Smith, who was Secretary of State to Queen Elizabeth, wrote that 'the most high and absolute power of the realm of England is in the Parliament'. The royal prerogative, he said, was 'declared . . . in the books of the laws and lawyers of England'.[14]

Force of personality and political, not constitutional, factors enabled the Tudor monarchs to exercise their powers so fully and vigorously. No new principle was invoked in support of royal powers. The Tudor kings and queens did not deny that they were *sub lege*. The supremacy of law was accepted, and this was coming to mean the supremacy of statute. When a case arose concerning a royal servant's claim to the parliamentary privilege of freedom from arrest, Henry VIII is said to have accepted in the course of his opinion that 'we at no time stand so highly in our estate royal as in the time of Parliament, wherein we as head and you as members are conjoined and knit together as one body politic'.[15] At one time it was customary to regard the Statute of Proclamations of 1539 as evidence of Tudor despotism.[16] Modern scholarship tells a different story. Within limits, the Crown could supplement the law by proclamations. The Act codified the common law interpretation of those limits. It 'preserved and indeed increased the supremacy of statute over the prerogative'.[17]

Elizabeth had not quite the cleverness of her father, and by the end of her reign disagreements with Parliament were becoming more frequent. But it was during the seventeenth century that the system broke down. The breakdown is sometimes explained by reference to growing causes of social stress: price inflation made the monarchy short of money; religious diversity was divisive; a rising bourgeoisie threatened the aristocracy; a more powerful

13 Sir John Fortescue *The Governance of England* (ed by C Plummer, 1926) p 109.
14 Sir Thomas Smith *De Republica Anglorum* (ed by M Dewar, 1982) pp 78, 87.
15 *Ferrers' Case* (1543): R Holinshed *Chronicles of England, Scotland and Ireland* (1577) III, pp 824–826.
16 Dicey propounded this fallacy, although it was common to the time: *Law of the Constitution* (10th edn) pp 50–53.
17 G R Elton *Reform and Reformation* (1977) p 286.

House of Commons was asserting itself. Under the 'Whig view of history', it might more simply be explained by the Stuart kings' betrayal of constitutional principles. Neither explanation is adequate, although neither is entirely invalid.

The royal prerogative, in a variety of its aspects, was central to the crisis. In *Bate's Case*[18] in 1606, Chief Baron Fleming, in upholding the king's power to tax imported currants, described the prerogative as comprising two kinds, the ordinary and the absolute. The ordinary powers were those such as the king's advantages in litigation and entitlement to certain revenues which were clearly defined at common law. The absolute powers were those discretionary rights to act for the benefit of the people, which were of necessity less restricted or defined. Under Tudor constitutional theory, such a distinction had scarcely been perceived, for prerogatives of all kinds had been regarded as subject to the common law, and in any event the Tudor monarchs avoided confrontations, by showing due regard for parliamentary consent.

The Stuarts, however, ruled in more difficult times; they were not so tactically astute nor nearly so competent in managerial skills; and they had less compunction about parliamentary consent, because they held a different conception of kingship. Certainly, the Stuarts could more justifiably claim to rule by hereditary right, and by their way of thinking that was divine right. James VI and I, addressing Parliament in 1610, told his audience that kings were 'God's lieutenants upon earth'.[19] Small wonder that the more enthusiastic exponents of royal power seized upon Fleming's judgment as supporting their view that the king was, in the exercise of his discretionary powers at least, above the law.

A reckoning was inevitable. Whether kings were answerable to the law in all respects or answerable to God only, was a question of political theory, incapable of tidy resolution. The courts could provide a resolution of sorts, but legal answers would tend to be inconsistent and inconclusive. Lawyers are tempted to make much of cases like *Prohibitions del Roy*[20] (when the king was told that he must dispense justice only through his judges, and could not himself act as a judge) and the *Case of Proclamations*[1] (in which the inability of proclamations to alter the general law of the land was firmly restated) on the one hand, or *Darnel's Case*[2] (when it was held sufficient answer to a writ of habeas corpus to state that a prisoner was detained by special order of the king, even though the king was using detention to enforce taxation levied

18 (1606) 2 St Tr 371.
19 Speech to Parliament, 21 March 1610: extract in J P Kenyon *The Stuart Constitution: Documents and Commentary* (1966) p 12.
20 (1607) 12 Co Rep 63.
 1 (1611) 12 Co Rep 74.
 2 Also known as *The Five Knights' Case* (1627) 3 St Tr 1.

without parliamentary consent) or the *Case of Ship Money*[3] (in which a tax imposed for the purpose of strengthening the navy was upheld as justifiable in a war emergency, of which state the king was sole judge) on the other. Most of these famous cases, however, are misleading, if viewed in isolation. They are better seen as moments of drama in the midst of an untidy and continuing altercation.

Political events provided a more lasting resolution. Charles I's attempt to dispense with Parliament in governing led to rebellion, and a period of constitutional experiment. In 1660, with the restoration of the monarchy, there was a restoration of the more acceptable parts of 'the ancient constitution', but not of the conciliar system which had been the main engine of executive authority and, through its prerogative courts such as the Star Chamber, had reliably supported the wider views of the king's powers. Charles II adjusted successfully. The Catholic King James II did not. In *Godden v Hales*,[4] a favourable bench had upheld his grant to Sir Edward Hales, permitting him to be colonel of a regiment without taking the oath required by the Test Act. Thus fortified, the King was encouraged to waive religious penal laws by further dispensations and suspensions, and displace Protestant by Catholic advisers and officials. The predominantly Anglican establishment felt threatened. Unwisely, James sought to weaken their ascendancy, and brought upon himself a successful revolution in favour of a Protestant, and limited, monarchy.

Lawyers look to the Bill of Rights (or in Scotland its counterpart, the Claim of Right) as the centrepiece of the Revolution settlement. The provisions of the Bill of Rights were essentially the terms of a contract under which the throne was offered to William and Mary. The preamble recited that James II 'did endeavour to subvert and extirpate the protestant religion, and the laws and liberties of this kingdom', and instanced twelve objectionable practices as evidence. Some of the more controversial prerogatives were dealt with. The suspending power was declared illegal, and the dispensing power 'as it hath been assumed and exercised of late'. Taxation without parliamentary consent was declared illegal. Yet these rules were little more than declaratory of existing law. There was the abolition of one undoubted prerogative power, that of keeping a standing army in peacetime without parliamentary consent. Another significant practical diminution of royal power was in the provisions about the meeting of Parliament, strengthened in the Triennial Act of 1694, which obliged the monarch to summon Parliament at least every three years and prevented Parliaments from lasting longer than three years.

There was a fundamental transition in 1688, but it is better looked for in events and thinking than in legal instruments. Take, for example, the

3 Also known as *R v Hampden* (1637) 3 St Tr 826.
4 (1686) 11 St Tr 1166.

prohibition of taxation without consent. There had been a similar provision in the Petition of Right enacted in 1628 and a number of other statutes, yet these had not affected the result in the *Case of Ship Money*. What matters is whether an arrangement holds, and after the Revolution settlement certain principles were established more firmly than ever before, even if they had been asserted previously. These included the supremacy of Parliament; that the prerogatives were not above the law, but were only such as admitted and allowed at common law; and that title to the Crown was founded in parliamentary enactment. These principles were occasionally explicit, but by and large merely implicit. They were none the less real and of the utmost significance.

Our scamper through the centuries has taken us to the beginnings of the modern constitution. The Revolution settlement left many important prerogatives in the hands of the Crown. But it also opened up two clear avenues of control, in case of further abuse. In conformity with the principle of the supremacy of Parliament, there was the threat in the background of a statute, to abolish or regulate the exercise of prerogative powers. In conformity with the rule of law, there was the subjection of executive power to what was accepted as law by the courts. We shall bring the story up to date, and make it more complete, by examining the prerogative and statute, and the prerogative in the courts. But first it is appropriate to consider how another means of control developed, which made the issues involved quite different.

CONVENTIONAL LIMITATIONS

The legal relationships between legislature, executive and judiciary within the British constitution have altered little in form since 1688. But the legislature and the executive, and the relationship between them, altered greatly in practice during the eighteenth and nineteenth centuries.

Nobody saw this change more clearly than Walter Bagehot, who drew attention to the gap between appearance and reality in the constitution in his book published in 1867.[5] With considerable insight and skill, he set out to describe the true workings of the British political system of his day, as distinct from the legal forms. Dicey admired Bagehot's work, and did not neglect the lesson. A few years later, in opening *Law of the Constitution*, he savaged the 'lawyer's view of the constitution', as represented by the unfortunate Blackstone, for its unreality:

> Its true defect is the hopeless confusion, both of language and of thought, introduced into the whole subject of constitutional law by Blackstone's habit – common to all the lawyers of his time – of applying old and inapplicable terms to new institutions, and especially of ascribing in words to a modern and constitutional King the whole,

5 *The English Constitution* (1867).

and perhaps more than the whole, of the powers actually possessed and exercised by William the Conqueror.[6]

In short, the chief fault lay in talking about the king's powers as if they were the king's powers.

What Bagehot and Dicey appreciated, but Blackstone had failed to underline, was that most of the prerogatives of government, which in the seventeenth century had been in the hands of the monarch, were being exercised by or in accordance with the advice of the leaders of the majority in Parliament. The transformation was perhaps just sufficiently observable by 1765 for Blackstone to be justly criticised. It was certainly obvious by the later nineteenth century (although sometimes the obvious requires to be stated, and herein lay the genius of Bagehot's work).

The process happened, as we know, through the operation of constitutional conventions. That is at least a convenient shorthand for encompassing a series of political events, out of which grew some practices sufficiently regular to be so regarded. There were many strands: the greater dependence of the monarch upon Parliament; the continuing growth in importance of the House of Commons; the beginnings of a party system there; the practice of holding Cabinet meetings, after 1717 rarely attended by the monarch, and the emergence of their chairmen as chief or 'Prime' ministers; the gradually declining role of the monarch in the conduct of government; the responsibility of individual ministers to Parliament, which could force their dismissal; the development of the government's collective responsibility to Parliament. These did not all happen simultaneously, but in fits and starts. By the middle of the nineteenth century, they had coalesced into some well-settled practices and doctrines, which are essentially still in operation today. There is a constitutional, or limited, monarchy. There is Cabinet government, with the political arm of the executive being drawn from and located in Parliament. There is ministerial responsibility to Parliament.

Let us see what these developments mean, so far as the royal prerogative is concerned. First, there is a problem of nomenclature. The 'royal' tag is misleading. We may say that the powers are exercisable by the Crown, on the understanding that 'the Crown' has come to be used as a convenient symbol for the central government, as well as the monarch in person or 'Sovereign'. Yet legally the prerogatives are vested in the Crown, and there is no need to discard the monarchical associations, provided we remember the reality.

The reality is that some prerogatives have gone out of the monarch's hands altogether: the court's power to make an infant a ward of court, and the Attorney General's powers of nolle prosequi and in relation to public rights and duties, are examples of this class. Most of the important remaining

6 *Law of the Constitution* (10th edn) p 7.

168 *The royal prerogative*

prerogatives are exercised upon the advice of ministers, and generally through ministers. Sometimes the Sovereign is involved in a formal capacity: for example, a pardon under the prerogative of mercy comes from the Crown, although the decision has been reached by the Home Secretary or the Secretary of State for Scotland. More often, as with acts involved in the negotiation of treaties or the control of the armed forces, for example, the Sovereign has no part to play at all, but the powers are purportedly exercised in his or her name. Thus, as to the largest class of prerogatives, the monarch today is little more than a cypher. Perhaps just a little more, for, as Bagehot wrote, the monarch has 'the right to be consulted, the right to encourage, the right to warn',[7] and conceivably this may occasionally be significant, depending on such factors as the personality of the monarch and the receptiveness of the ministers.

There are at most a few prerogatives where the monarch's personal discretion remains important. The conferment of certain honours and awards (such as the Order of Merit, and the Orders of the Garter and the Thistle) is treated as within the Sovereign's personal choice. More importantly, it is possible to conceive of circumstances in which a monarch's personal role could be of influence in the appointment of a Prime Minister, the dismissal of a government, the dissolution of a Parliament, a decision not to dissolve Parliament, and the giving of the royal assent to legislation.[8] In all of these matters, there are conventions which in most circumstances would require the Sovereign to act in a particular way. But there might be exceptional circumstances not covered by the conventions, or the supposed conventions may not be so clear, or for that matter could be ignored.[9]

By and large, however, prerogative powers are exercised by the government of the day, not by the monarch. With that change, the way in which we view the prerogative also has to be changed. Different persons exercise it: not a king by virtue of heredity or a mixture of heredity and selection, but the leaders of a parliamentary majority, owing their position to election. The most obviously objectionable aspect of the prerogative is thereby removed, for its exercise then accords with the democratic process (or at least that degree of democracy which the system allows). To an extent, different persons have the function of challenging the exercise of the prerogative. The political contest is no longer between king and Parliament, but between some members of Parliament who comprise the government, and others who are not part of the government. The accountability of ministers to Parliament, which has developed, provides a means for the

7 *The English Constitution* (1963 ed with Introduction by Richard Crossman) p 111.
8 See Geoffrey Marshall *Constitutional Conventions* (1984) chs 2 and 3; S A de Smith *Constitutional and Administrative Law* (5th edn by Harry Street and Rodney Brazier, 1985) pp 127–134.
9 See also ch 3.

challenge to be made, but the dominance of governments within Parliament provides ministers with some measure of protection. As to the further abolition of prerogatives, there has been an ironic reversal of positions. Whereas the seventeenth century Parliaments were eager to curtail the prerogatives, the interests of those parliamentarians who at any particular time comprised the government of the day, now lay in preserving, not in curtailing, what powers remained.

In short, our perspectives are greatly altered. We shall still have to consider how the prerogative has been controlled since 1688 by statute, and by the courts. But control became less of a problem, or at least a different problem, when the exercise of the powers passed into ministerial hands. Political accountability seemed to provide a solution. Whether it is an entirely satisfactory solution will also have to be considered.

STATUTES AND THE PREROGATIVE

As we have seen, the supremacy of Parliament was a central feature of the Revolution settlement. From 1688 onwards, prerogative powers could undeniably be controlled, or even abolished, by parliamentary enactments. The Bill of Rights itself was such an enactment. It abolished one or two prerogatives and regulated others. When, as with the levying of taxes or the keeping of an army in peacetime, it made the exercise of power subject to parliamentary consent, regulation was tantamount to extinction. Once something could be done by the king only with Parliament's approval, then it would be unlikely deliberately to be attempted otherwise than under statutory powers.

By comparison with the high drama of the seventeenth century, however, subsequent moves to abolish or control prerogative powers by statute have been uncontroversial and infrequent. In part, this is because some of the chief causes of contention had been dealt with by the beginning of the eighteenth century. In part, it is because, as we have seen, the powers changed hands, which ensured their survival if that was desired. Remember that the prerogative is the residue of authority which of necessity inhered in the Crown, attributes which it was essential for the executive to possess if it was to carry out its responsibilities for the protection of the subjects and in the interests of the subjects. It is easy to see some prerogatives in this light, such as the disposition of the armed forces or the requisitioning of property for military purposes. It is not surprising that modern governments have found it useful to retain such broad discretionary powers to act, which enable action to be taken without the necessity of prior parliamentary approval.

Sometimes, however, it has been thought desirable to replace, or at least temporarily displace, the prerogative by statutory powers. There are prerogative powers to do what is necessary for the waging of war, but in 1914 and 1939 governments put war powers on a statutory footing, for reasons well explained by Viscount Radcliffe:

> Several different considerations must have argued for the change – the feeling that the extreme actions that might be required ought to receive explicit parliamentary approval, the desirability of defining and, very likely, of extending and supplementing the range of admitted executive powers and, thirdly, the advantage of Parliament imposing whatever conditions or consequences it thought proper upon the exercise of such powers.[10]

Similar considerations will often apply, and in some fields the displacement of prerogative by statute has become semi-permanent. There is, for example, a prerogative power to exclude aliens from the realm, or perhaps more accurately amidst the uncertainty, there may be. But it is practically inconceivable that a government would carry out its immigration policy other than under statutory powers. We ought to remember that 'it is not easy to discover and decide the law regarding the royal prerogative and the consequences of its exercise', as Lord Reid observed in 1965, while noting that there had been 'practically no authority' in the centuries since 1688.[11] This helps to explain why some of the questions concerning the effects of statute upon the prerogative are regarded as problematical.

Of course, some matters are perfectly clear, because they are consequences of the supremacy of Parliament. Thus there is no doubt that Parliament may expressly abolish or restrict the prerogative. An important instance occurred with the enactment of the Crown Proceedings Act 1947. Before its passing, the Crown had an immunity from being sued in contract and tort. This was taken away by the Act or, to be strictly accurate, restricted to the monarch in a private capacity, for section 40 provides that the Sovereign's own position is unaffected. Parliament may abolish or restrict or preserve aspects of the prerogative, as it chooses.

What is less certain is the position when a prerogative is neither expressly abolished nor preserved, but a statute is passed which covers all or part of the same ground, so that statute and prerogative seem to overlap or co-exist. If they co-exist, might the Crown then act under either power, selecting whichever is more favourable to it as the occasion demands? That argument was advanced in *A–G v De Keyser's Royal Hotel Ltd*,[12] but rejected by the House of Lords. During the 1914–18 war, the respondent's hotel had been requisitioned for the use of the Royal Flying Corps. The requisition had taken place under the Defence of the Realm Acts and Regulations, and these incorporated provisions in the Defence Act 1842, providing for statutory compensation as of right. It was later argued for the Crown, however, that there was a prerogative to take the land of the subject in case of wartime

10 *Burmah Oil Co v Lord Advocate* [1965] AC 75 at 121, [1964] 2 All ER 348 at 367.
11 Ibid at [1965] AC 99, [1964] 2 All ER 353.
12 [1920] AC 508.

emergency, involving perhaps no compensation or only compensation ex gratia. The court had little difficulty in deciding that, since possession had been taken under statutory powers, compensation as of right was payable. The House also held that the Crown was not in any event entitled to act under the prerogative, in a context where the prerogative had been superseded by statute, as it had here.

The principle that is clear is, that to the extent that a prerogative power is inconsistent with statutory powers, the former is abrogated by necessary implication. As Lord Atkinson said in that case:

> It is quite obvious that it would be useless and meaningless for the legislature to impose restrictions and limitations upon, and to attach conditions to, the exercise by the Crown of the powers conferred by a statute, if the Crown were free at its pleasure to disregard these provisions, and by virtue of the prerogative do the very thing which the statutes empowered it to do.[13]

But other matters are often thought to be left unclear. The relationship between statute and prerogative remains 'strangely abstruse',[14] according to two commentators. The questions considered especially puzzling are these:

> Suppose a statute merely covers the same ground as prerogative without expressly restricting the Crown's competence. Do statute and prerogative then co-exist, or is the prerogative swallowed up and superseded? If superseded, does it revive when the statute is repealed?[15]

However, nothing here should cause difficulty, for the answers are perfectly plain. They were given in the *De Keyser's Royal Hotel* case by Lord Atkinson:

> It was suggested that when a statute is passed empowering the Crown to do a certain thing which it might theretofore have done by virtue of its prerogative, the prerogative is merged in the statute. I confess I do not think the word 'merged' is happily chosen. I should prefer to say that when such a statute, expressing the will and intention of the King and of the three estates of the realm, is passed, it abridges the Royal Prerogative while it is in force to this extent: that the Crown can only do the particular thing under and in accordance with the statutory provisions, and that its prerogative power to do that thing is in abeyance.[16]

In other words, in such a situation, the prerogative is temporarily superseded, or displaced, or supplanted by the statute, which is the highest form of law known to our courts, and when the government exercises the

---

13 Ibid at 539.
14 S A de Smith *Constitutional and Administrative Law* (5th edn by Harry Street and Rodney Brazier, 1985) p 144; B S Markesinis 'The Royal Prerogative Re-visited' (1973) CLJ 287 at 299.
15 S A de Smith *Constitutional and Administrative Law* (5th edn by Harry Street and Rodney Brazier, 1985) p 144.
16 [1920] AC 508 at 539.

relevant powers, 'it must be presumed that they are so exercised under the statute'.[17]

However, if the statute is later repealed, the prerogative power will still exist as it did before the statute was enacted. This was the clear implication of Lord Atkinson's remarks in *De Keyser's Royal Hotel*, and it was also accepted by Lord Pearce in *Burmah Oil Co v Lord Advocate*.[18] No doubt confusion has been sown by the variety of terms used to describe what happens to the prerogative when a statute is passed. Sometimes differences of opinion have been attributed to judges, when it is by no means clear that they differ other than in choice of words.[19] It does not seem to have been judicially advanced that a prerogative power would be extinguished were a statute covering the same field to be repealed. Principle is against such an argument too. If the repealing statute has not expressly abolished the prerogative, then the argument must be that it is abolished by implication. But the courts generally lean against repeal by implication, and it is the less likely because they also employ the rule of interpretation, derived from the prerogative, to the effect that the Crown is not bound by statute except by express words or necessary implication.[20] In the leading case, the Privy Council was concerned that 'necessary' should not be 'whittled down', and held that the Crown was bound by necessary implication only 'if it can be affirmed that, at the time when the statute was passed and received the royal sanction, it was apparent from its terms that its beneficent purpose must be wholly frustrated unless the Crown were bound'.[1] To sum up, neither authority nor principle suggests that prerogatives are abolished other than by express statutory provisions.

It should be remembered that these supposed difficulties only arise when there is room for doubt concerning Parliament's wishes. Sometimes Parliament takes care to provide for the matter, by expressly preserving any powers exercisable by virtue of the prerogative.[2]

POLITICAL ACCOUNTABILITY

Parliament, in its supremacy, could always take away the prerogatives, but, as we have seen, many have been allowed to survive. The price of this was their transfer to ministerial hands. After that happened, their employment

---

17 Ibid at 554, per Lord Moulton.
18 [1965] AC 75 at 148, [1964] 2 All ER 348 at 385.
19 Eg in discussions of *Sabally and N'Jie v A–G* [1965] 1 QB 273, [1964] 3 All ER 377, CA, as well as the speeches in *A–G v De Keyser's Royal Hotel Ltd* [1920] AC 508.
20 See further Peter W Hogg *Liability of the Crown* (1971) ch 7.
 1 *Province of Bombay v Municipal Corpn of Bombay* [1947] AC 58 at 63.
 2 See eg s 9 of the Emergency Powers (Defence) Act 1939, or s 33 of the Immigration Act 1971.

was subject to parliamentary scrutiny, for the exercise of powers by ministers could give rise to question and debate in Parliament, as part of the general responsibility of government to Parliament.

Political accountability, through the supervision of Parliament, is thus heavily relied upon as a means of control. Any backwardness of the courts in reviewing the exercise of the prerogative need hardly concern us, Professor Heuston implies, for the 'mode of user can be called in question on the floor of the House of Commons by way of parliamentary question or a debate on the adjournment, and every student of politics knows how potent these weapons are'.[3]

This balm does not entirely reassure. It is true, of course, that in principle the exercise of prerogative powers by ministers is as amenable to parliamentary supervision as any other governmental actions. Thus the disposition of the armed forces is part of the prerogative power, and the government's decision to send them to the Falkland Islands to repel the Argentinian invasion was one which could be (and was) the subject of parliamentary debate, discussion and questioning, and Select Committee investigations. No doubt the supervision which members of the House of Commons are able to exercise is sporadic and imperfect, hindered by lack of knowledge, and made less effective by reason of the government's usual dominance of the House. But these are qualifications which apply equally to the supervision of statutory powers and other matters.

In practice, however, the supervision of prerogative powers does seem to be attended by greater than average difficulty. The very nature of these powers makes them less readily subject to challenge. As the authors of a study of parliamentary questions noted, 'there is a very big difference' between questioning a minister about matters for which he is statutorily responsible and about other matters: 'It is a different level of answerability, there is less opportunity to use it and even when used the results are likely to be less definite.'[4]

In fact, it is sometimes more than just a difference of degree. When a member sought in 1955 to ascertain by way of a question in Parliament what advice the Prime Minister had given the Queen as to the dissolution of Parliament, the question was ruled out on the ground that the Prime Minister was not responsible to Parliament for that advice. 'Dissolution appears', it was remarked, 'to be one of a small number of subjects clearly within the Government's responsibility but anomalously shielded from parliamentary questioning.'[5] The number, however, is not so small. Exercises of the personal prerogatives, where discretion still resides in the

---

3 R F V Heuston *Essays in Constitutional Law* (2nd edn, 1964) p 63.
4 D N Chester and Nona Bowring *Questions in Parliament* (1962) p 294.
5 G Marshall and G C Moodie *Some Problems of the Constitution* (5th edn, 1971) p 127.

Sovereign, are shielded from questions and discussion.[6] The advice given to the Sovereign about some wider matters has similarly been ruled out of bounds: not only the dissolution of Parliament, but also the grant of honours, the ecclesiastical patronage of the Crown, the appointment and dismissal of Privy Councillors, and the prerogative of mercy in relation to capital sentences.[7] These are the subjects of specific rulings, but more generally ministers may simply refuse to answer questions, if there are reasons of national security, confidentiality, relations with other states, or public interest, which in their view justify a refusal. On some topics, the consistency of refusals has created a clear precedent, and from time to time governments issue a list of matters with regard to which questions will not be answered.[8] Thus the Secretary of State for Defence will decline to provide information on (inter alia) operational matters, details of arms sales, contract prices, and numbers of foreign forces training in the United Kingdom, the Attorney General on judicial and other appointments, investigations by the Director of Public Prosecutions, and so on. Exercises of prerogative and non-statutory powers figure prominently, although not exclusively, in the list.

It is interesting to note that the picture is similar with regard to the jurisdiction of the Parliamentary Commissioner for Administration (or Ombudsman, as he is popularly known).[9] The Department of the Law Officers is not subject to his investigations, so that the exercise of prerogatives by the Attorney General may not be reviewed. A large number of matters are listed which the Commissioner is barred from investigating. These include actions taken outside the United Kingdom, actions taken for the protection of the security of state, the issue of passports, the prerogative of mercy, the grant of honours and privileges, and action taken in respect of pay and personnel matters in the Civil Service, armed forces, or other Crown employment. The correlation between the matters excluded from the Commissioner's jurisdiction and the spheres of activity in which governments exercise prerogative powers is striking.

To sum up, the exercise of prerogative powers is imperfectly subject to parliamentary control, and in most cases removed from the Parliamentary Commissioner's purview (ironically, since the office was supposedly created to supplement the deficiencies of existing controls). If there are deficiencies in the judicial control of their exercise (and we shall see that there are), then we must have reservations about the adequacy of these other means.

---

6 Thomas Erskine May *Treatise on the Law, Privileges, Proceedings and Usage of Parliament* (20th edn by Sir Charles Gordon, 1983) pp 338, 430.
7 Ibid, pp 338–339.
8 See eg App 9 to the Evidence of the Report of the Select Committee on Parliamentary Questions, HC 393 (1971–72), p 114.
9 Parliamentary Commissioner Act 1967.

THE PREROGATIVE AND THE COURTS

The courts' claim that they had jurisdiction to determine the existence and extent of prerogative powers had been vigorously asserted in cases like the *Case of Proclamations*,[10] and was indisputable after 1688. Yet something survived of the notion that the king's discretionary powers were 'absolute'. From cases such as *Darnel's Case*[11] (where the king's warrant for detention of a prisoner, although giving no reasons, was accepted as conclusive) and the *Case of Ship Money*[12] (when the king's judgment as to the existence of an emergency was held to be unchallengeable), was derived a view that courts lacked jurisdiction to review the manner of exercise of prerogative powers, or the adequacy of the grounds upon which they had been exercised.

This view survived the Revolution, and found judicial acceptance long afterwards. In *R v Allen*,[13] it was argued that the Attorney General had entered a nolle prosequi irregularly because he had failed to give the prosecutor and the accused the opportunity to state their views. The court was not interested. 'The power . . . is entrusted to the Attorney General, who is the great law officer of the Crown', said Blackburn J, 'and whether he is right or wrong this court cannot interfere.'[14] In *Engelke v Musmann*,[15] the House of Lords, accepting that the recognition of envoys of foreign states was a matter for the Crown, ruled that a ministerial certificate as to the entitlement of an individual to claim diplomatic privilege was conclusive.

In *Chandler v DPP*,[16] supporters of the Campaign for Nuclear Disarmament had been convicted of conspiracy to commit a breach of section 1 of the Official Secrets Act 1911 by entering a prohibited place 'for any purpose prejudicial to the safety or interests of the state'. They had undoubtedly plotted to enter Wethersfield air base in rural Essex and immobilise it by sitting down on the runways. But was their purpose prejudicial to the interests of the state? The trial judge had not allowed them to call evidence to argue otherwise, and the House of Lords held that this was right. Lord Reid said:

> It is . . . clear that the disposition and armament of the armed forces are and for centuries have been within the exclusive discretion of the Crown and that no one can seek a legal remedy on the ground that such discretion has been wrongfully exercised.[17]

---

10 (1611) 12 Co Rep 74.
11 (1627) 3 St Tr 1.
12 (1637) 3 St Tr 826.
13 (1862) 1 B & S 850, 121 ER 929.
14 (1862) 121 ER 929 at 932.
15 [1928] AC 433, HL.
16 [1964] AC 763, [1962] 3 All ER 142, HL.
17 [1964] AC 763 at 791, HL.

Viscount Radcliffe agreed:

> If the methods of arming the defence forces and the disposition of those forces are at the decision of Her Majesty's Ministers for the time being, as we know that they are, it is not within the competence of a court of law to try the issue whether it would be better for the country that that armament or those dispositions should be different.[18]

Some other more recent attempts to impugn the manner of exercise of non-statutory powers have been just as firmly repulsed. In *Hanratty v Lord Butler of Saffron Walden*,[19] the Home Secretary's advice as to the prerogative of mercy in relation to a man condemned to death for murder was the issue. In *Blackburn v A–G*,[20] it was the signing of the Treaty of Rome, by which the United Kingdom might enter the European Economic Community. In *Jenkins v A–G*,[1] it was the government's distribution of a pamphlet about its policy on the EEC. In *Secretary of State for Home Department v Lakdawalla*,[2] it was the government's refusal to grant a passport.

It would appear, given such a weight of authority, that the manner of exercise of prerogative powers lies outside the scope of judicial review. Certainly that conclusion was generally accepted, until recently. Yet its correctness may be questioned.

In the first place, some of the decisions must be viewed with reservation because, properly regarded, they do not seem to concern the prerogative at all. It is surely not a power peculiar to the Crown that it may spend money in distributing information about its intentions; in fact, it does not involve a power at all, in the legal sense of a capacity to affect the rights or liabilities of others. Similarly, the issue of passports is merely an administrative act, not a legal one, however important they may be in facilitating foreign travel. Even the negotiation of a treaty is, on one view, not a prerogative power since 'the making of treaties by itself has no legal effect on the law of this country, so that there is no exercise of legal power at all'.[3] Thus the true explanation of some of the decisions might be not that exercises of the prerogative are unreviewable, but that some government actions are unjusticiable for the simple reason that they do not have legal consequences.

Of course, there cannot be any doubt that matters such as the nolle prosequi or the policies of the armed forces are truly prerogatives. But perhaps the true inference to be drawn from the decisions in *R v Allen* and *Chandler v DPP* was not that the manner of exercise of a prerogative is invariably outside the courts' powers, but rather the more limited one that

---

18 Ibid at 798.
19 (1971) 115 Sol Jo 386, CA.
20 [1971] 2 All ER 1380, [1971] 1 WLR 1037, CA.
 1 (1971) 115 Sol Jo 674.
 2 [1972] Imm AR 26.
 3 H W R Wade *Administrative Law* (5th edn, 1982) p 350.

the courts will not undertake inquiries of the kind asked into such exercises of prerogative powers as were involved in those cases. The courts' reluctance to be involved in areas such as the prerogative of mercy or the Attorney General's powers might be explained on policy grounds. With matters such as defence policy and foreign relations, the questions are essentially political, and the courts have effectively decided that the control of such matters should be left to political mechanisms. However, if this is right, the true explanation of the courts' inhibition lies in the nature of the matter involved, not in the circumstance that the power in question is prerogative. There was a hint of this in Viscount Radcliffe's approach to the problem in *Chandler*, when he said, 'I can think of few issues which present themselves in less triable form.'[4] Equally, we may point to cases involving statutory powers where the courts have been prepared to concede a wide, almost uncontrolled, degree of discretion to the Crown, for reasons of policy. One thinks of cases like *Liversidge v Anderson*[5] (detention in wartime), *Schmidt v Secretary of State for Home Affairs*[6] (entry permits), and *R v Brixton Prison Governor, ex p Soblen*[7] or *R v Secretary of State for the Home Department, ex p Hosenball*[8] (deportation). These are looked on as distinct because they arise in their statutory contexts, but they may plausibly be viewed in the same light as some of the cases on the prerogative.

So it was not necessary to conclude, on the basis of the authorities, that the manner of exercise was in all circumstances outside the courts' purview. On the basis of principle too, that proposition did not seem sound. The fundamental reasons which account for the courts' control over abuse of statutory powers are equally able to justify the same degree of control over prerogative powers. In fact, that this should even have to be stated represents an historical irony. For, if we ask from where derived the courts' power to review actions under statutory powers, the answer lies in such authorities as the *Case of Proclamations*.[9] As a distinguished writer put it in explaining the origins of the ultra vires doctrine,

. . . from the proposition that it was for the courts to determine the legal limits of the royal prerogative, it followed inevitably that it was for them to determine whether statutory powers claimed by the Crown or its servants to have been conferred upon them existed in law, and, if so, whether such powers had been validly exercised.[10]

---

4 [1964] AC 763 at 798, [1962] 3 All ER 142 at 151.
5 [1942] AC 206, [1941] 3 All ER 338, HL.
6 [1969] 2 Ch 149, [1969] 1 All ER 904, CA.
7 [1963] 2 QB 243, [1962] 3 All ER 641, CA.
8 [1977] 3 All ER 452, [1977] 1 WLR 766, CA.
9 (1611) 12 Co Rep 74.
10 S A de Smith *Judicial Review of Administrative Action* (4th edn by J M Evans, 1980) p 94.

This shows that any general distinction which turned on the source of the power being statutory or prerogative was ill-founded in principle. It also shows that by recourse to earlier authorities, courts could rediscover the correct path.

In fact, there are in the last twenty years some indications of a growing judicial willingness to review prerogative acts. In *Burmah Oil Co v Lord Advocate*,[11] the issue was whether the destruction of the company's oilfields by the departing British forces, in order to prevent them from falling into the advancing enemy's hands, gave any legal right to compensation for the loss suffered. There is a loosely defined war prerogative, which includes a right to take property in appropriate circumstances. But by a majority of three to two, the House of Lords held that if, in the exercise of the prerogative in relation to war, a subject was deprived of property otherwise than by damage in the course of battle, then he was entitled to compensation from the Crown. The decision may be viewed as merely defining the extent of prerogative power. But it could just as easily be regarded as a judicial regulation of the way in which prerogative powers are exercised. In practice the distinction between determining the ambit of a prerogative (as to which the courts have jurisdiction) and reviewing the manner of its exercise (as to which they were thought to lack jurisdiction) is hazy, not clear-cut.

Another thing which is sometimes hazy is what may be classed as prerogative, and what may not. The Crown's right to have admissible evidence withheld from a court when it claimed that the public interest so demanded was known as Crown privilege. Crown privilege was generally regarded as an aspect of the prerogative, and had been treated as such by courts.[12] Under the House of Lords decision in *Duncan v Cammell, Laird and Co*,[13] the rule appeared to be that the Crown's claim was conclusive. But in *Glasgow Corpn v Central Land Board*,[14] the House of Lords held that in Scotland the courts retained the power to override the Crown's claim in the interests of justice. In *Conway v Rimmer*[15] the House, in a striking reversal of policy, decided that in England too the courts, while giving full weight to any claim made by a Minister of the Crown, had the power to overrule it when the public interest in the administration of justice outweighed the public interest in non-disclosure. Thus, apparently the courts were claiming the right to supervise the manner of exercise of a prerogative, and correct abuses of the power. But all is not always what it seems. In *Conway v Rimmer*, the House of Lords did not refer to Crown privilege as a prerogative; the matter was viewed rather as a rule of public policy within the inherent jurisdiction of

11 [1965] AC 75, [1964] 2 All ER 348.
12 Eg in *Conway v Rimmer* [1967] 2 All ER 1260, [1967] 1 WLR 1031, CA; and *Glasgow Corpn v Central Land Board* 1956 SC (HL) 1 at 8, per Viscount Simonds.
13 [1942] AC 624.
14 1956 SC (HL) 1.
15 [1968] AC 910, [1968] 1 All ER 874.

courts. Later in *R v Lewes Justices, ex p Home Secretary*,[16] the term 'Crown privilege' was said to be a misnomer, since a request for non-disclosure of evidence might be made by anyone, not only by the Crown. In the same case, Lord Simon of Glaisdale expressly declared that 'the right to demand that admissible evidence be withheld . . . is not one of the prerogatives of the Crown.'[17] That is plainly said, but, as has been noted, inconsistent with some earlier dicta. In reality, there has been a subtle reclassification, enabling the courts to check abuses of a particular executive power, without being seen to attack prerogatives as such. Perhaps we are bound to accept as correct the recent judicial view that the claim to withhold evidence is not a prerogative. But we might then wonder which other prerogatives are liable to be reclassified as part of a similar process of bringing them under wider review.

Neither in *Burmah Oil* nor in *Conway v Rimmer* did the courts directly deny the orthodoxy that the manner of exercising prerogative powers is outside the scope of review. The same must be said of *Carl Zeiss Stiftung v Rayner and Keeler (No 2)*,[18] where the Crown's certificate as to recognition of a foreign state (to the effect that the German Democratic Republic was not recognised) was accepted as conclusive by the House of Lords, which nonetheless attributed legal effect to a decree of the unrecognised government.

But in *Chandler v DPP*, Lord Devlin, although he concurred in the result, did seem to deny the orthodoxy, for he said that in relation to prerogative as well as statutory powers, 'the courts will not review the proper exercise of discretionary power, but they will intervene to correct excess or abuse'.[19] Then, a similar line was taken by Lord Denning in *Laker Airways Ltd v Department of Trade*.[20] A previous government had given approval for Sir Freddie Laker's Skytrain service to operate on the transatlantic route in competition with the nationalised British Airways. In 1975 another government decided to reverse that policy. The Secretary of State for Trade effectively directed the Civil Aviation Authority to withdraw Laker's licence. That was held by the Court of Appeal to be ultra vires, as contrary to the objectives set out in the Civil Aviation Act 1971. As well as being granted a licence, Laker had had to be accepted as a designated carrier under the Bermuda Agreement, a treaty made between the British and United States governments. The minister's second argument was that a withdrawal of that designation, a treaty matter, was within the prerogative, and therefore unreviewable by the court. Lord Denning would have none of it:

16 [1973] AC 388, [1972] 2 All ER 1057, HL.
17 [1973] AC 388 at 407.
18 [1967] 1 AC 853, [1966] 2 All ER 536, HL.
19 [1964] AC 763 at 810.
20 [1977] QB 643, [1977] 2 All ER 182, CA.

The law does not interfere with the proper exercise by the discretion of the executive in those situations; but it can set limits by defining the bounds of the activity; and it can intervene if the discretion is exercised improperly or mistakenly. That is a fundamental principle of our constitution.[1]

The attempt to invoke the prerogative power so as to sidestep the protection afforded to parties under the Act was, in his view, an improper exercise. The other members of the Court of Appeal reached the same result, but preferred to rely on the *De Keyser's Royal Hotel* principle, from which they inferred that the prerogative could not be exercised so as to nullify the statutory licence.

Shortly afterwards, in *Gouriet v Union of Post Office Workers*,[2] Lord Denning had a further opportunity to put his 'fundamental principle' into practice. There was a possibility that postal workers, in response to a call from their trade unions, would boycott South African mail as a protest against apartheid. Mr Gouriet claimed that such action would be criminal conduct under the Post Office Act 1953, and asked the Attorney General to grant his consent for relator proceedings. When this consent was refused, Mr Gouriet succeeded himself in obtaining an interim injunction from the Court of Appeal. Within the next few days, the court heard further argument. The Attorney General contended that the court had no jurisdiction to question his decision, and that the plaintiff lacked standing to bring the action in his own name since it was a matter of public rights and duties, in which he had no special interest at stake, over and above the general public.

The court held that it had jurisdiction to grant an interim injunction to the plaintiff. Lord Denning held that the Attorney General's discretion to grant consent to relator proceedings was absolute, but his discretion to refuse was not. Where he had misdirected himself, his decision could be 'overridden by the courts, not directly, but indirectly',[3] as by allowing an ordinary citizen to come to the court and ask that the law be enforced. Again Lord Denning's colleagues preferred a different approach. Lord Justices Lawton and Ormrod said that the Attorney General's discretion was not reviewable, but in appropriate circumstances an individual citizen could be allowed to restrain threatened breaches of the criminal law by seeking a declaration or interim injunction, even although the Attorney General had not consented to relator proceedings. On either ground, the finality of the Attorney General's decision would have been lost.

On the face of it, however, there was a very different approach in the House of Lords, to which the case went on appeal.[4] There it was held that it was for the Attorney General to vindicate public rights, and an individual had no standing to do so unless his private rights were affected or he would

---

1   [1977] QB 643 at 705, CA.
2   [1977] QB 729, [1977] 1 All ER 696, CA.
3   [1977] QB 729 at 759, [1977] 1 All ER 696 at 716, CA.
4   [1978] AC 435, [1977] 3 All ER 70, HL.

suffer special damage. Four of their Lordships also declared that the refusal of the Attorney General to give his consent to a relator action was not subject to review by the courts. Yet in affirming this unreviewability the court emphasised the political nature of the Attorney General's role rather than its origin in the prerogative. As one commentator observed, 'it is surely unlikely that a different result would be reached were the Attorney General's refusal of a statutorily required consent to a prosecution brought into question in legal proceedings'.[5]

To sum up the position as it then appeared, the view seemed to be gaining ground, at least in academic circles, that the reviewability of the exercise of powers depended on the nature of the question, and not on the source of the power. On that view, the propriety of exercise of prerogative powers was not, as had previously been thought, unreviewable per se. However, judicial support for that view, the iconoclastic Lord Denning apart, was more doubtful and had to be inferred, if it could be, from acts rather than words.

Judicial views became clearer with *Council of Civil Service Unions v Minister for the Civil Service*[6] in 1984. The government, concerned about the effects or possible effects of industrial action on national security, decided to take away from Civil Service employees working at the Government Communications Headquarters (GCHQ) the right of belonging to a trade union. It was done not directly by the Crown but under a power to regulate the Civil Service conferred on the Minister for the Civil Service by a prerogative instrument, the Civil Service Order in Council 1982. The Minister for the Civil Service, who was the Prime Minister, had issued the instruction orally and without consultation, and it was argued that she had acted unfairly.

But was the government's action reviewable? Their Lordships were unanimous that it was. Lords Fraser and Brightman put it on the narrower ground that *delegated* powers emanating from a prerogative power were not immune from review, for judicial control was there to ensure that the purpose, scope and limits of the delegation, whether expressed or implied, were not exceeded. That was sufficient for the present case, and they preferred to leave open the question whether there could be review of the manner of exercise of powers exercised *directly* under the prerogative, although Lord Fraser observed that 'an impressive array of authority'[7] held otherwise.

However, a majority of the House (Lords Scarman, Diplock and Roskill) thought that the time was ripe to answer that very question, and their answer, as put by Lord Scarman, was that:

> . . . the law relating to judicial review has now reached the stage where it can be said with confidence that, if the subject matter in respect of which prerogative power is exercised is justiciable, that is to say if it is a matter on which the court can

5 S A de Smith *Judicial Review of Administrative Action* (4th edn by J M Evans, 1980), p 287.
6 [1985] AC 374, [1984] 3 All ER 935, HL.
7 [1985] AC 374 at 398, [1984] 3 All ER 935 at 941, HL.

adjudicate, the exercise of the power is subject to review in accordance with the principles developed in respect of the review of the exercise of statutory power.[8]

So, by this view, it is confirmed that reviewability depends not on the source of executive power, but on its subject matter. As to the occasions when exercises of the prerogative will be justiciable, Lord Roskill had this to say:

> It must, I think, depend on the subject matter of the prerogative power which is exercised. Many examples were given during the argument of prerogative powers which as at present advised I do not think could properly be made the subject of judicial review. Prerogative powers such as those relating to the making of treaties, the defence of the realm, the prerogative of mercy, the grant of honours, the dissolution of Parliament and the appointment of ministers as well as others are not, I think, susceptible to judicial review because their nature and subject matter is such as not to be amenable to the judicial process. The courts are not the place wherein to determine whether a treaty should be concluded or the armed forces disposed in a particular manner or Parliament dissolved on one date rather than another.[9]

Their Lordships did not provide a positive list, to accompany the negative list, but did consider that the regulation of Civil Service conditions was susceptible to review. To complete the story, the Lords thought that the government's failure to consult was unfair; but, on being satisfied that the decision not to consult was taken for reasons of national security, they held that requirements of procedural fairness had to give way to considerations of national security.

The more general significance of the case lies in the majority view concerning the prerogative. Lord Roskill's remarks provide an explanation of the earlier decisions such as *Chandler v DPP* and *Hanratty v Lord Butler of Saffron Walden* which is consistent with the newly stated view. But those remarks also suggest that, even if the reason is different from that formerly understood, the propriety of most exercises of prerogative power will continue to be unsusceptible to challenge in the courts. Interesting although the case is in terms of principle, it would be a mistake to overrate its practical consequences.

ABOLITION OR REFORM?

The court's willingness to assume a greater role, in certain cases, in the control of exercises of the prerogative is understandable. It has been plausibly explained as a response to a constitutional imbalance:

> It is as if the courts had seen the new domination of Parliament by the Executive (or, rather, the restoration of an almost eighteenth century or even Tudor domination) and had decided to reinforce the other constitutional pillar, the Rule of Law.[10]

---

8 [1985] AC 374 at 407, [1984] 3 All ER 935 at 948, HL.
9 [1985] AC 374 at 418, [1984] 3 All ER 935 at 956, HL.
10 P Allott 'The Courts and the Executive: Four House of Lords Decisions' (1977) CLJ 255 at 282.

The need for this response was the greater because of the deficiencies in the practice of ministerial responsibility. In the past, courts have sometimes referred approvingly to ministerial responsibility, as if it were the complete answer, in cases where they have conceded, so far as judicial review was concerned, a virtually uncontrolled discretion to the executive.[11] But ministerial responsibility is not a complete answer. It sometimes assumes a fictive aspect, and in reasserting their powers to supervise the prerogative, the courts are perhaps beginning to recognise this.

However, if there are deficiencies in political accountability, there are also, as already observed, limits to the courts' willingness and capacity to intervene. Perhaps the answer lies in a return to the 1688 solution: legislation, to abolish or reform.

A couple of examples will serve to show the desirability of change. Consider first the prerogative power of dissolving Parliament. A statute puts the maximum duration at five years, but within that period a Parliament may be dissolved, and a general election held, at any time. The prerogative, nominally exercised by the Crown, is in reality exercised on the Prime Minister's advice, at least in the ordinary course of events. This effectively enables the Prime Minister to choose the date of the next general election, and it is notorious that the choice is influenced not by considerations of the public interest but by calculations of party advantage. That is surely an abuse of power, but it is a power the exercise of which cannot be effectively challenged.[12] It is one of the subjects, as noted earlier, on which governments simply refuse to submit themselves to parliamentary questioning, and it is, according to Lord Roskill's guidance, unamenable to challenge in the courts. The force of any public criticisms which opposition parties might tender is undercut by their own past record. Only legislation could remove the opportunity for abuse, for example by providing for a fixed term, although legislation would require a government sufficiently disinterested to embark on it.

Then consider the surviving prerogative immunity, that the Crown is not bound by statutes, unless it is so provided. This might not have mattered so much in the seventeenth century, but in the twentieth century the government is a very large employer, an important landowner, an owner of factories, prisons, and hospitals, a manufacturer, a builder, a landlord, and much more besides. Even so, legislation which imposes requirements or controls or penalties in the interests of health, hygiene, or safety, or in protection of employees, consumers or tenants, or for the sake of the

---

11 Eg *Liversidge v Anderson* [1942] AC 206, [1941] 3 All ER 338, HL; *R v Secretary of State for the Home Department, ex p Hosenball* [1977] 3 All ER 452, [1977] 1 WLR 766, CA; *Gouriet v Union of Post Office Workers* [1978] AC 435, [1977] 3 All ER 70, HL.

12 For a more general criticism of uncontrolled Prime Ministerial powers, see A Benn 'The Case for a Constitutional Premiership' (1980) 33 Parliamentary Affairs 7.

environment, is presumed not to apply to the government unless there is a clear indication to the contrary. In fact, important pieces of legislation are sometimes made applicable to the government, and sometimes not. Unfair dismissal legislation applies to the government, but government employees do not enjoy the protection provided by the Contracts of Employment Act 1972. The Occupiers' Liability Act 1957 applies, but the Health and Safety at Work etc. Act 1974 does not. The Town and Country Planning Act 1971 does not, in spite of the significance for the environment of some government activities. It is difficult to justify the exemption of the government from any of these laws, and the removal of the immunity by statute would be desirable, as it would throw the onus of proof on those who argue for special treatment. The issue came to public notice in 1986, when a food poisoning outbreak at the Stanley Royd Hospital in Wakefield resulted in 19 deaths, but the immunity from the food hygiene laws attaching to NHS hospitals prevented any prosecutions. The government responded to criticisms by agreeing to make hospitals subject to the hygiene laws, not by sweeping away the immunity altogether.

If some prerogatives are ripe for abolition, there are others which must either remain or be replaced. There must be some legal powers for the regulation of the Civil Service, the control of the armed forces, and the conduct of foreign policy. But there would be several advantages in replacing the existing prerogatives with statutory powers, such as the government more usually acts under. If that were done, the purposes and extent of the powers could be clearly set out, whereas much of the law concerning the prerogative is obscure and derived from ancient precedents. Supervision of the exercise of the powers could be more efficiently carried out in Parliament and by the courts. The opportunity for members of Parliament to consider and debate the appropriate limits of such powers would also provide an occasion for other arrangements to be mooted. It is not self-evident, for example, that the government should be involved in the appointment of archbishops and bishops in the Church of England; nor is it obvious that the honours system is best, or most appropriately, administered by the government. These last may be thought relatively minor issues. What is more important is that behind the phrase 'royal prerogative' lie hidden some issues of great constitutional importance, which are insufficiently recognised.

9 Legislature, executive and judiciary

Constitutional law is concerned with government in a state. If we ask what 'government' is, we are likely to think first of the various official powers which are exercised over us, or the decisions which are made on our behalf. If we are drawn towards the major political issues of the day, we might consider the present policies on nuclear weapons, or law and order, or trade and industry, or education. Or we might have in mind the small change of official power, such as the reminder in our mail that a television licence fee is due or the 'parking ticket' which a traffic warden has attached to our illegally parked car.

Our thoughts are naturally formed by our own time and place, but we should notice that the activities of government are neither universal nor the same as in other periods of history. When the Duke of Wellington was Prime Minister from 1828 to 1830, there were no motor cars, televisions or nuclear weapons, and such educational institutions as existed were not publicly funded. His administration was concerned with some particular matters such as the removal of religious disabilities and the establishment of a police force to deal with London's street crime and disorder; and, like others of the period, it tried to improve trading conditions, manage and preserve the British Empire, and conduct external relations to the country's best advantage.

However, even if the particular activities involved in government are variable, there are certain regularities in the pattern to be observed. The establishment of the Metropolitan Police required legislation in 1829, just as did the increases in police powers contained in the Police and Criminal Evidence Act 1984. Nineteenth-century governments, through the Admiralty and the War Office, sought to arm our military forces sufficiently to protect against and deter aggressors, just as present-day governments do with different weaponry. The criminals captured by Sir Robert Peel's Metropolitan Police were brought before the magistrates for trial, just as their present-day counterparts would be, or for that matter persons evading payment of a television licence fee or failing to pay the fixed penalty for a parking offence.

It would be simple enough to classify the activities referred to above as legislative, executive, or judicial. As the term is generally employed, the legislative activity involves the enactment of general rules for the individuals and groups in a society. The executive function is harder to define, but includes actions taken for the maintenance of order, in the implementation of the law, for the defence of the state, in the conduct of external affairs, and in the administration of internal policies. The judicial function involves the determination of issues of fact and the interpretation of law, and dealing with crimes or civil causes by the application of the law to them.

Sometimes the three functions may be viewed as a combination or sequence. For example, it was a legislative act (the Wireless Telegraphy Act 1949) which provided authority for the raising of a special tax to be levied on persons applying for the requisite licence for the reception of television programmes. Executive action is involved in the arrangements for the collection of the licence fees and the detection of offenders, which is done under the auspices of the Home Office. Judicial proceedings may be involved when persons are found to have installed or used television receiving equipment without, or outside the terms of, a licence. In some instances, such as this, the three functions might be described as making law, applying law, and enforcing law. But some of the activities which we would classify as 'executive', including the general conduct of foreign policy, do not involve the execution of law at all.

The vocabulary which we have been using, which categorises the functions of government as legislative, executive or judicial, has become commonplace in the description of constitutional arrangements. The terms have been derived from a doctrine which was developed in the seventeenth and eighteenth centuries, the doctrine of the separation of powers. It is also natural to use the terms because in many states there seem to be institutions or agencies whose primary functions correspond to one of these three kinds of activity, whether it is under the influence of the doctrine or not.

THE DOCTRINE OF THE SEPARATION OF POWERS

The doctrine of the separation of powers is not a legal principle, but a political theory. It prescribes what *ought* to happen, if a particular goal is to be achieved. Of course, we may ask to what extent the doctrine has been put into practice, or to what degree the constitution of a state conforms to it, and we shall do this presently with regard to the British constitution. First, let us consider how and why the doctrine was developed and propounded.

Origins[1]

The doctrine of the separation of powers is most often associated with the French writer Montesquieu, but it would be a mistake to think that he invented it. The doctrine includes a proposition about the functions of

---

1 See generally M J C Vile *Constitutionalism and the Separation of Powers* (1967); W B Gwyn *The Meaning of the Separation of Powers* (1965).

government, and discussions of the forms and functions of government may be traced back to ancient Greece. In Aristotle's *Politics*, he distinguishes three elements in every constitution, which he classified as the deliberative, the magisterial and the judicial.

Another related theme, which has as long a history in political thought, is the problem of ensuring that the exercise of governmental power, if it is necessary for the promotion of a society's values, may nonetheless be subject to limits so that it does not itself destroy those values. That is the principle of constitutionalism, which became central to the western democratic tradition. One of the contributions of the ancient Greeks to that tradition was the notion of government according to law, under which the procedures and values implicit in rational law-making and law-enforcement are enjoined on rulers, so that legal process is employed as a means of subjecting governmental power to control. That notion, elevated into the principle of 'the rule of law', has become a measure of procedural fairness in government, despite Dicey's attempt to hijack it for the purpose of claiming it as distinctively British.[2]

Another theory which was first developed in ancient Greece and Rome was the theory of mixed government, which held that the major interests in society must be allowed to participate jointly in government, so preventing any one interest from being able to dominate entirely. The interests in question were recognised in the types of government being classified as monarchies, aristocracies, and democracies. The Greek city-states exhibited a variety of possible arrangements, and different mixtures were recommended in the works of Aristotle, Plato and Polybius, amongst others.

The theory of mixed government was obviously designed to ensure some division of power, but it was a division that was based upon numbers or classes, rather than upon functions. Some distribution of power along these lines was characteristic of the councils and assemblies of many countries in the middle ages. In this country, as we know, by the thirteenth century the English Parliament was composed of the three estates of King, Lords, and Commons. One part of the government of the country could thus be presented as a compound of monarchy, aristocracy, and democracy.

Like the theory of mixed government, the doctrine of separation of powers which was to develop was aimed at avoiding absolutism by preventing a monopoly of power. But what had to be perceived, for it to be developed, was a need for particular functions of government to be distributed amongst different hands.

It is hardly surprising that ideas of that sort first became prominent in England. Between the fourteenth century and the seventeenth, the distinction between the king-in-Council and the king-in-Parliament had become ever clearer, and the contest between king and Parliament in the

2 *Law of the Constitution* (10th edn, 1961) Part II.

middle of the seventeenth century naturally concentrated minds upon the proper roles of each. There was interest too in the independence or otherwise of the judges' position in this, and particularly in the judicial powers of the Houses of Parliament. Against this background, classifications of the functions of government were commonplace in the constitutional writings of that period. Most often, a twofold division of legislative and executive functions was made, but some tract writers such as John Sadler, Charles Dallison, and George Lawson made threefold divisions. Dallison in a work dated 1648 wrote that 'It is one thing to have power to make Lawes, another to expound the Law, and to governe the people is different from both'.³ What is more, he went on to argue that a satisfactory system of government required these powers to be placed in different hands so that 'every one is limited, and kept within his owne bounds'.⁴ However, elements of the theory of mixed government were combined in Dallison's proposals, for he considered that the King should retain an important part in the legislative process.

The separation of powers emerged, briefly, in a purer version when the execution of the King made it imperative to design a new institutional structure. It will be recalled that the Instrument of Government of 1653 may properly be regarded as a written constitution.⁵ It was besides a constitution which embodied a well-developed separation of the functions assigned to different bodies. In the official defence of the Instrument which was published, a doctrine of separation of powers is prominently deployed, as in arguments that 'placing the legislative and executive powers in the same persons is a marvellous in-let of corruption and tyranny'.⁶ The authorship of the defence was generally attributed to Marchamont Nedham, who adduced similar arguments in a longer work in 1656.⁷

It is evident, then, that the doctrine of separation of powers was first formulated in England. After 1650, it was part of the general currency of political thought, but it was only one of a number of strands which had to be interwoven into the texture of the changing constitution. With the Restoration, the theory of mixed government re-emerged, and after the Revolution of 1688 the supremacy of Parliament had to be accommodated. John Locke, whose *Second Treatise of Civil Government* may be read as a justification of the Revolution, insisted upon the supremacy of the legislative function. But his legislature was not unlimited, but confined to the exercise of its proper functions, so that, for example, its enactments should be of general application and were not to be 'varied in particular cases'.⁸ Locke

---

3 *The Royalists Defence* (1648) p 70.
4 Ibid, p 126.
5 See ch 1.
6 *A True State of the Case of the Commonwealth* (1654) p 10.
7 *The Excellencie of a Free State* (1656).
8 *Two Treatises of Government* (ed by P Laslett, 1960), Second Treatise, XI, para 142.

recommended that the legislative and executive functions should be placed in separate hands, for the sake of efficiency as well as for the protection of liberty. His classification of functions was into the legislative, the executive, and the federative, but the last of these, involving foreign relations, was not a separate function but rather part of the executive.

Locke's work was abstract. In the writings of Viscount Bolingbroke, a purposeful practicality is combined with an appreciation of the realities of the British constitution as it was in the first half of the eighteenth century. Concerned as he was to oppose the 'ministerial system' of Sir' Robert Walpole, with its reliance on 'influence' or corruption for the securing of a ministry's parliamentary majority, he presented a clear delineation of functions:

> A King of Great Britain is that supreme magistrate, who has a negative voice in the legislature. He is entrusted with the executive power, and several other powers and privileges, which we call prerogative, are annex'd to this trust. The two Houses of Parliament have their rights and privileges, some of which are common to both; others particular to each. They prepare, they pass bills, or they refuse to pass such as are sent to them. They address, represent, advise, remonstrate. The supreme judicature resides in the Lords. The Commons are the grand inquest of the nation; and to them it belongs to judge of national expences, and to give supplies accordingly.[9]

Yet Bolingbroke had the wisdom to see that 'In a constitution like ours, the safety of the whole depends on the balance of the parts'.[10] He recognised too that the balance was achieved by a 'mutual dependency', of which he approved, provided that it did not turn into a 'constant dependency of one part'.[11] It was the constitution which Bolingbroke described which Montesquieu was to take as his model, when restating the doctrine of the separation of powers more explicitly and more influentially than any earlier writers.[12]

Montesquieu

Charles Louis de Secondat, Baron Montesquieu, inherited from an uncle his title and an office of judgeship which he held for nine years. However, at the age of thirty-six, he decided to spend the rest of his life as a man of letters, and embarked on a series of travels. From 1729 to 1731 he stayed in England. He was presented at court, visited Parliament, and moved amongst the leading figures in political and literary circles. He renewed his acquaintance with Bolingbroke, whom he had met in France. When he

9 *Remarks on the History of England* (1743) p 82.
10 *The Craftsman* 27 June 1730.
11 *Remarks on the History of England* (1743) p 84.
12 See R Shackleton 'Montesquieu, Bolingbroke and the Separation of Powers' (1949) 3 French Studies 25.

returned home, he was a confirmed admirer of the English love of liberty and the political arrangements to which it had given rise.

An essay on the British constitution was written by him in 1733, but it was to be another fifteen years before it was published as part of his major work, *De L'Esprit des Lois*. The book was conceived as a scientific study of government. With a wide sweep of historical and comparative examples, Montesquieu attempted to show how the laws of a society were related to the nature and type of its government, to the climate and physical environment of the country, to its economy, and to its manners and customs. His method was original and important, and his imagination fertile, even if he may be accused of credulity, inconsistency, and lack of judgement.

In classifying the forms of government, Montesquieu ignored the traditional typology of monarchies, aristocracies and democracies, and instead suggested a different one: republics, monarchies and despotisms. The classification does not appear very satisfactory. It seems strange for aristocracies and democracies, so different in many ways, both to be classed as republics. It seems surprising that monarchy and despotism, apparently similar, are so firmly distinguished. Moreover, it is difficult to interpret Montesquieu's application of these distinctions, as when he describes this country as 'a nation that may be justly called a republic, disguised under the form of a monarchy';[13] and it is unclear how he would relate his distinctions to the theory of mixed government or to the doctrine of separation of powers which he develops later in the book. In one respect, however, the distinction between monarchies and despotisms plays a significant role. Montesquieu characterises despotism as government by a single person according to his will and caprice, and monarchy as government by a single person according to fixed and established laws.[14] It follows that in a monarchy the king never acts as a judge, and justice is independently administered. The separation of the judicial function thus assumes an importance which earlier theorists had not given it, in the prevention of illegal oppression.

But Montesquieu realised that there could be oppression by means of the law, as well as outside it, and that is why further and more practical recommendations for the organisation of government had to be made, in order to ensure the liberty of the subject. These are put forward in Book XI, and especially in chapter VI, which is entitled 'On the English Constitution'.

It is there that the doctrine of the separation of powers is propounded, although Montesquieu himself does not use that term. He begins with a classification of the functions of government: 'In every government there are three sorts of power: the legislative, the executive in respect of matters involved in the law of nations, and the executive in respect of matters of

13 *De L'Esprit des Lois* (1748) Book V, ch 19.
14 Ibid, II, ch 1.

domestic law'.[15] However, the third function, under which the magistrate punishes criminals or decides disputes between individuals, is then immediately re-named as 'the power of judging'. A little later, the three functions are 'that of making laws, that of executing public affairs, and that of adjudicating on crimes or individual causes'. In this final sense, the executive function apparently refers to internal affairs as well as external relations, and so the definitions seem to correspond to the modern use of the terms 'legislative', 'executive' and 'judicial'.

So the trinity of governmental functions was established in a recognisably modern form. But that involved only a descriptive proposition. Montesquieu carried the argument further by stipulating that there should be three branches or agencies of government to correspond to the three functions:

> When the legislative and executive powers are united in the same person, or in the same body of magistrates, there can be no liberty . . . Again, there is no liberty if the power of judging is not separated from the legislative and executive. If it were joined with the legislative, the life and liberty of the subject would be exposed to arbitrary control; for the judge would then be the legislator. If it were joined to the executive power, the judge might behave with violence and oppression. There would be an end to everything, if the same man, or the same body, whether of the nobles or of the people, were to exercise those three powers, that of enacting laws, that of executing public affairs, and that of trying crimes or individual causes.

The third stage of Montesquieu's argument may be expressed as being that the three agencies should perform their respective functions of government *separately*. That is certainly the essence of the doctrine, but it is not entirely clear which of several forms of separation the author is prescribing as necessary. It is tolerably clear that he advocates, at the minimum, that one agency of government should not be performing the function appropriate to another. But whether he would insist on a complete separation of personnel in the different agencies is less obvious. There is no blanket prohibition to that effect, but it is perhaps implied in the passage above and in his contention that if the executive power were committed 'to a certain number of persons drawn from the legislative body, there would be no more liberty, because the two powers would be united, as the same persons would sometimes possess and always be able to possess, a share in both'.

However, Montesquieu also gave some support to the notion of there being 'checks and balances', by which the branches of government might legitimately influence or even impose certain limits on each other's actions. The independence of the judiciary was not to be compromised in such a way. But he thought that the chief executive should have a veto over legislation, and should have the power to summon and to regulate the duration of meetings of the legislature. The legislature, he suggested, should have the

15 Ibid, XI, ch 6. The following quotations in this section are from the same chapter.

power to examine the manner in which its laws have been put into effect, and should have the power to impeach ministers, but not the chief executive.

A system of checks and balances obviously involves one agency encroaching on the preserves of another. You might wonder whether that is inconsistent with a 'pure' doctrine of separation of powers. The answer must be that whether checks and balances are compatible with or infringe the doctrine of separation of powers depends upon what 'the doctrine' is. The trouble is that different interpretations may be attached to the doctrine and even, as we see with Montesquieu, to one person's exposition of it.

However, the doctrine entered the world stage at the beginning of a period of accelerating change, when in Europe and America old institutions were under threat and new forms and systems of government were being discussed. Its open texture, which enabled people to see in it what they liked, and take from it what they wanted, was no disadvantage to its reception or to its employment. It was influential in revolutionary France, but even more so in the United States of America, where its effects are apparent in the Constitution promulgated in 1787.[16]

THE DOCTRINE AND THE BRITISH CONSTITUTION

The doctrine of the separation of powers was put forward as a *prescription* of what ought to be done for the promotion of certain values, and the question of its validity is a question of political theory. A question of particular interest to British constitutional lawyers is the extent to which as a matter of *description* our constitution exhibits the kind of separation which the doctrine would require.

Two initial observations may be made. The first is that the British constitution, with its long and largely unbroken history, is above all the product of experience and experiment.[17] Its development has been characteristically pragmatic rather than principled, and so it is hardly likely absolutely to conform (or not to conform) to any ideal type. A second and related point is that the outlines of the modern British constitution had already been formed by the late seventeenth century. Therefore, even if earlier versions of the doctrine may not have been without some effect, Montesquieu's formulation of it in the mid-eighteenth century could only have affected such developments as occurred after that date.

In fact, as may be recalled, the initial influence seems to have been the other way round. The chapter in which Montesquieu elaborated the doctrine was entitled 'On the Constitution of England', so it is reasonable to assume that he regarded that as a model of the sort of arrangements he was advocating.

16 See M J C Vile *Constitutionalism and the Separation of Powers* (1967) chs 6, 7, 9 and 10.
17 See ch 1.

In this respect, many later commentators have taken issue with Montesquieu, considering that his interpretation of the eighteenth century constitution was mistaken.[18] Their criticisms are probably unfair. In the chapter in question,[19] despite the impression conveyed by its title, the author did not purport to give an account of the British constitution, but presented an ideal type of the constitution appropriate to a liberal state, with occasional complimentary references to the British constitution or derogatory remarks concerning others. Besides, it may be argued that, relative to others in the early eighteenth century at least, the British constitution did exhibit a separation. In France, where there was no parliamentary assembly, the king was the chief law-maker and the supreme executive. In this country there was an independent judiciary, which as early as 1607 had told the King, in Sir Edward Coke's words, that 'His Majesty was not learned in the laws of his realm', and so could not judge disputes;[20] and which, since the Act of Settlement in 1700 enjoyed tenure of office during good behaviour, and not at the pleasure of the executive. There was a legislature which by the Bill of Rights in 1688 had established its ascendancy over the Crown, and by the assertion of its privileges had achieved a practical independence. The king, along with his ministers and counsellors, was still the governor of the country.

It is easy, with hindsight, to criticise Montesquieu for paying insufficient attention to the developing Cabinet system. But when Montesquieu visited England, ministers still owed their position more to the king's confidence in them than to support in the House of Commons. It only became clear much later in the century that the monarch's own executive powers had sharply declined in favour of the ministers, who had been transformed into a Prime Minister and Cabinet, all of whom sat in one or other of the two Houses.

What about the twentieth-century constitution? Writers on the constitution seem to speak almost with one voice in denying that the separation of powers is a feature of the constitution. In his *Principles of British Constitutional Law* in 1925, C S Emden employed the vocabulary of the separation of powers in a scheme designed to show the constitution's disconformity to the doctrine, with chapters devoted to the functions of the legislature which could not properly be classed as legislative, the non-executive functions of the executive, and the non-judicial functions of the judiciary.[1] W A Robson, whose *Justice and Administrative Law* was first published three years later, likened Montesquieu's doctrine to 'a rickety chariot' and claimed that:

---

18 Eg Sir William Holdsworth *A History of English Law* (1938) vol X, pp 713–724.
19 Montesquieu also deals with the British constitution in Book XIX, ch 27.
20 *Prohibitions del Roy* (1607) 12 Co Rep 63.
 1 C S Emden *Principles of British Constitutional Law* (1925).

. . . the division of powers enunciated in this theory, and their allocation to separate branches of the government has at no period of history borne a close relation to the actual grouping of authority under the system of government obtaining in England.[2]

Moreover, he thought, 'when we come to the present day, we find a mingling of functions more extensive than any that has existed since the sixteenth and early seventeenth centuries'.[3] In *Halsbury's Laws of England*, Sir William Holdsworth denied that the doctrine had ever 'to any great extent corresponded with the facts of English government'.[4]

These views seemed still to represent the academic orthodoxy forty years later. Griffith and Street considered that 'the doctrine is so remote from the facts that it is better to disregard it altogether'.[5] Hood Phillips believed that the negation of the doctrine in most of its meanings was 'generally acknowledged' by students of the British constitution.[6] S A de Smith obviously thought likewise:

> Mention the theory of separation of powers to an English constitutional lawyer, and he will forthwith put on parade the Lord Chancellor, the Law Lords, the parliamentary executive, delegated legislation and administrative adjudication and shift the conversation to more significant topics. He tends to regard the theory as a somewhat tiresome talking-point, appropriate for political philosophers and inquisitive experts on comparative government, but an irrelevant distraction for the English law student and his teachers.[7]

In his textbook, the verdict was short and sharp: 'No writer of repute would claim that it is a central feature of the modern British constitution'.[8]

However, in recent years some distinguished judges have risked incurring disrepute. In a Privy Council appeal in 1977, Lord Diplock referred to some of the Commonwealth constitutions as having been drafted by persons 'familiar . . . with the basic concept of separation of legislative, executive and judicial power as it had been developed in the unwritten constitution of the United Kingdom'.[9] He returned to the theme when the House of Lords, in a case concerning an industrial dispute, felt it necessary to rebuke the Court of Appeal for having strayed beyond its proper constitutional function:

> At a time when more and more cases involve the application of legislation which gives effect to policies that are the subject of bitter public and parliamentary

2 W A Robson *Justice and Administrative Law* (3rd edn, 1951) p 16.
3 Ibid, p 22.
4 *Halsbury's Laws of England* (2nd edn, 1932) vol 6, p 385.
5 J A G Griffith and H Street *Principles of Administrative Law* (5th edn, 1973) p 16.
6 O Hood Phillips 'A Constitutional Myth: Separation of Powers' (1977) 93 LQR 11.
7 S A de Smith 'The Separation of Powers in New Dress' (1966) 12 McGill LJ 491.
8 *Constitutional and Administrative Law* (5th edn by Harry Street and Rodney Brazier, 1985) p 31.
9 *Hinds v R* [1977] AC 195 at 212, [1976] 1 All ER 353 at 359.

controversy, it cannot be too strongly emphasised that the British constitution, though largely underwritten, is firmly based on the separation of powers: Parliament makes the laws, the judiciary interpret them.[10]

Lord Scarman, in his speech in the same case, also remarked that 'the constitution's separation of powers, or more accurately functions, must be observed if judicial independence is not to be put at risk'.[11] In another case later, an applicant was seeking to determine the prospective validity of a draft Order in Council which had yet to be laid before the Houses of Parliament as required. The Court of Appeal held that there was jurisdiction to entertain such a challenge, although it had to be exercised with great circumspection and due regard to the dangers of encroaching on any functions of Parliament. Sir John Donaldson MR said:

> Although the United Kingdom has no written constitution, it is a constitutional convention of the highest importance that the legislature and the judicature are separate and independent of one another, subject to certain ultimate rights of Parliament over the judicature which are immaterial for present purposes. It therefore behoves the courts to be ever sensitive to the paramount need to refrain from trespassing on the province of Parliament . . .[12]

There is something of a puzzle here, which we shall have to try to unravel. On the one side, there is distinguished judicial support for the view that our constitution is 'firmly based' on the separation of powers. On the other, there is the weight of academic judgment these fifty years past, almost wholly to the opposite effect.

Of course, the differences might be explained by differences in usage. As we have already seen, the separation of powers doctrine is susceptible to a variety of meanings, and this is apt to bedevil discussions of it. But these difficulties, although real, should not be exaggerated. What Lord Diplock seems to have had in mind is a version of the doctrine which would require that the persons who exercise one kind of governmental function should not also exercise another; and from the evidence which they individually adduce, that is a formulation which, as regards British government, Hood Phillips, de Smith and the others took to be negated. The disagreement seems to be real, and not merely apparent.

In order to explore this further, we should make a survey of the extent to which, in the constitution of the present day, the legislature, executive and judiciary are separated or mixed. It is necessary to define these terms. In speaking of 'the legislature', we are thinking of Parliament. In speaking of 'the executive', we would include the Sovereign as its nominal head, the Prime Minister and other members of the government, and the Civil Service.

---

10 *Duport Steels Ltd v Sirs* [1980] 1 All ER 529 at 541, [1980] 1 WLR 142 at 157, HL.
11 [1980] 1 All ER 529 at 551, [1980] 1 WLR 142 at 169, HL.
12 *R v HM Treasury, ex p Smedley* [1985] QB 657 at 666, [1985] 1 All ER 589 at 593.

'The judiciary' consists of the judges who preside in courts of law. We shall have these definitions in mind, but mention some other persons and bodies in the waygoing. We shall consider to what extent the same persons compose the legislature, executive and judiciary; and consider the extent to which these branches of government perform functions which, according to the doctrine, are inappropriate to them. In order to give a more complete picture, we shall consider also the extent to which these branches control or check each other. Bear in mind, however, that on one view of the doctrine, checks and balances are not inconsistent with a separation of powers, but represent the doctrine in its highest form.

LEGISLATURE AND JUDICIARY

The legislature and the judiciary do not overlap significantly in their membership. Most importantly, in the case of the House of Commons, an overlap cannot arise because judicial offices are amongst those offices disqualifying for membership of the House under the House of Commons Disqualification Act 1975. The specified offices include judges of the Court of Appeal and High Court in England, and of the Court of Session in Scotland and High Court in Northern Ireland, as well as circuit judges in England, sheriffs in Scotland, resident magistrates in Northern Ireland and stipendiary magistrates in England. In addition, the chairmanship or membership of many tribunals, such as the Lands Tribunal or industrial tribunals, also involves disqualification. Justices of the peace are not disqualified.

Of course, one part of Parliament is the Sovereign. Parliament is properly the Queen-in-Parliament (or King-in-Parliament, as the case may be), which should remind us that the third element in the process of enactment is the signification of royal assent. As was noticed earlier,[13] a constitutional convention has developed which constrains the Sovereign's discretion in the matter. In practice, the Sovereign's part in the process is that of a rubber-stamp. Only occasionally, and in unusual circumstances, is the Sovereign's role in legislating likely to be of any more importance than that. But the Sovereign's role in the judicial process is even more of a formality. It was the Crown's prerogative to be 'the fountain of justice'. Historically, that was of great importance, and there are reminders of the Crown's association in nomenclature (the 'Royal Courts of Justice') and some legal forms and procedures (the 'prerogative orders'). But today the Sovereign in person plays no part in the judicial process. The Crown's responsibilities and powers with regard to justice and the administration of the law have passed either to a

13 See ch 3.

judiciary which operates independently or to ministers, including the law officers.

The Lord Chancellor may more realistically be viewed as part of the legislature and the judiciary. As Lord Chancellor, he is a member of the House of Lords. In fact, when it is sitting in its legislative capacity, he presides in it, rather as the Speaker does in the House of Commons. However, he does not exercise similar disciplinary powers to the Speaker's, because he has not been given such powers by the House, which did not elect him. Another contrast is that he may cast off the mantle of impartial chairmanship. The Lord Chancellor is often the principal spokesman for the government in the chamber, and when he wishes to participate partially in the House's debates, he may vacate the Woolsack and move to another spot to do so. [14]

The Lord Chancellor is also the head of the judiciary. He is the titular head of the Supreme Court and president of the Chancery Division. He sits from time to time in the Appellate Committee of the House of Lords, which discharges the judicial work of the House as a final court of appeal, and in the Judicial Committee of the Privy Council. When he sits, he presides. He is also responsible for arranging who shall hear cases in the Appellate Committee and Judicial Committee. In practice, because of the expansion of their other responsibilities and changes in the parliamentary timetable, there is less opportunity nowadays for Lord Chancellors to sit frequently as judges. When Lord Gardiner was Lord Chancellor between 1964 and 1970, he sat in only two appeals. Lord Hailsham has managed to sit more frequently.

The Lord Chancellor is part of a wider overlap in membership of the legislative and judicial branches. Since the enactment of the Appellate Jurisdiction Act 1876, there has been provision for the appointment of Lords of Appeal in Ordinary, who are expected to enable the House to discharge its judicial responsibilities. There is currently provision for 11 to be paid a salary, and they have peerages for life. Besides, at any one time there will be a few former Lords of Appeal and Lord Chancellors and a few other peers who hold or have held high judicial office. All these persons, known as Law Lords, may sit as judges in the House of Lords and in the Judicial Committee of the Privy Council. But, as members of the House of Lords, they may also participate in the other activities of that body. In fact, when matters of criminal law or punishment or technical law reform are being considered, they may contribute significantly and valuably to the work of the House. However, a convention has developed to limit their participation, to the effect that they should only concern themselves with subjects which fall outside the arena of party political controversy. A survey of the Law Lords' participation in the House's legislative activity confirmed that they 'confine

14 He moves two paces to the left, a spot assigned by Henry VIII: Lord Hailsham *The Door Wherein I Went* (1975) p 248.

themselves largely to acting as resident technical consultants to the legislature on legal points arising out of proposed legislation'.[15]

There is a convention, too, which operates to limit the other members of the House. There is nothing in law to prevent any member of the House from participating in the exercise of its judicial functions. But in 1844, when Daniel O'Connell's appeal against a conviction was heard, the lay peers who had initially voted were persuaded to withdraw; and since then it has been accepted that the decision should be left to the professional judges present.[16]

Aside from the judicial functions of the House of Lords, are there other occasions of which it might be said that the legislature is performing a judicial function?

There is another respect in which parts of the legislature participate in a process of a judicial nature, and that is in enforcing parliamentary privileges.[17] In this limited area of law, the Houses act like a criminal court in considering whether somebody is in contempt of Parliament and deciding what punishment should be imposed. The function of interpreting the law seems to have been assumed by the Houses as well, when they claim to be the sole judges of the extent of their own privileges. It is precisely because the Houses in these respects do seem to be like courts of law, that there are objections because they do not in other respects act like courts. The central criticism is of the conflict of interest involved when the House is victim, prosecutor, judge and sentencer. The arguments against that conflict of interest have much in common with those which underlie the separation of powers doctrine.

Parliament as a whole could exercise a judicial function if it took it upon itself to try, convict and sentence someone for the commission of a crime. Parliament did just that on occasions from the fifteenth century onwards when it passed Acts of Attainder. These were technically legislative measures, but they effectively provided that a person was guilty of an offence (usually of a political nature) and prescribed a punishment. Consistently with the sovereignty of Parliament, it was not necessary that the offence of which a person was attainted was a crime at the time when he committed it. The last Act of Attainder was in 1715, and it may be presumed that the practice is obsolete. The personal Acts which Parliament occasionally passes nowadays are of a less repugnant kind, being employed to allow exceptional marriages or divorces, for example. But they could also be looked on as judicial in nature.

When we ask whether the judiciary legislates, much depends upon the meaning which we give to that term. If the definition of legislation is confined to enactments in fixed verbal form, then it applies only to Acts of

15 L Blom-Cooper and G Drewry *Final Appeal* (1972) p 203.
16 See Robert Stevens *Law and Politics* ch 1.
17 See ch 7.

Parliament and subordinate legislation. The judges are involved in the passing of Acts only to the extent that the Lord Chancellor and other judges in the House of Lords are influential. However, there are some instances where Parliament has delegated legislative powers to the Lord Chancellor and to judges. For example, the power to make rules for procedure in courts has been given to Rule Committees under various statutes, which consist mainly of judges.[18]

If the essence of legislation is the declaration of general rules, then there is a much more important sense in which judges legislate, for their creation and exposition of the common law could then be regarded as 'legislative' in nature. Admittedly, that process has taken place only within the limits allowed by Parliament, but there is no denying its importance. Indeed, it is interesting to consider why this aspect of judicial activity, despite being the object of so much legal study, is not widely recognised as 'legislative'. In part, it is perhaps because the customary distinction between legislation and common law as sources helps to obscure their similarities in nature. No doubt, another reason lies in the myth fostered by judges to the effect that they are only discoverers, and not makers, of law. That myth continues to influence legal rhetoric and perceptions of the law, even although it is palpably false. Even judges have sometimes come clean, as when Lord Reid admitted it was a 'fairy tale'.[19]

It is time to ask whether the legislature and judiciary exercise any checks or balances upon each other. As between these institutions, the picture is rather one-sided. The sovereignty of Parliament entails that the courts have the duty to ascertain and give effect to the will of Parliament, and no power on any ground to declare an Act of Parliament invalid.[20] In practice, as students of law find out, the courts are not invariably so docile as the constitutional doctrine would imply. There is a kind of balance in the discretion left to judges, when they are called upon to interpret and apply often imperfectly drafted legislation to the diverse circumstances presented before them. Yet, if this is real, it should not be exaggerated.

The legislature may check judges and the activities of judges. Parliament is not involved in the appointment of judges, but may have a hand in the removal of judges of the higher courts. Lords of Appeal, and judges of the High Court and the Court of Appeal are removable by the Crown upon an address presented by both Houses of Parliament.[1] It has only happened once, when an Irish judge's dereliction of duty was such as to require intervention.

Parliamentary motions for the removal of judges have been unsuccessful on a few occasions. In 1973, over 180 Labour MPs signed a motion calling

---

18 Eg Courts Act 1971, s 15.
19 Lord Reid 'The Judge as Law Maker' (1972) 12 JSPTL 22.
20 See ch 5.
 1 Appellate Jurisdiction Act 1876, s 6; Supreme Court Act 1981, s 11.

for the dismissal of Sir John Donaldson, who was then President of the National Industrial Relations Court, but time was not found to debate it.[2] Under parliamentary rules, aspersions should not be cast upon the conduct of particular judges, nor judges generally, except upon a substantive motion or in speeches supporting an address for removal.[3] But members have not always been able to resist commenting on judicial remarks or judicial decisions to which they have taken objection. In 1982 the Prime Minister herself declared that she found incomprehensible the decision of a judge to impose a suspended sentence on the rapist of a six-year-old girl.[4] There are also parliamentary sub judice rules, designed to prevent comment on cases while they are pending or being tried.[5]

There can be no doubt that Parliament, if it wishes, has the last word. If Parliament disapproves of judicial lawmaking or interpretation, it can change the law, prospectively or retrospectively. An extreme example of this was the War Damage Act 1965. In form it was a public general Act excluding the possibility of claims for compensation against the Crown in certain circumstances. In reality, the government had used its dominance in Parliament in order to have reversed an inconvenient decision in the courts,[6] with retrospective effect.

EXECUTIVE AND JUDICIARY

Do the same persons form part of the executive and the judiciary? The Sovereign, who is at the head of executive government, is nominally involved in the administration of justice, since the courts are the Queen's courts and criminal indictments are brought in her name. But there is no real involvement. In *Prohibitions del Roy*, James I was told that although he might be present in court, he could not give an opinion.[7] Since the beginning of the seventeenth century, it has been clear that the royal prerogative of administering justice has been exercisable only through duly appointed courts and judges.

The Lord Chancellor is indisputably a member of the executive, as a Cabinet minister, and of the judiciary, of which he is the head. As we have seen, the opportunity for a Lord Chancellor to sit in the Appellate Committee is limited in practice, and it would appear that holders of that office avoid hearing any appeals in which the government is directly

---

2 866 HC Official Report (5th series) col 42.
3 See Erskine May's *Treatise on the Law, Privileges, Proceedings and Usage of Parliament* (20th edn by Sir Charles Gordon, 1983) ch 18.
4 34 HC Official Report (6th series) col 123.
5 See Erskine May ch 19.
6 That in *Burmah Oil Co v Lord Advocate* [1965] AC 75, [1964] 2 All ER 348, HL.
7 *Prohibitions del Roy* (1607) 12 Co Rep 63.

involved. As a minister, the Lord Chancellor has a small department staffed by civil servants, and is responsible for appointments of judges and magistrates, for administering the Crown Court centres, for law reform and statute law revision, and a number of other matters which in many countries would fall to a Minister of Justice.

The only other overlap between the personnel of the executive and the judiciary would be found in the Privy Council. A Judicial Committee of the Privy Council acts as a court to hear appeals from colonies and some Commonwealth jurisdictions and from the courts of the Channel Islands and the Isle of Man. It also hears appeals from some professional disciplinary tribunals and in some ecclesiastical causes. The composition of the Judicial Committee is laid down in statute.[8] It is wider than that of the Appellate Committee of the House of Lords, but in practice it is usually present or former Lords of Appeal who sit in the Judicial Committee. The same persons, being Privy Councillors, are also members of that body which is technically an instrument of executive government. However, the Privy Council today, which consists of about 380 members, is not an important part of government. It has a few miscellaneous functions, mostly exercised through committees, and it is used as an organ for giving formal effect to certain acts done under statutory or prerogative powers. It meets in plenary session only on rare ceremonial occasions, and otherwise operates by the summoning of three or four members (usually government ministers) to the Queen's presence.

Do members of the judiciary perform executive functions? Certainly, courts have some ancillary powers for the prevention of interference with their proceedings and for the enforcement of their decisions. These might be considered executive in nature, but are hardly central to the government of the country. At the lower court levels, there is often a mingling of functions. Justices of the peace were until the nineteenth century the principal agents of local administration and have a few surviving functions such as licensing which could be classed as executive rather than judicial. Similarly, the sheriffs in Scotland retain some administrative functions.

It might be thought to threaten judicial independence if members of the judiciary provided advice to the executive on questions of law. There is a procedure which would allow for this, under section 4 of the Judicial Committee Act 1833, which enables the Crown to refer any matter (not necessarily arising out of litigation) to the Judicial Committee of the Privy Council for an advisory opinion. In practice, it has been used only infrequently and uncontroversially, the last occasion being in 1957 at the request of the House of Commons, which was anxious to know whether its privileges had been affected by a statute passed in 1770.[9]

---

8 Judicial Committee Act 1833; Appellate Jurisdiction Acts 1876, 1887, 1908; Judicial Committee Amendment Act 1895.
9 *Re Parliamentary Privilege Act 1770* [1958] AC 331, [1958] 2 All ER 329, PC.

Members of the judiciary do sometimes perform non-judicial functions at the behest of the government. Since the 1920s it has become increasingly common for judges to preside over or participate in commissions, inquiries and law reform committees. Evidently, judges regard duties of this sort as part and parcel of public service, and there are some kinds of inquiry where judicial expertise may be invaluable, as when the causes of the Aberfan disaster or the Bradford City football ground fire are investigated. But there is perhaps a distinction to be drawn between inquiries such as those and subjects of political controversy. It is precisely because judges may be recognised as impartial that governments may find it useful to ask them to report on thorny political problems. However, it may be thought that judges should not be asked to, or should not agree to, become involved in such issues as the Profumo affair, the activities of the intelligence services, industrial disputes, and the troubles in Northern Ireland.[10] Their involvement may endanger their individual reputations for impartiality, or even lower respect for the judiciary as a whole. It will be a sad reflection on Lord Diplock's judicial career, if he is better remembered for recommending jury-less trial courts in Northern Ireland than for the quality of his judgments.

Members of the executive do not perform the function of judging in courts, except to the extent of overlaps of personnel already discussed. However, ministers and others do have some important powers with regard to judicial proceedings and the administration of justice. The Home Secretary is entrusted with the exercise of the prerogative of mercy, by which he may pardon offenders, or remit or reduce judicial sentences. The law officers have a variety of important functions.[11] The Attorney General is the principal legal adviser to the government, and appears on its behalf in major cases. He also exercises supervision over criminal justice. He may institute criminal proceedings, and by use of the nolle prosequi may stop proceedings on indictment, whether instituted by himself or another. In civil matters, the Attorney General represents the Crown as *parens patriae*, and has standing to vindicate public rights. He is assisted by the Solicitor General, and the Director of Public Prosecutions, an official with particular functions regarding criminal proceedings, is under his superintendence. The Scottish law officers, the Lord Advocate and the Solicitor General for Scotland, have special functions in connection with legal proceedings there.

The law officers are members of the government, but not normally of the Cabinet. However, the Attorney General is usually a member of some Cabinet committees concerned with proposed legislation. Some

---

10 See J A G Griffith *The Politics of the Judiciary* (2nd edn, 1981) ch 2; G Zellick 'Comment' [1972] PL 1.

11 See J L J Edwards *The Law Officers of the Crown* (1964), J L J Edwards *The Attorney General: Politics and the Public Interest* (1984).

constitutional conventions come into play in order to separate the law officers' various roles.[12] In his functions in connection with proceedings, the Attorney General should not take orders from the government (although the views of other ministers may be given or sought) and should not be influenced by party political factors, although he is entitled to have considerations of public policy in mind. A possible breach of the convention in 1924, when the Attorney General stopped a prosecution for sedition, apparently on the advice of the Cabinet, led to the downfall of the first Labour government. Another convention obliges ministers not to disclose advice given confidentially by the law officers, and it was a disclosure of that kind attributed to his department which led to Mr Leon Brittan's resignation in 1986.

It could certainly be granted that some adjudication is performed other than by the courts. We are perhaps in some terminological difficulty here. There are many issues which are potentially justiciable, in the sense that they could be resolved in the courts, but which are actually disposed of in another way. Some kinds of decision, involving interpretation and application of the law, are entrusted primarily to specialised tribunals, such as industrial tribunals, social security appeal tribunals, and traffic commissioners. The members of these tribunals are usually appointed by the relevant minister or the Lord Chancellor, or both jointly, but they are not government officials in the ordinary sense. The members are mostly part-time, and sometimes must have a legal or professional qualification. Appeals lie to the courts from most tribunals, usually on questions of law only, and their decisions besides are subject to review within the supervisory jurisdiction of the High Court.

There are other questions and disputes which are resolved by government departments. This will be appropriate when aspects of public policy are relevant. When executive action is involved, then ministers will be responsible to Parliament in respect of it, and it will be reviewable by the courts. It is impossible to draw hard and fast distinctions between the kinds of decision appropriately left to the executive, the kinds most suitably consigned to tribunals, and those properly for the courts. The force of the separation of powers doctrine seems to lie in the principle that decisions which should be taken free of political influence, and which require the application of rules to individual cases, should be entrusted to courts or tribunals.

What checks and balances do the executive and the judiciary exercise upon each other? In the first place, judges owe their appointment to the executive. The Lord Chancellor, the Lord Chief Justice, the Master of the Rolls, the President of the Family Division, the Lords of Appeal and the Lords Justices of Appeal are all appointed by the Sovereign, but by convention on the advice of the Prime Minister (who no doubt consults the Lord Chancellor on the

12 See Geoffrey Marshall *Constitutional Conventions* (1984) ch 7.

other appointments). High Court and circuit judges are appointed by the Sovereign, by convention on the Lord Chancellor's advice. In practice, party political considerations do not influence these appointments,[13] which seem to depend upon the competence, judicial qualities and necessary integrity of eligible persons, normally senior barristers. However, the tradition of non-political appointments has only developed in the twentieth century and only been firmly established since 1945.[14]

Security of judicial tenure has been firm for much longer, since the Act of Settlement in 1700. As we have noted, only one judge of the higher courts has been removed from office in two hundred years. Circuit judges are removable by the Lord Chancellor 'on the ground of incapacity or misbehaviour'.[15] There was an instance in 1983, after a judge was convicted of smuggling.

The judiciary checks the executive by being available to review its actions. This extends to the executive in its widest sense, including local authorities, public corporations, the police, and other public authorities, as well as central government. The High Court in its supervisory jurisdiction may declare the acts of these bodies invalid, on well-established grounds of illegality, procedural impropriety, and irrationality.[16]

LEGISLATURE AND EXECUTIVE

To some degree the same persons do belong to the legislative and the executive branches of government. There is first the Sovereign, who is at the head of the executive and who is part of Parliament. However, as we have noted already, these are roles which have diminished in practical importance, as constitutional conventions have developed to limit the monarch's powers.

Much more important is the fact that the Prime Minister and government ministers are members of one or other House of Parliament. We have a parliamentary executive. There is no law which requires that ministers must be parliamentarians, but that became the practice in the eighteenth century, and is a firmly established convention today. When Mr Harold Wilson became Prime Minister in 1964, he was able to give ministerial offices to Mr Patrick Gordon Walker (who had failed to retain his seat at the general election) and Mr Frank Cousins, a trade union leader, only on the expectation

---

13 This, at least, is the generally held view. Arguably there are some exceptions, and for a more sceptical view see J A G Griffith *The Politics of the Judiciary* (2nd edn, 1981).

14 See S Shetreet *Judges on Trial* (1976).

15 Courts Act 1971, s 17.

16 Judicial review of executive action is a central topic in administrative law. This classification of the grounds of review was suggested by Lord Diplock in *Council of Civil Service Unions v Minister for the Civil Service* [1985] AC 374, [1984] 3 All ER 935, HL.

that the two would shortly become MPs after contesting by-elections. In fact, Mr Cousins won a by-election and remained in office, but Mr Gordon Walker resigned office after a second election defeat. More usually, a Prime Minister who wishes to have someone as a minister who is not a member of the House of Commons would recommend the creation of a life peerage, as Mrs Thatcher did in 1984 for Mr David Young, afterwards Lord Young of Graffham. The ministerial office of Lord Chancellor, which is almost invariably a Cabinet post, must obviously be held by a member of the House of Lords.

Therefore Cabinet ministers and other ministers and junior ministers, numbering a little over a hundred, who are the most important persons in the executive branch of government, will also be members of the legislature. Interestingly, however, there is a limitation on this overlap. Concern over the effects of executive influence on the legislature is long-standing, for it goes back to the battles between Crown and Parliament in the seventeenth century. But it is still felt today, when the executive appears in a different guise.

The relevant legislation now is the House of Commons Disqualification Act 1975, which specifies particular offices which are legally incompatible with membership of the House. Ministerial offices are dealt with in section 2(1), which provides that 'Not more than ninety-five persons being the holders of . . . Ministerial offices shall be entitled to sit and vote in the House of Commons at any one time'. Since some twenty to thirty parliamentary private secretaries may also be appointed, who are expected to support the government although they do not hold ministerial offices, in practice the government may count on about 120 supporters out of 650 MPs. Of course, the government would normally have the general support of a majority of the 650 (for that is how governments are formed in the first place), but the backbench supporters or allies, who are not members of the government, are not constrained by the doctrine of collective responsibility, and so tend to act rather more independently. That is the tendency which the limitation on numbers is designed to guarantee and encourage. It is no longer the monarch, but the Prime Minister, whose powers of patronage have to be restrained, but the rationale remains the same, and the aim is essentially that of ensuring that the legislature is not entirely dominated by the executive.

Notice also that the overlap between members of the legislature and the executive is strictly confined to ministers. The executive includes not only the politicians who are ministers, but the members of the Civil Service who staff their departments. The House of Commons Disqualification Act 1975 disqualifies from membership of the House civil servants, whether established or not, and whether full-time or part-time. It also disqualifies members of the armed forces, the police, and the members of specified commissions, boards, authorities and tribunals. In the case of civil servants, it is taken further: there are rules requiring their resignation if they should become parliamentary candidates, and other restrictions on their political activities, depending upon their kind of employment.[17]

Does the legislature, Parliament, perform any executive functions? Certainly, it must be acknowledged that the enactment of legislation is only one of its functions, occupying about half of its time. A Select Committee of the House of Commons in 1979 considered that the House had four main tasks, the other three being the scrutiny of the activities of the executive, the control of finance, and the ventilation and redress of grievances.[18] That is only a rough guide, but it is interesting for what it omits. As John Stuart Mill said, 'there is a radical distinction between controlling the business of government, and actually doing it'.[19] England had unhappy experience of a Parliament's efforts to govern the country in 1648 and 1649 when the Long Parliament proved to be so inefficient, intolerant, and meddlesome, as to provoke Cromwell's further intervention. That experience was perhaps in Mill's mind when he expressed the view that a representative assembly was 'radically unfit' to govern. In practice, the parliamentary body is not organised in such a way as would enable it to execute foreign policy or implement domestic policies. When it is said that we have 'parliamentary government', this must be understood as referring not to government by Parliament, but by an executive drawn from and accountable to Parliament.

However, we cannot acquit the executive of performing legislative functions. Much of the legislative output consists of subordinate or delegated legislation, made by someone other than Parliament. The recipients of these powers are most often ministers or government departments or the Privy Council (which is effectively under ministerial control).

In fact, the volume of subordinate legislation produced in a year exceeds that of primary legislation. But it is far from commensurate in importance. It is accepted that it is for Parliament to determine the general principles of the law. Subordinate legislation is appropriate for supplementation or detail. Besides, it is subordinate precisely because Parliament is supreme and may always repeal the legislation or take away the powers. Ministerial legislation generally has to be laid in draft form before the Houses of Parliament, and there is some scrutiny of delegated legislation by parliamentary committees. The purposes and limits of any delegation will be specified in an Act of Parliament, and judicial control may be asserted to ensure that the delegate has not acted ultra vires.

What checks and balances are exercised by the legislature and the

---

17 Servants of the Crown (Parliamentary Candidature) Order 1960; Civil Service Pay and Conditions of Service Code.
18 HC 588-1 (1977-78).
19 John Stuart Mill *Representative Government* (1861) ch 5.

executive upon each other? First, by law the meeting of Parliament is dependent on the will of the Sovereign, who summons it and dissolves it. However, the Meeting of Parliament Act 1694 requires that not more than three years must elapse after a dissolution before the summoning of a new Parliament, and convention requires that a Parliament be summoned annually. The Parliament Act 1911 fixes the maximum duration of a Parliament at five years. Subject to that, the Sovereign has the power of dissolution, but by convention it is exercised on the Prime Minister's advice.

When Parliament is in session and a government has been formed, Parliament, or more particularly the House of Commons, ultimately controls the government. It is a fundamental convention of the constitution that a government is entitled to continue in office only so long as it enjoys the confidence of a majority in the House of Commons. In consequence, a Prime Minister is obliged to tender his resignation or advise the dissolution of Parliament if his government is defeated in a vote on a matter of confidence, being an issue designated as such or so important as to be regarded as such. That expectation became clear in the nineteenth century, and especially after 1832, and in the years between 1852 and 1859 no fewer than five governments lost office in this way. Mr James Callaghan had to advise a dissolution in 1979 when his government lost on a vote of confidence by one vote. The Labour Party no longer had an overall majority of seats in the House at the time. There was also a minority government on the previous occasion when a vote of confidence was lost, in 1924.

As may be seen, defeats of that kind have become rare in modern times. The reasons for that are the same reasons as explain why, if there is one sense in which the legislature controls the executive, there is another sense in which the executive often appears to control the legislature. The key to it all is that one party normally has an overall majority in the House of Commons. That is the more likely because in our national politics, there have usually been two principal competing parties, and because our electoral system encourages it. If one party has an overall majority, then the government will be formed from that party. Party discipline today is much stronger than in the 1850s, and so a government with a working majority may expect that, on major issues at least, it will invariably win the day.

Under conditions such as described, it has to be accepted that the government is able to dominate in Parliament. The point could be demonstrated in a variety of ways, but perhaps is most easily shown by reference to the legislative programme. With its majority and its ability to shape the business of the House of Commons, the government is able to ensure that the vast majority of its Bills become law, and substantially in the form it wishes. For example, in the 1983–84 session, 60 of the 73 public Bills which were passed were government Bills; there were no Bills passed by the House of Commons, but not by the House of Lords; and there were no

Bills introduced by the government which did not receive the royal assent, whereas there were 105 public bills introduced by individual members of the Commons or Lords which did not.[20]

It is on these grounds that it may be said that 'legislation is largely a function of government', or that Parliament is merely used by the government as a means of securing those changes in the law which it wishes. It was this tendency which was perceived by Bagehot as 'the close union, the nearly complete fusion, of the legislative and executive powers'.[1] What Bagehot praised, others have found objectionable or dangerous, at least when it becomes an 'elective dictatorship'.[2]

Yet that depiction of the relations between legislature and executive is often overdrawn.[3] For one thing, the case is altered radically when governments do not have a safe overall majority, and that is not too unusual. There was no party with an overall majority following the February 1974 general election, and overall majorities of fewer than five following the 1964 and October 1974 general elections. But in any event the executive's legislative and other activities are subject to continuing public scrutiny in Parliament, through the traditional means of motions, debates, parliamentary questions and committees. These are pressures on all governments, whatever their majority. For example, the Conservative government had a secure majority when it introduced the Police and Criminal Evidence Bill in 1983. Its proposals met with considerable reservations, expressed in Parliament and outside, by politicians of all parties, pressure groups, and academic and professional opinion. Without changing its mind about the ends to be pursued, the government made or accepted a large number of amendments in concession to these pressures, and the Police and Criminal Evidence Act finally passed in 1984 differed significantly from the original version. That is evidence of democracy rather than dictatorship, and it suggests that generalisations about 'fusion' or 'domination' should not be swallowed too readily.

CONCLUSION

Does our survey support the academics or the judges? We must grant, of course, that there is no absolute separation of powers in this country. However, to rest one's case there would be to be satisfied with the form and to miss the substance.

In fact, the nature of the evidence usually relied upon should make us

20 HC 16 (1984–85).
 1 Walter Bagehot *The English Constitution* (1867) ch 1.
 2 Lord Hailsham 'Elective Dictatorship' (1976) 120 Sol Jo 693.
 3 See L S Amery *Thoughts on the Constitution* (1947), for a balanced account which is still valid.

sceptical of the academic orthodoxy. It is easy enough to portray the Lord Chancellor ('certainly the spectacular exhibit in the museum of constitutional curiosities')[4] as a sort of dangerous one man band, but a consideration of constitutional practice might be more informative. When some jurors complained to the Lord Chancellor about a judge's conduct of a trial, Lord Hailsham, in his reply to them, observed that he was a member of the Cabinet, and that if he were to comment upon the conduct of controversial trials, 'the distinction, which is vital to the whole system, between the courts and the government would be destroyed'.[5]

Many other matters deserve to be put under a similarly searching spotlight. Yes, the Law Lords are members of the legislature and of a court; but no, they do not participate crucially, or even freely, in legislative business. Yes, the Privy Council is an executive body which (through a committee) exercises a judicial function; but its judicial tasks are specialised, and its largely ritual executive functions carried out by different members. Yes, the Houses of Parliament have a penal jurisdiction; but the House of Lords does not seem to use it, and even the House of Commons has not imprisoned anyone for more than a hundred years. In the British constitution, where conventions and practice count for such a lot, it is all the more necessary to see behind the forms.

There are substantial, and not merely trivial, links between the legislature and the executive, because of there being Cabinet government with a parliamentary executive. But this is not to show that the separation of powers doctrine has been without effect. True, members of the government may sit in the Commons – but only up to a statutorily limited number. True, a large volume of legislation emanates from the executive. But by convention primary legislation is the appropriate embodiment for matters of principle, and over subordinate legislation Parliament retains a number of controls. Thus, even where the doctrine is apparently breached, it has had an important effect in limiting the extent of the breach. The same may be argued with respect to administrative tribunals. The protection of their members from dismissal and the improved rights of appeal conferred in the Tribunals and Inquiries Act 1958[6] were designed to bring them closer to a 'judicial' model. It was doubtful anyway whether their members could be considered part of the executive, so that representing the work of the tribunals as the executive exercising judicial functions was strained, to say the least.

In fact, it is significant that features of modern government such as delegated legislation and adjudication by tribunals should have been perceived as problematic. In the 1920s and 1930s that perception was

---

4 C K Allen *Law and Orders* (3rd edn, 1965), p 16.
5 *The Times*, 1 February 1980.
6 Replaced by Tribunals and Inquiries Act 1971, ss 8, 13.

widespread. In books such as *The New Despotism* by Lord Hewart of Bury[7] (who was Lord Chief Justice at the time) and *Bureaucracy Triumphant* by C K Allen,[8] there were dire warnings of the dangers involved in the increasing use of these techniques. It was in response to these concerns that the Committee on Ministers' Powers[9] was set up in 1929 and the Committee on Administrative Tribunals and Enquiries[10] in 1956. The two Reports were reassuring. Delegated legislation and adjudication by tribunals were regarded as necessary and useful features of a developed state, provided that they were accompanied by safeguards to prevent abuse. The thinking behind the Reports has been immensely influential in modern public administration and administrative law.[11] What is interesting for our present purpose is the underlying concern and the stress laid on safeguards to allay it. In this there is eloquent testimony to the depth of separation of powers ideas in our political consciousness.

When one looks around today, there are plenty of other examples to the same effect. It was early in Lord Denning's judicial career when he was accused by Viscount Simonds of 'a naked usurpation of the legislative function'.[12] But at the end of that career, Lord Denning was still being criticised regularly, by politicians and the media as well as by fellow judges and lawyers, for assuming a role which properly belonged to the legislature. The merits of the criticisms do not concern us here. What is instructive is that they should be made in these terms.

Whenever governments anxious to reduce the prison population try to influence sentencing policy, there are objections raised on constitutional grounds. Even a sensitively phrased circular addressed to magistrates' clerks, which asked for the co-operation of courts in keeping custodial sentences to a minimum, was criticised by Professor Michael Zander as 'an unprecedented example of the executive trying to influence the courts' judicial decision-making'.[13]

When in the European Communities Act 1972 Parliament provided for Community obligations to be implemented by ministerial legislation, it was careful not to transfer some of its traditional functions, so that subordinate legislation may not be used for the imposition of taxes or for the creation of major criminal offences.[14]

In a variety of important ways, ideas of the separation of powers have

---

7 Lord Hewart *The New Despotism* (1929).
8 C K Allen *Bureaucracy Triumphant* (1931).
9 Cmd 4060.
10 Cmnd 218.
11 See D G T Williams 'The Donoughmore Report in Retrospect' (1982) 60 Public Administration 273.
12 *Magor and St Mellons RDC v Newport Corpn* [1952] AC 189 at 191.
13 *The Guardian*, 23 October 1980.
14 See European Communities Act 1972, s 2; and ch 6.

shaped constitutional arrangements and influenced our constitutional thinking, and continue to do so. The separation in the British constitution, although not absolute, ought not to be lightly dismissed.

Index